BIG GAME
HUNTER

A Biography of Frederick Courteney Selous

BIG GAME HUNTER

Norman Etherington

ROBERT HALE

First published in 2016 by Robert Hale, an imprint of
The Crowood Press Ltd, Ramsbury, Marlborough
Wiltshire SN8 2HR

www. crowood.com

www.halebooks.com

British Library Cataloguing-in-Publication Data
A catalogue record for this book is available from the British
Library.

ISBN 978-0-7198-0828-9

Typeset by Catherine Williams, Knebworth

Printed and bound in India by Replika Press Pvt Ltd

Contents

Note on Orthography

Present-day historians of Africa and the British Empire generally use the term Ndebele to denote subjects of the founding king Mzilikazi and his successor, Lobengulor, in the early nineteenth century. This was not a term liked by either man. Both insisted that the proper name of their people was Zulu. The term Matabele, meaning 'alien intruders from the lowlands', was conferred on them by the Tswana-speaking people of the South African Highveld in the 1830s. Ndebele is the way Matabele is rendered in the Zulu language. F.C. Selous was a good self-taught linguist and in early writings used the term Ndebele. Later, following the practically universal practice of his time, he writes exclusively of the Matabele and Matabeleland. Using the term Zulu would honour the wishes of Mzilikazi and Lobengula but confuse readers used to thinking of the Zulu exclusively in terms of people living in the South African province of KwaZulu-Natal. Matabeleland refers to a particular territory and is never written Ndbeleland. Because it would be inelegant and cumbersome to switch between Matabele in quotations from my sources and Ndebele in my own text, I have conformed to Tswana usage in this book.

The names Courteney and Selous are also orthographically unstable forms. Some of Frederick Selous's ancestors spelt the name as Slus. His grandfather spelt his name Slous, as did one of his uncles. Another family name Courteney was sometimes spelled Courtney. Understandably confused, two of Frederick's biographers (Millais and Tidrick) misspelt the name as Courtenay.

Preface

At the time of his death in 1917 Frederick Courteney Selous stood out among big game hunters as an international celebrity. Today his name barely registers with the public outside circles of people who still hunt with guns. Historians of European imperialism know him primarily as an exemplar of outmoded masculine virtues and as a participant in the Scramble for Africa.

That is not to say that he has fallen into complete oblivion. A company in Missouri makes a Courteney Selous Boot with Cape buffalo uppers and 'velvety soft collars of impala skin'. A German firm manufactures the Blaser R8 Selous Rifle, 'technical perfection' for sale at $US15,453. In 2010 a rifle Selous once owned sold at auction in Norfolk, England for £23,000, a premium of £17,500 over the cost of the same model without the Selous provenance. South African artist Gary Owen will paint you a full-colour original portrait of Selous with rifle and elephant in acrylic on canvas. Another artist offers a twelve-inch circular engraving on crystal, also with elephants.[1]

Had Lytton Strachey written a sequel to *Eminent Victorians* in the 1920s Selous would have been a hands-down favourite for inclusion as an example of a once-revered personage who failed to strike a chord with later generations. As a recent study of his public reception points out, he:

> gathered together in himself all the finally evolved and admired elements of the Victorian and Edwardian officer-hunter. He forged the hunting field and the battlefield into a melded unity: honourable killing. After his 'glorious death' in 'the line of duty' in the East African Campaign in 1917, he was exalted as the masculine archetype of his era.'[2]

Selous's life falls into rather neat, slightly overlapping phases. As a schoolboy at Rugby he was the kind of rule-breaking but fundamentally sound character celebrated in the wildly popular Victorian novel *Tom Brown's Schooldays*. Like the eponymous hero Tom Brown, Selous was good at games, always up for an escapade or fight, the prince of a boy's world that was practically devoid of females. In the next phase Selous ran off to Africa and spent a decade earning his living as an elephant hunter. The book he wrote about his experiences in 1881 was largely responsible for the reputation he acquired as 'Africa's greatest hunter'. Over the next decade he made a name for himself in scientific circles by collecting specimens of African mammals for museums and exploring little-known parts of central Africa. In the 1890s Selous was caught up in Cecil Rhodes's schemes for the colonization of the country then called Southern Rhodesia and now known as Zimbabwe. During the first decade of the twentieth century he emerged as the world's best-known safari guide, thanks largely to the part he played in the organization of his friend Theodore Roosevelt's African expedition of 1909–10. At the outbreak of World War I he managed, at the age of sixty-three, to be commissioned as an officer in Britain's East African Campaign, where he died leading troops into battle in January 1917. That event elevated him for a time to the upper circle of the pantheon of British heroes and saw his bust enshrined alongside the statue of Charles Darwin on the central staircase of the Natural History Museum in South Kensington.

A Man for No Seasons?

Judged from the perspective of the twenty-first century every phase of his life provokes boos rather than applause. His elephant hunting reminds us of the holocaust of wildlife wrought by the nineteenth-century ivory trade and the ongoing poaching of elephants and rhinoceros from African game reserves. Robin Brown writes in his book *Blood Ivory*, that Selous was 'the most deadly elephant hunter of all time'. The *Rough Guide to Tanzania* tells travellers that he is thought to have killed more than a thousand elephants in the reserve that bears his name.[3] Neither statement is true. Many other hunters killed far more elephants than Selous; he killed no elephants at all in Tanzania. Thus the outlandish claims made for his achievements in the nineteenth century become today's badge of infamy.

In 1911 the public acclaimed George V of Great Britain for killing tigers, bears and rhinoceros in Nepal. A century later, a newspaper photograph of the Spanish king, Juan Carlos, alongside a slain elephant led to that monarch's abdication. In 2015 an American dentist who killed a lion named Cecil with a crossbow outside Zimbabwe's Hwange National Park provoked such a firestorm on social media that he was forced to close his practice. Most twenty-first century people have a zero tolerance for big game hunting.

Selous's decade of collecting specimens tends to be seen through the same lens, even though tourists and schoolchildren still crowd through natural history museums where the specimens are displayed. In an era when David Attenborough's wildlife documentaries give television viewers insights into the behaviour of living animals beyond anything experienced by Selous, the mammal galleries seem more like mausoleums than educational facilities. Indeed, they are often maintained for the specific purpose of illustrating outmoded attitudes. Selous's association with prominent taxidermists supplying trophy heads for gentlemen's clubs and homes reminds us uncomfortably of a truly weird episode in interior decoration.

Any association with Rhodes and the failed experiment with the colonization of Southern Rhodesia carries a taint. Selous's role in the overthrow of the Matabele King, Lobengula, who had done so much for him in his elephant hunting days looks like a gross betrayal of trust. His participation in parcelling out the conquered territory to white settlers has been characterized by one historian as 'robbery under arms'. The book he wrote about the second Matabele campaign in 1896 reads today like a racist apologia for conquest, made worse by his own sexual relations with African women. Legends persist that he fathered children by three different African women, even though documentation is thin and may be based on mistaken identity. He certainly did have at least two children with one African woman, so the charge of double standards sticks.

At the end of the 1890s he took a principled stand against the second Anglo-Boer War, which temporarily turned British public opinion against him. However, the reason he gave for opposing this extension of colonialism – that the Afrikaners of Dutch descent deserved to govern the country they had seized from its original African owners

– wins him few friends in post-apartheid South Africa. In fact, in 1987 a successful campaign was waged in the north London suburb of Camden Town to change the name of Selous Street to Mandela Street (the activists being unaware that the street was originally named in honour of Selous's artist uncle, Henry Courtney Selous).[4]

The final act of his life, leading troops into battle at the age of sixty-five, is grudgingly admired as an example of splendid physical fitness, but one qualified by the contribution men like him made to the militarist ethos that pushed the nations of Europe into a paroxysm of killing in World War I.

Selous and the Scholars

After many decades of neglect, towards the end of the twentieth century serious scholars began to pay attention to Selous as a pivotal figure of his era. Up to that time he had figured in historical works only in relation to the British South Africa Company's colonization of Southern Rhodesia.[5] John MacKenzie's ground-breaking study, *The Empire of Nature: Hunting, Conservation and British Imperialism*, showed how hunters like Selous were in the forefront of the modern wildlife preservation and nature conservation movements.[6] Before Selous, the hunting frontiers that drove big game toward extinction in many regions of the globe were the product of uncontrolled capitalist development and settler colonialism. Many intellectuals treated extinctions as a regrettable but inevitable consequence of the Darwinian struggle for existence. Selous's first book, *A Hunter's Wanderings in Africa*, alerted people to the retreat of the elephants into ever-more inaccessible country. The contradiction at the heart of the book is that the thrill Selous felt in hunting down elephants was tempered by the knowledge that unless something was done soon to kerb the slaughter, the African elephant would go the way of Europe's woolly mammoths. The involvement of Selous and his friends Theodore Roosevelt, Edward North Buxton and H.A. Bryden in movements for the preservation of wildlife was a logical consequence of their shared passion for hunting. John MacKenzie also introduced scholars to the paradoxical links between imperialism and conservation. The conservation of wildlife in the modern era dispossessed indigenous people of their accustomed hunting grounds and proclaimed that big game belonged to all mankind rather than the native inhabitants of the land over which they roamed.

The debate over hunting and conservation continues to this day, with some contending that managed hunting has done more for the preservation of large fauna than outright bans because it provides economic incentives for conservation. Whether public bonfires of elephant tusks do more to break the back of the ivory trade than the regulated sale of tusks from managed herds is still the subject of impassioned debate.

Similar observations have been made on zoos and natural history museums in relation to conservation. Keith Thomas, in *Man and the Natural World* (1983) showed how the urbanization and industrialization that alienated people from agricultural landscapes paradoxically spurred research in zoological science that led to a less anthropocentric view of nature. Tom Griffiths's book *Hunters and Collectors* (1996) details the process by which museums, taxidermy and zoos made city folk take an interest in wild nature. Selous's progress from collector of butterflies and birds' eggs to provider of specimens for natural history museums in London and Cape Town charts an epochal transformation. Urban dwellers brought face to face with caged, living and stuffed, dead animals were more likely to become vegetarians or conservationists than those who read about them in books.[7] Though the nineteenth-century dioramas of mounted animal specimens no longer serve the purposes for which they were intended, Selous's collecting activities were a necessary way station on a long road towards the photographic safari, the open range zoo and the protected game reserve.

Victorian and Edwardian valorization of the hunter-soldier as the highest form of manly man – derided and ridiculed for much of the twentieth century – has now become the subject of scholarly enquiry. In a world where gender roles are no longer taken for granted, the question of what makes a man a man has been subjected to unprecedented scrutiny. Historical works on masculinity have begun to accumulate on library shelves previously populated by feminism and women's studies. R.W. Connell's *Masculinities* (1995) attempted to set the theoretical parameters of the field. A landmark in African history was a 1998 issue of the *Journal of Southern African Studies* devoted to the subject of various historical forms of masculinity.[8]

Selous and the Biographers

Selous has been the subject of two full-length biographies and one penetrating character study. The first biography was written by his friend John Guille Millais in 1919 as part of the memorial celebrations that followed his death.[9] Millais was no historian, so he makes many forgivable mistakes of fact and chronology. He did, however, have the advantage of having at his disposal a cache of Selous's letters written to him and other close friends that were later lost or destroyed. Because he quoted extensively from the later correspondence, Millais's book stands as an historical source in its own right. He shared Selous's passion for hunting and natural history and so presents the man as he might have wished to see himself, ignoring contradictions, blemishes and blunders.

In the 1980s would-be biographers competed to produce a new work. James Casada, then a university professor of history, lost the race to journalist Stephen Taylor. Raised in South Africa, Taylor viewed Selous's life primarily in the context of southern African history. His book, *The Mighty Nimrod*, is distinguished by its lively prose but suffers from a lack of references and footnotes. It concentrates on the first forty-five years of Selous's life, barely touching on his experiences between the Boer War and the outbreak of World War I. Although James Casada did not complete his projected biography, he did produce two useful compendia of material by and about Selous: *Frederick C. Selous, A Hunting Legend: Recollections by and about the Great Hunter*, and *Africa's Greatest Hunter: The Lost Writings Of Frederick C. Selous*.[10] A shorter but intellectually penetrating character study appears as a chapter in psychologist Kathryn Tidrick's *Empire and the English Character*.[11] It focuses on the contradiction between Selous's public self-presentation as a simple, honest hunter and his devious behaviour during his involvement with Cecil Rhodes from 1889 to 1896.

In an uncrowded field the present book for the first time brings an historian's eye to bear on Selous's life, career and legacy. Like previous biographers, I found my most important sources among the letters and papers presented to what were then the National Archives of Rhodesia by his widow prior to her death in 1951. These include letters to his parents dating from 1867 until his marriage in 1894, the Roosevelt side of correspondence with Selous and an assortment of other correspondence. The ability to search many newspaper archives online has been a godsend, enabling me to sort out the chronology of events more thoroughly than was previously possible. Paying close attention to his life from year to year allows us to see Selous as a more conflicted and multidimensional character. It is all too easy to be taken in by the persona of unchanging simplicity and honesty he projected in his first book and a series of studio photos. He altered his opinions and allegiances over time. Money was a worry and a beacon for him. He craved the public attention he affected to despise. Even his attitude to hunting animals shifted over time.

The present book is aimed at the general reader and makes no claims to theoretical innovation or revolutionary findings. It reinforces rather than challenges the work done by scholars on the cutting edge of research into environmental, imperial, cultural and gender history. My hope is that it will stimulate further work on the many-sided career of Frederick Courteney Selous.

Norman Etherington

Acknowledgments

I particularly acknowledge my commissioning editor, Alexander Stilwell, for conceiving the project and keeping faith during the months I spent turning my research into chapters. Stephen Taylor helped by providing a vital archival reference. The eminent South African historian and my valued friend Jane Carruthers pointed me to useful sources. The staff of the Brenthurst Library in Johannesburg, The Royal Geographical Society, the Natural History Museum in South Kensington, the British National Archives and the British Library made every effort to assist with my research. So did Mr I. Murambiwa, Director of the National Archives of Zimbabwe and the staff of the reading room. Staff at the Selous River Camp in Tanzania were unfailingly courteous and helpful, especially my guide Dennis, who made the expedition to the Selous grave site an unforgettable experience.

I have benefited greatly from advice, encouragement and careful proofreading by my wife Peggy and my long-time friend and colleague Robert Dare.

1

Birds' Nests, Butterflies and Mischievous Boys

When Queen Victoria opened the Great Exhibition at the Crystal Palace on May Day, 1851, a fashionable history painter was engaged to record the occasion on a large canvas. Henry Courtney Selous shone the spotlight of his luminous oils on the 31-year-old queen, her wonder-struck children and the towering figure of her consort. Prince Albert strikes a proprietary pose appropriate to his role as the mastermind of the exhibition. Neglecting the serried rows of dignitaries on the upper balconies, Selous's painting draws our eyes irresistibly to a vista of trees, foliage, fountains and a sunny sky beyond the royal couple. Joseph Paxton's stupendous glass and iron structure had miraculously tamed and enclosed wild nature, including a tropical palm as alien to Hyde Park as any of the foreign gentlemen on the sidelines.

Conquering and containing the natural world was a major theme in an exhibition showcasing the achievements of industrial Britain. Hunters found a great array of firearms and knives available for inspection. Manufacturers like Colt, Smith & Wesson, Remington and Winchester supplied a gun for every quarry. Britain's expanding empire opened new worlds for hunters in every corner of the globe, as evidenced by the exhibits of individual colonies. The Cape Colony in South Africa sent an assortment of 'carouses, or cloaks made of the skins of wild animals skilfully dressed', along with ostrich feathers and an enormous elephant's tusk weighing 163 pounds.[1] A note in the exhibition catalogue explained that 'ivory is chiefly bought of the natives' rather 'than obtained by white hunters'. One hunter who had shot African elephants at close range contributed many specimens to the exhibition, though not a whole beast. Roualeyn George Gordon Cumming had published his sensational account of *Five Years of a Hunter's Life in the Far Interior of South Africa* the previous year. A flamboyant Scottish aristocrat, Cumming had begun collecting hunting trophies even before he entered Eton College. Military service took him to India and then to South Africa where he took up ivory trading and hunting for profit. His accounts of the chase pulsate with animal bloodlust: 'It is a heart-stirring sight to behold one bull elephant; but when five gigantic old fellows are walking slowly along before you, and you feel that you can ride up and vanquish whichever one you fancy, it is so overpoweringly exciting that it almost takes a man's breath away.'[2] On his return to Scotland Cumming set up a private museum on his estate and arranged for the best of his stuffed and mounted specimens to be shown all over Britain.[3]

His contribution to the Crystal Palace extravaganza included species of big African animals never before seen in England. Thanks to recent advances in taxidermy, they could be represented by more than skulls, horns and fur. Their professionally stuffed hides could be made to stand in lifelike positions and arranged in tableaux with painted backdrops suggesting their distant habitats. The Great Exhibition has been called 'the birthplace of Victorian taxidermy' owing to the large number of practitioners whose work was on display. The burgeoning market for animal heads had by now extended beyond the traditional hunting and shooting aristocracy. Demand for African elephants' ivory had likewise soared. Ivory figured not only in exhibits of ladies' fans and decorative carvings but also in its more practical role on pianos, where its unique capacity to deal with moisture increased players' dexterity on the keyboard. As an instrument ideally suited to the parlour, the piano became an essential feature of 'the woman's sphere' in bourgeois homes. The Crystal Palace and subsequent international exhibitions enabled manufacturers to show off their products to a mass audience. Between 1850 and 1890 world production of pianos rocketed from 50,000 to 232,000 per annum.[4] Ladies' drawing room recitals would help push the African elephant to the brink of extinction in most parts of the continent.

By the time the Great Exhibition closed in October 1851 six million paying customers had trooped through Paxton's glass and iron marvel. Profits amounted to £186,000 (£18 million in today's money), which was used to found the great museums of South Kensington: the Science Museum, the Natural History Museum and the Victoria and Albert Museum of applied arts and science, where Henry Courteney Selous's painting resides today.

In 1851 Henry Selous the artist was easily the best-known of three talented brothers. His younger sibling Angiolo had his first play produced in the West End the previous year, but his greatest success would come fifteen years later with *True to the Core: A Story of the Armada*. The elder brother, Frederick, took up a less glamorous career in finance, which led him eventually to election as Chairman of the London Stock Exchange. The brothers' closeness was evident in the adjoining houses they built in Gloucester Road in Regent's Park. Here, while Henry worked away at his Crystal Palace painting, the first-born son of his stockbroking brother came into the world on New Year's Eve 1851. He was christened Frederick Courteney Selous, most probably as a mark of respect for his father's brother, Henry Courtney Selous.

Few would have imagined that Frederick would forsake his privileged, cultured London life for Gordon Cumming's trade of elephant hunting. Or that his life would revolve around ivory, guns, and stuffed animals like those exhibited at the Crystal Palace. His father was anything but the rugged outdoorsman. Friends regarded him as the quintessential 'City man', though his interests ranged far beyond stocks and bonds. He was a recognized master at chess and an accomplished clarinettist. Young Fred could hardly have grown up in a more stimulating cultural environment. From the age of ten he attended Bruce Castle School in North London, perhaps the most progressive educational institution in the country. Its founders were the radical utilitarian philosopher, Jeremy Bentham, and Rowland Hill, who went on to become head of the General Post Office, where he introduced the penny postage stamp. Corporal punishment was forbidden at the school and boys accused of serious offences were tried by a court of pupils. Unlike conventional schools which concentrated on Greek and Roman classics, the curriculum included contemporary foreign languages, science and engineering.

Fred said little in later years about his time at Bruce Castle, except that it was there that he 'was initiated into some of the mysteries of football, and laid the foundation of my career as naturalist'.[5] This suggests lessons in natural science as a source of inspiration. Another possible influence was the London Zoo, only a short walk from his home. When he was thirteen the zoo acquired its most celebrated resident, Jumbo the elephant. No African elephant had been seen alive in Britain since Roman times, so Jumbo's arrival in London drew enormous crowds. It seems highly likely that around this time Fred began to collect birds' eggs and butterflies.

Most of what we know about Selous's schooling comes from him. One of the earliest written accounts appeared in *Chums*, a magazine for boys that Cassells publishers had launched in 1892, hoping it might rival the success of *The Boys' Own Paper*. Selous told the *Chums* reporter that very early in life he began to study natural history and read books of adventure – not fiction but 'books of travel and actual experience in far lands'.[6] Soon after his arrival, aged fourteen, at Rugby School he was elected captain of his house football team, the youngest ever. Rugby football in the 1860s was a rough-and-tumble affair that included a great deal of intentional shin-kicking, or 'hacking'. 'I was weekly hacked', Selous recalled, but he gave as good as he got. Apart from football, his great passion was collecting bats, beetles, butterflies and birds' eggs. As keeper of the ornithological notebook for the newly founded Rugby Natural History Society, he was granted special leave to go into nearby woodlands to collect specimens. He also kept his own gun, a so-called pea rifle. This was nothing like the modern air rifles or BB guns that are sometimes called pea rifles. This was a serious field piece with a flintlock mechanism and rifled barrel, firing round bullets of .32 to .45 calibre, which Selous used to shoot 'rabbits, moor-hens and various flying and creeping creatures'. Swimming, he told *Chums*, was another notable accomplishment. The aquatic skills that won him second prize at Rugby would stand him in good stead in later life when he had to cross African rivers carrying a heavy rifle in one hand.

'Crocodiles in those rivers, may I ask?'

'Sometimes', he replied, with wrinkles at the corners of his mouth; adding, 'I am not a bad swimmer now, at forty-two.'

In this version of his boyhood Selous emphasizes his predestined life as a big game hunter. 'One of his preparations' for his future career was sleeping next to the open dormitory window to accustom himself to 'sleeping in the open'. The *Chums* interview concluded by saying that 'poaching of all kinds was dear to him: bathing in forbidden waters had for him a fascination, but besides all this, he was good at books, at games, knew no fear, and was universally loved'.

From a twenty-first-century perspective these confessions strike a discordant note in an article aimed at adolescent boys. Poaching was and is a criminal activity, associated nowadays with illegal hunters seeking tusks and rhino horns in African game parks. In Georgian England the Game Laws imposed severe penalties on poachers who took game from private parks. By the early Victorian era poaching had emerged as a symbolic frontline of class warfare. Unemployed and poorly paid workers poached game to supplement their families' meagre diet. The cry of the upper classes that crime must be punished was answered by trade unionists and Methodist parsons insisting on the right of the poor to live.[7] Why, then, should a privileged Rugby schoolboy glory in his exploits as a poacher? The answer seems to be that rule-breaking and even law-breaking were expected from boys who would grow up to be real men. In a lecture at London's Exeter Hall in 1895 Selous told a distinguished audience including Lord Chelmsford and the Duke of Teck that, at Rugby, 'he earned the reputation of being the biggest poacher in the school'.[8] In a speech to Rugby boys he told how gamekeepers on nearby estates used to chase him through the hedgerows while he clutched stolen birds' eggs to his bosom. At the conclusion of the talk the headmaster 'said it was a great privilege to the school' to have heard so distinguished an explorer. Selous did not present himself as a reformed bad boy, but rather as someone whose mature manliness was prefigured in his adolescent feats of strength and daring. 'Mr Selous said there was an old saying that the boy was father to the man, and believed the sort of life he led at Rugby—wandering about after birds' nests and investigating points of natural history—gave him kind of fitness for the life of adventure he had led since for 25 years in the interior of Africa.'[9]

The repetition of this youthful autobiography on so many eminently respectable occasions tells us that his boyhood was considered fairly normal, even admirable in English society. In fact, it conforms closely to a template laid down in the most famous of all nineteenth-century public school novels, *Tom Brown's Schooldays*. From his infancy Tom is a rebel, escaping from his nurse and running wild with the village boys. On his way to Rugby he hears astonishing tales of Rugby pupils' crimes and misdemeanours: assaults on coaches, punch-ups with Irish labourers and any number of other 'desperate and lawless' escapades. 'He couldn't help hoping that they were true.' He soon falls in with a group of like-minded fellows, 'as full of tricks as monkeys'. They treat neighbouring squires, landlords and gamekeepers as enemies. Illegal poaching, swimming and fishing are their favourite pursuits. Temperance for them means drinking beer in their rooms rather than laying into hard liquor at the village pub. Led by 'Madman Martin', whose room abounds in live animals, dangerous chemicals and natural history collections of all kinds, Tom and his gang venture into the woods to steal eggs from a kestrel's nest set high in a towering fir tree. Not long afterwards Tom gets into a set-piece fight with 'Slogger Williams' behind the chapel. Round after round he stands up to a flurry of blows until the headmaster arrives to break up the forbidden affray. Author Thomas Hughes is anything but disapproving:

> After all, what would life be without fighting, I should like to know? From the cradle to the grave, fighting, rightly understood, is the business, the real highest, honestest business of every son of man. Every one who is worth his salt has his enemies, who must be beaten, be they evil thoughts and habits in himself, or spiritual wickednesses in high places, or Russians, or Border-ruffians, or Bill, Tom, or Harry, who will not let him live his life in quiet till he has thrashed them.
>
> It is no good for Quakers, or any other body of men, to uplift their voices against fighting. Human nature is too strong for them ...[10]

As might be expected, Tom Brown makes some progress in religion and morality as he nears graduation. He even allows himself to be persuaded not to use cheat sheets in recitations of Greek and Latin. But when asked what he would like to be remembered for, he stammers out his wish to have 'the name of a fellow who never bullied a little boy, or turned his back on a big one'. The book ends with his entry to Oxford while his friend 'Scud' East goes off to India with his regiment and 'Madman Martin' embarks on a voyage to the south Pacific to collect specimens of natural history. From start to finish Tom Brown lives in a man's world. Women are rarely mentioned and girls, not at all.

The novel appeared in 1857, just nine years before Selous arrived at Rugby. There can be no doubt he knew the book well. When old Rugby friends gave a dinner in his honour in 1895, he said – quoting almost verbatim – the school taught him 'to despise the strong boy who bullied the weak one, and to admire the strong boy who guarded the weak one'.[11] A few years later, in 1908, he approached his publisher, Macmillan, with a proposal to write a boys' book along the lines of *Tom Brown's Schooldays*.[12] He was still working on the project in 1914, casting a thinly disguised version of himself as the hero (John Leroux, not Fred Selous) – who in turn is an amalgam of characters from *Tom Brown's Schooldays*. On his first day he takes on an older boy in a classic fight. From there he progresses to raiding rooks' nests on lofty elms, playing practical jokes on policemen, and expanding his voluminous collection of butterflies and birds' eggs. Like the maturing Tom Brown he 'never used a crib to assist him with his Greek and Latin translations'. All of 'his most interesting experiences were connected with his passion of birds'-nesting, and the pursuit of sport, at first with a saloon pistol and subsequently with a pea-rifle, on the domains of neighbouring landowners.'[13] Needless to say Leroux conducts a low-level guerrilla war against gamekeepers and comes perilously close to apprehension and punishment.

The wonder to modern eyes is that Selous's own exploits made him, not a pariah, but a favourite with teachers. His first housemaster at Rugby, J.M. Wilson, recalled the letter of recommendation received from his previous school:

> 'Take my advice,' was the gist of the letter, 'and say your house is full; the boy will plague the life out of you.... He breaks every rule; he lets himself down out of a dormitory window to go birds'-nesting; he is constantly complained of by neighbours for trespassing; he fastened up an assistant master in a cowshed into which he had chased the young villain early one summer morning; somehow the youngster scrambled out, and fastened the door on the outside, so that the master missed morning school.'
>
> Such were his crimes; so, of course, I wrote back and said that he was the boy for me.[14]

The conclusion to be drawn from these memoirs is that Selous set out at some stage to make his life conform to a prevailing Victorian ideal of the good mischievous boy. The older he got, the more he presented his adolescent self as 'a regular Tom Brown'. It was not so much a case of life imitating art as Selous writing and rewriting his youth to suit the spirit of the times, which made heroes of fighters, rule-breakers, mischief-makers, soldiers and hunters. The passage of time has dimmed, but not altogether extinguished, the popularity of the good bad boy. Han Solo of *Star Wars* and Harry Potter enact for present-day audiences versions of the Tom Brown/John Leroux/Fred Selous model of youthful masculinity.

Less typical was Selous's passion for natural history. In this respect he resembles 'Madman Martin' and twenty-first-century geeks more than Tom Brown. His clergyman housemaster, Wilson, wrote that, on their first encounter, Selous said 'I mean to be like Livingstone'. Collecting butterflies and eggs was not a casual pastime for him. There was a genuine urge to understand 'the order of things' and the underlying forces at work in nature. He was a founding member of the Natural History Club at Rugby. Whether or not he actually spoke of Africa and Livingstone at age fourteen, the urge to interact with little-known fauna in unfamiliar places was strong. It seems less likely that the figure of Livingstone the missionary held any appeal. There is scant evidence to indicate any interest in organized religion or theology. On the contrary, his reading of Darwin and other scientists inclined him to a personal materialism at odds with the earnest Christianity of most of his contemporaries.

It is hard to say when Fred first began to handle firearms, but by the end of his time at Rugby he was proficient at shooting with saloon pistols and pea rifles.[15] He had also learned to heft the heavy army issue Enfield rifle, thanks to his membership of the school's Volunteer Rifle Corps. Following the Crimean War in the late 1850s, the Volunteer movement sprang up as a way of preparing civilians for military service in times of national emergency. With support from celebrities like Thomas Hughes, Rugby was one of several leading schools to organize rifle corps. Selous's fictional John Leroux recounts the problems of carrying the cumbersome Enfield 9 ½ lb muzzleloader.[16]

Surviving letters to his parents show no clear intention to be a Livingstone, or to be anything in particular as he prepared to leave Rugby. At some stage the family decided that he would not go on to university but would study medicine, probably in Germany. As a preparation he would improve his knowledge of modern languages, beginning with French studies in Switzerland. Writing to his mother from Neuchâtel in November 1868, he said his progress had been slow. However, the following month he sent her another letter in perfect French, explaining why he intended to study medicine at Wiesbaden rather than Dresden. His chemistry tutor told him that he could provide letters of introduction to an eminent chemist in Wiesbaden. Not only would he receive a fine medical education, he would find plenty of opportunities for hunting all kinds of game in the surrounding countryside and enjoy far more personal liberty than in Dresden.[17] Some accounts of Selous's life imply that he lived the life of an idle young gentleman in Switzerland. His letters home tell a different story of diligent study in French, chemistry and the violin. When his mother suggested he had reached 'the age of irresponsibility', he protested that he had been very responsibly going about the business of 'learning these infernal languages'.

On the other hand, he did not look forward with any great enthusiasm to his medical career:

> I do not want particularly to be a doctor, but I shall go in for that as I can't see anything else that I should like better except sheep farming or something of that sort in one of the colonies, but I suppose I must give up that idea; however if I become a surgeon I do not intend to practice in England but I should try and get a post as ship's surgeon, or army surgeon in India if I could get any leave of absence which would give me a little time to myself, but anyhow I am certain I shall never be able to settle down quietly in England. ... How glad I shall be when my education is finished and I have got into my profession. 5 years more of it is something awful to contemplate.[18]

Back in London the following year he told his sister 'Locky'(Florence) that he had met a German who had made his fortune in Natal, South Africa, and who had never tired of singing its praises. The climate was superb, there was no winter and 'society there is very good'. Fred read R.J. Mann's book on Natal and longed to go, but that meant getting money. 'But how?'[19] There seemed no alternative to medical studies at Wiesbaden.

Like the English city of Bath, Wiesbaden built its reputation on hot springs that had drawn visitors since Roman times. Under the Duchy of Nassau the city flourished in the early nineteenth century when renewed interest in the health-giving properties of mineral springs spurred the development of hotels and clinics. It was this concentration of doctors that made it attractive to aspiring medics like Selous. No surviving letters describe the nature of his studies, except that they were wide enough to embrace German language and music. Not long before his arrival the Duchy lost its independence when it allied itself to the losing side in the Austro-Prussian War of 1866. Indirectly, this contributed to the abrupt termination of Selous's premedical training.

In December 1869 he made friends with Charley Colchester, an English boy of about his own age whose family lived in Wiesbaden. Soon Fred drew Charley into birds'-nesting raids in the wooded parks and reserves on the fringe of the town. Early in the summer of 1870 a forester, Herr Keppel, caught the pair as they were making off with honey-buzzards' eggs. Threatened with prison, Fred and Charley chose to stand and fight. In the course of the struggle Fred knocked the gamekeeper to the ground and scampered home. This time there was no question of the escapade being written off as boys being boys. Fred had not only broken the law but obstructed an official in the performance of his duty, a far more serious offence than stealing eggs.[20] Before 1866 the consequences would not have extended beyond Wiesbaden, but as the town was now part of Prussia, Fred and Charley were wanted men all over Germany. On the advice of a lawyer, Fred hurriedly packed his belongings and fled to Salzburg, Austria.

In any case, it is unlikely that Selous would have stayed much longer in Wiesbaden, because the very next month Prussia went to war with France and most foreigners fled the city. At this point his parents dropped their insistence that he patch up his differences with the German authorities. From his own point of view as a fairly dutiful son, Selous thought:

> it was rather too much to expect me to go back to Wiesbaden which I must emphatically refuse to do, but except this I will do anything else you wish, go to Luxembourg or anywhere else you may think fit but at the same time I express a hope that you will allow me to remain here [in Salzburg where he had already paid a month's rent].

I shall lose a great deal by interrupting my studies so often but about this you shall decide as you like and I will obey, the only thing is I wish you would not take on so about such a trifle, making a molehill into a mountain which you seem to me to be doing.[21]

There would be no more talk of medical examinations thanks to the outbreak of war. It seems to have come as a complete surprise to Fred, who confessed he had been 'in the most sublime ignorance that there was any misunderstanding between the two countries'.[22] Throughout his life Selous remained profoundly indifferent to the course of politics or international relations. Some see this as evidence for an admirable simplicity and honesty of character. However, his failure to appreciate the moral and practical complexities of politics would more than once land him in hot water. His first reaction to the Franco-Prussian War was to worry that his stockbroking father might lose money on investments. Later, influenced by reports of atrocities printed in the Austrian newspapers, he told his mother he had ceased to 'believe any more in the humanity of the Germans'. Almost in the same breath he thanked his mother for forwarding copies of *The Field*, which kept him up to date on the world of hunting, fishing and natural history.[23]

In Salzburg he pursued his own specimen-collecting with a passion seldom evident in other aspects of his life. He flew into a temper when bad weather thwarted his search for Purple Emperor butterflies:

Why I feel the absence of the sun so very acutely is because, when the sun is not shining no butterflies or none worth having are to be got. Now this is just the time for the purple Emperors, some specimens of which I want very much to get and so I have been exceedingly provoked ... you can't think how I put my whole soul into egg and butterfly collecting when I'm at it, and how I boil up and over with impotent rage at not being able to attain the object of my desires on account of the weather over which I have no control.[24]

Meanwhile, his mind was turning more and more to Africa. In a letter to his father he revealed his plan to go to Natal as a colonist 'in a year or so'. The best preparation would be practical training in agriculture. As it happened, a rich Hungarian then residing in Salzburg had taken a liking to him. Hearing of Fred's plans, he offered to take him on as an apprentice on one of his many farms when he returned to Hungary in January 1871. He 'offers to take me as a pupil and teach me farming just as would be done in Scotland or England'. What is more the Hungarian 'says he will treat me like a son'. Father must have, at one time or another, offered financial support, because Fred said any money problems could be overcome by sending a 'letter of credit to a bank in Vienna from which I can draw money as I require it'.[25]

This letter, more than any other he wrote home, reveals tensions in his relationship with his father. Financial dependency limits his options even as he expresses in the strongest possible terms his wish to be free. Telling dad about a Hungarian who offers to treat him 'like a son' sounds like a taunt, hinting at defects in his natural parent. He follows this up with the warning that 'if you do require me to return [to England] you will be doing me a positive wrong'. Fred then launches into an imaginary conversation, anticipating his father's objections:

> Although when in Switzerland, Prussia or here I might have shirked work and spent my money on pleasures such as shooting and fishing (when I went to Switzerland you said to me, 'I know you'll never learn French but spend all your time in shooting and fishing') yet I learnt more French in a year than 9 fellows out of ten would have done in three and German I have polished off at the same pace. I have never abused the trust you placed in me but always attended diligently to my studies.
>
> While father might say that at eighteen Fred was too young to go off on his own to Hungary, 'my answer is that as everybody says I appear about two or three and twenty not only in looks but in thoughts and manners, I think I ought to be considered of that age.'

Although no letters survive that detail the negotiations, father and son did work gradually toward a compromise. Fred would not learn farming in Hungary, but he would go to Africa after finishing his gentlemanly studies in Austria. These included German language and quite a lot of music. By the time he left Mozart's home city of Salzburg he was reasonably proficient on the violin and piano – and had also learned to play the Austrian zither, an instrument that gave him great pleasure because it required no accompaniment and could be carried on his travels.

With every passing year Selous grew more settled in his antipathy toward orthodox religion. His open profession of philosophical materialism set him apart from the conventional Anglican piety that gradually exerts its hold over fictional Tom Brown and his Rugby friends. When his sister Locky wrote to him about Chinese Buddhist teachings on reincarnation and the transmigration of souls, Fred replied that her letter 'almost tempts me to commit suicide. If I can't get good shooting and fishing in this world, I'll have it in the next if what the Chinaman says is true'.[26] He warned his mother against associating with 'bigoted fanatical church-going idiots', and regularly contrasted the stifling atmosphere of religion with the pleasures of the hunt.[27] Speaking of European travel, he said he 'wouldn't care to go to Rome and see the Holy Week', but 'should like to go to Russia, Sweden or some other country where some shooting or fishing is to be had'.[28]

Toward the end of June 1871 he spent a week in Vienna, drinking in all the delights the imperial city could offer a cultivated, multilingual young gentleman of nineteen. He saw the crown jewels, the emperor's stables (by which he meant the Spanish Riding School), and went several times to the opera. He loved *Martha, oder Der Markt zu Richmond* by Flotow, but found – as do many opera-goers – the plot of Wagner's *Tannhäuser* completely baffling. Worse still, there were 'no pretty arias'. Gounod's *Faust* was more to his liking, 'as near to perfect as possible'. A few days later he was back in Salzburg, resuming piano lessons and reading Dickens's *Bleak House*. Two months later he would land in South Africa to seek his fortune.

This abrupt break cries out for an explanation, on which existing sources are silent. None of the surviving letters tell of his trip home or the arrangements for a passage to South Africa. On 27 June he is writing about the Vienna Opera and *Bleak House*. On 1 September he stepped ashore at Cape Town after a passage of thirty-seven days from England, which means he shipped out on 24 July.[29] He must have wound up his affairs in Austria, transported his goods to London, and booked his passage to South Africa all in the space of a month. None of the interviews he gave to various newspapers in later life say anything about his time in Wiesbaden or Salzburg. His first biographer, John Guille Millais, confuses matters by writing that Selous returned to London in August 1871 'and during the next three months he attended classes at the University College Hospital

(London) to gain some knowledge of medical science preparatory to going to Africa'.[30] In the very next chapter Millais records Selous's arrival at Algoa Bay, South Africa, on 4 September 1871. Either the medical studies were misremembered by Fred's family or they happened at some other time. Another biographer, Stephen Taylor, resorts to supposition. Africa must have 'suddenly loomed large', because Fred had finally won his father over.[31] But won him over to what? His family were well aware of his intention to live in one of Britain's colonies, with farming in Natal uppermost in his mind. There is no evidence that either of his parents resisted the plan. Father must have bankrolled the enterprise, including the voyage out, his 300 pounds of baggage and the £400 he carried in cash when he landed at Algoa Bay. This was a tidy sum, more than a high-ranking colonial official would earn in a year, and four to six times the annual salary of educated missionaries.

In everything Selous subsequently wrote he presents his big game hunting in Africa as if it were preordained from childhood. It is all too easy to fall in with his script, even though letters to his family tell a different story – one of indecision about a future career apart from a strong desire to live an outdoor life in one of the colonies. Once arrived in Africa he sets about writing his life anew. He begins Chapter 1 of his first book with the words, 'On the 4th of September 1871, I set foot for the first time upon the sandy shores of Algoa Bay, with £400 in my pocket, and the weight of only nineteen years upon my shoulders.' There is not a word about his parents, his schooling, or the source of his money. It is as though, like Athena, he sprang to life as an adult in full armour. No one would guess that nine weeks earlier he had been living the life of a cultured connoisseur in Central Europe.

It is striking that practically everything we know about his life from September 1871 to February 1876 comes from the book he published in 1881, *A Hunter's Wanderings in Africa*. We know he kept journals, but only a fragment of one survives in the National Archives of Zimbabwe: a bound volume that begins in September 1871 and runs up to February 1872.[32] The rest of the pages were used by Selous to write out part of the first draft of his book, which is clearly shown by references to events that took place after his return to England. For this reason it needs to be treated as literature as much as reportage. Just as he would cast his childhood as a version of *Tom Brown's Schooldays*,

he modelled his chronicle of his life as a hunter on his literary predecessors. He says as much on the opening page of *Hunter's Wanderings*
(1881):

> Having carefully read all the works that had been written on sport
> and travel in South Africa, I had long ago determined to make my
> way to the interior of that country ... for the free-and-easy gipsy sort
> of life described by Gordon Cumming, Baldwin, and other authors,
> had quite captivated my imagination, and done much to determine
> me to adopt the life of ever varying scenes and constant excitement,
> which I have never since regretted, and for which an inborn love of
> all branches of Natural History, and that desire so common amongst
> our countrymen of penetrating to regions where no one else has
> been, in some degree fitted me.

Just as *Tom Brown's Schooldays* describes how a mischievous boy
grows into a manly man, *A Hunter's Wanderings* recounts the making
of a hunter who is, in every particular, a man's man.

Though Selous underplays the imperial context of his enterprise,
it was unthinkable without the continually expanding network of
political, technological and economic forces that had entangled South
Africa with the British Empire. The Cape Colony's exhibition at the
Crystal Palace had made that plain the year he was born. The search
for ivory, ostrich feathers and animal skins drove hunters and traders
ever further into the interior. By the time Fred arrived in September
1871 another prize was in view: diamonds. For the previous eighteen
months men had been scrambling to stake claims on what had previously been the arid and isolated De Beers brothers' farm. With 'New
Rush' booming, Fred abandoned his dream of Natal, and headed for
the diamond fields. About the same time an even younger man named
Cecil Rhodes made the same decision – moving on from cotton
farming in Natal. Two years' experience of African agriculture gave
Rhodes the know-how to manage black workers whose assistance in
dragging diamond-bearing clay to the surface was indispensable.
Speed was of the essence in sorting the diamonds from the dirt. The
more claims a man could manage, the more money he could make.
On the very day Selous landed at Cape Town, newspapers reported
that Rhodes had found diamonds weighing 110 carats.[33] He built on

his luck by devising an ambitious plan to consolidate ownership of the entire field.

By the time Selous arrived, upwards of 5,000 men were at work on the two main fields. Though they did not know it, they were probing the dead cores of volcanoes that long ago had packed enough heat and pressure to turn black carbon into translucent gems. As the diggers plunged deeper, the diamonds just kept appearing. Because the structure of diamond pipes was then unknown to geologists, the miners had no idea that they were engaged in the impossible task of approaching the centre of the earth through the square holes of their claims. Down and down they went, using simple tools – picks, shovels and bucket hoists – creating a landscape that grew ever more hellishly dangerous. Cave-ins of roads and claims increased, claiming hundreds of lives. Every day it was easier for cashed-up men like Rhodes to buy out adjoining claims, until monopoly control was a real possibility for his De Beers Consolidated Company.

Diamond mining profoundly altered the geographical, political and social landscape of southern Africa. Young African men came from far and wide, attracted by the comparatively high wages on offer. They returned to their rural homes with money, guns and tales of wicked, lawless life in a primitive maelstrom of cowboy capitalism. The balance of political and economic power shifted from the coast to the interior. Who knew what other sources of mineral wealth might be discovered? For their part, African chiefs strove to consolidate and expand their power by tapping the earnings of their young men and controlling access to their territories by fortune hunters of all sorts.

Selous had only a dim understanding of the large forces at work around him. But gazing upon the diamond diggings, which awestruck observers described as like a scene from Dante's *Inferno,* he knew this was not the reason he had come to Africa.

2

Not-so-great White Traders

Had Selous intended to try his luck at the diamond fields, he would have booked the fast coach from Port Elizabeth, which could make the journey in two to three weeks.[1] The trouble was that he had landed about 300 pounds of luggage, and for that he would need an ox wagon. Within a few days he had found a driver who would do the trip for £8. The only drawback was that by ox wagon the trip took nearly two months. This shows that, unlike the aspiring diggers, Selous was in no hurry. Perhaps, as a devoted reader of *The Field* magazine, he had seen a letter from an old South African hand published in November 1870. It advised the young man who wanted to shoot or do business in the South African interior 'to go up with a trader or elephant hunter for one or two trips before attempting a venture of his own'. Traders generally left Hopetown for the interior about the month of April, after the rainy season. Moreover:

A man must serve a short apprenticeship to become a Kaffir trader. He must thoroughly understand the native character, and if possible the language also. Don't by any means take out any things to trade with; for the chances are, if you do you will find they can be bought cheaper in Graham's Town than in London. Beads are among the chief articles the traders take up country with them; but so much does fashion in their colour change amongst the niggers, that what is all the rage one season – some slightly different shade having taken their fancy – they will not look at the next. The same may be said of blankets; indeed the only articles that a man may take up country with a certainty of finding a good market, are guns and powder, both of which have to be smuggled, as the colonial authorities don't believe in giving the Kaffirs guns to shoot us with.[2]

Both in tone and content this advice anticipated what Selous would hear from most white men in South Africa. The calculated use of racist slang – 'niggers' and 'Kaffirs' – underlines the settler's assumption of white supremacy. At the same time it is clear that there was good money to be made trading with Africans, who were by no means the simple savages most Europeans imagined them to be. Not only had Africans become accustomed to commercial capitalism, they were canny consumers whose tastes changed from year to year. Successful dealing required cultural awareness and facility in African languages. Lastly, all transactions were taking place within the context of a jumpy geopolitical atmosphere: 'the colonial authorities don't believe in giving the Kaffirs guns to shoot us with'. For most of the previous century the Cape Colony had been continuously at war with its African neighbours. Government attempts to limit interaction with people beyond the frontier had failed. Now, with black workers streaming to the diamond fields, new dangers loomed. Several of the more important African kingdoms and chieftaincies were known to be strengthening their arsenals. In a vain attempt to slow down the arms race, the colonial government banned dealings in guns and ammunition. However, as the correspondent of *The Field* noted, smuggling in defiance of the law was rife.

The few surviving pages of Selous's first African journal illustrate his style of note-keeping. He does not write every day, but when he does he keeps careful track of dates, names and places. Descriptive accounts of scenery and passages of personal introspection are rare. He records episodes of physical exertion and fatigue, but not malaise, anxiety or boredom. Along the wagon route to the diamond fields he notes that on 15 September he 'shot a hare; the first thing I shot in Africa'. Careful recording of fauna shot, fish hooked and birds' eggs collected had been a habit since early boyhood. It is a great pity that the rest of this and subsequent journals have been lost; without them there is no way of gauging the extent to which his published books omit significant personal details. Fortunately we have enough of his first diary to reconstruct the process by which he turned laconic journal entries into publishable books.

As the oxen plodded on, Selous kept his guns at the ready. He records several species of antelope killed, but says nothing of his thoughts or feelings until, on the last day of his journey, he gets into a ruckus with some Korannas. They were, he thought, 'about the ugliest people under the sun'. By this time the Kora, or Korannas, had lost any semblance of a defined ethnic identity. They were loosely associated groups of Afrikaans-speaking, mounted raiders once widely feared for their ruthless ways. Decades earlier a French missionary noted that 'the name of Koranna designates ... less a people than an association of brigands'.[3]

The journal says nothing of Selous's reaction to the physical and social chaos of the diamond fields. Neither does his finished first book, which merely notes that on the 29 October he bought a horse for £8 and met up with a young man who had come out on the ship with him to Cape Town. Arthur Laing had tired of looking for diamonds and persuaded Fred to join him in a trading expedition to African settlements lying west toward the Kalahari Desert. Within thirty-six hours they were on the road to Griquatown with a guide, a wagon and trade goods.

A Land of Tumult and Turmoil

This was hardly unknown territory. Sixty years earlier agents of the London Missionary Society (LMS) answered a call from the Griqua people who lived alongside scattered springs that provided the only reliable water in an otherwise arid and desolate landscape. They were a racially mixed population derived from aboriginal Khoi herders living at the Cape. Expansion of Dutch colonists since their first arrival in 1652 had driven them from their ancestral lands while at the same time giving them a new language and way of life. Gradually they made their way eastward along the Orange River valley and then turned north along the right bank of the Vaal River. Their horses and guns gave them an advantage in encounters with more established agriculturalists in the region. For thirty years the Griqua maintained a marginal existence, competing with similar groups for the spoils of herding, trading, raiding and occasional slaving. Soon a new threat emerged as a trickle of so-called *trekboeren* began to infiltrate the country. For two centuries they and their kind had formed the advance guard of the expanding colonial frontier. Called 'trek boers' from their habit of being constantly on the move, living out of their wagons or simple huts, they were hardly distinguishable from the Griqua, except in their insistence on a white identity. They cared little for borders, laws or land titles.

For defence against the newcomers, the Griquas relied on their guns, Bibles, and the treaties they negotiated with British governors of the Cape Colony, which had displaced the Dutch East India Company in 1806. The invitation to the London Missionary Society had been a calculated political act by people who saw the need for intermediaries. Their reward was the creation of a Christian Griqua state with a settled government and system of laws. From the point of view of the missionaries their Griqua stations gave them a jumping-off point for the evangelization of all Africa. Though the stations at the springs of the western Highveld were oases of Christian life in an otherwise desolate wilderness, they stretched north in the direction of the Limpopo River and the unknown lands of central Africa. The pick of their chain of stations was Robert Moffat's settlement at Kuruman. While it maintained close communications with the Griqua missions, the predominant population of the region were Tswana people who practised a mixed form of farming based on cattle and agriculture. Their language was spoken by people all over the central and eastern Highveld (the high country lying between the Kalahari and the Qathlamba or Drakensberg mountains). Tswana was one branch of the widespread Bantu language family whose closely related tongues are spoken by most African people living south of the equator.

Moffat's Kuruman mission thus found itself situated at a crossroads of economic, cultural and political interaction. Life got even more complicated in the late 1820s when a new kingdom arose not far from the site of the modern-day South African capital city of Pretoria. Chief Mzilikazi had led a formidable warrior band up from the lowlands of south-eastern Africa. Success in battle and cattle raiding soon won him a large following drawn from all parts of the eastern Highveld. The chief wanted his people to be known as Zulu, perhaps in imitation of the rising kingdom founded by the notorious Shaka. However, history decreed that they would be called by the name given to them by the Tswana people of the Highveld: Matabele or the 'alien newcomers from beyond the eastern mountains'. The name stuck, eventually being rendered in Mzilikazi's home language as Ndebele.

Mzilikazi was a complex character, by turns ruthless, tactful, cruel and charming. In 1829 he sent emissaries to Moffat who readily responded. Upon his arrival at the chieftain's capital the missionary found a tall, athletic, good-humoured man in his early thirties who spoke in a 'soft and feminine voice' and behaved with the impeccable manners of a gentleman.[4] Selous would have met Mzilikazi in the pages of William Cornwallis Harris's *The Wild Sports of Southern Africa*, the first of the great southern African hunting books. In 1836 Harris described him in terms similar to Moffat's:

> Attired in a handsome black leathern mantle; its ample folds, reaching to his heels, well became his tall and manly person; and he looked the very beau ideal of an African chief. [Soon he cast] aside that reserve and gravity which in a public assembly he had conceived most becoming, and now appeared in high good humour, joking, laughing, and familiarly pulling our beards, of which the luxuriant growth elicited his admiration and surprise. He frequently asked us how many wives we had, and whether they also had beards.[5]

By this time Mzilikazi had moved his headquarters further west to Mosega in the Marico River valley. From this capital he carried on the consolidation of his power through long-distance raids, primarily aimed at building up the stocks of cattle on which all chiefly power rested in this part of the world. His forces inflicted fearful losses on the Griqua and the other marauding groups whose guns and horses had previously ruled the western Highveld. They also overwhelmed the Hurutshe and other significant western Tswana chieftaincies. The key to Mzilikazi's success was the mobilization of fit young men into well-drilled regiments. Armed only with spears, their ability to run long distances and stage lightning attacks at dawn made them a match for the Griqua, Kora, Bergenaars and Hartenaars. Situated far from powerful kingdoms in the east and south-east, they were rarely threatened on their home ground. For several years they were the unchallenged great power of the region.

Nemesis arrived at last in 1836, when a mass movement of Boer settlers dragged their wagons up to the Highveld from the Cape Colony bent on establishing a white-ruled republic free from British influence. In later decades this would be called the Great Trek, but for the moment it was known simply as the movement of the emigrant farmers. On their own it was doubtful that the so-called *Voortrekkers* could have defeated Mzilikazi, but after years of terrifying Matabele raids there was no shortage of willing allies ready to join a grand coalition in a campaign of vengeance. Gradually the trekkers assembled their forces through a mixture of cajoling, promises and diplomacy. For example, commandant Hendrick Potgieter told the Griqua captains 'we are emigrants together with you', who 'dwell in the same strange land and we desire to be regarded as neither more nor less than your fellow-emigrants, inhabitants of the country, enjoying the same privileges with you'.[6] By December 1836 the allies were ready to ride. An allied force of Griqua, Kora, Rolong, Tlokwa and trekker commandos swept into Mosega wreaking havoc among the Matabele villagers. In October the following year another allied force struck as Mzilikazi was retreating northward and seized a huge swag of booty. By the end of the terrible year 1837 the Matabele king had lost upwards of 10,000 cattle and the equivalent of several regiments. At this point he decided to cut his losses and move his kingdom yet again somewhere his enemies could not strike him. Up until 1854 no one knew precisely where he had gone or even if he was alive.

Meanwhile, the Boers spread themselves in scattered farms and villages across the Highveld in loosely governed, self-proclaimed republics. All of them were engaged in more or less continual skirmishing warfare with their African neighbours. The British worried that turmoil beyond their frontiers would draw them into unforeseen and potentially very expensive military operations on the margins of their expanding South African dominion. In February 1848, Sir Harry Smith, High Commissioner for South Africa, announced the annexation of all the territory lying between the Orange and Limpopo Rivers – virtually all of the Highveld. At the same time he confirmed the Boer settlers in possession of their land titles and abrogated all the treaties the British had made with the Griqua and other chieftaincies beyond the Orange. Unsurprisingly, the Boers failed to appreciate Smith's generous gestures. After four tumultuous years of sporadic fighting and general turmoil, Britain had enough. Smith was recalled and the British handed back the Highveld, split into two republics: the Orange Free State south of the Vaal and the South African Republic or Transvaal to the north. Knowing nothing of the diamonds and gold lurking beneath the surface, the British government was glad to be rid of desolate, worthless, endlessly troublesome territories.

Directly and indirectly these turbulent decades cleared the Highveld of big game all the way to the Limpopo. Elephants, rhino, lions and many other species had been more or less wiped out from Cape Town to the Orange River by the end of the eighteenth century. In 1836 William Cornwallis Harris travelled hundreds of miles to Mzilikazi's capital at Mosega before he saw his first elephant in its wild habitat. Only when he pushed north of the Magaliesberg range did he find great herds in what he named a 'fairy land of sport'.[7] Twenty years later these too were gone. Some fell victim to dedicated hunters. In addition, many of the Boer settlers of 1836–7 supplemented their agricultural income by elephant shooting. Even more beasts were killed by Africans working to acquire trade goods and firearms for their chiefs.[8] In the year Selous arrived at the Cape, veteran missionary John MacKenzie summed up African bewilderment at the way frontier capitalism had transformed the Highveld. 'Who can understand the white man? First you clear off the elephants for the sake of the ivory, and the ostriches for their feathers; and when you have swept the country clean as to what is above ground, you then proceed to find treasures in the bowels of the earth.'[9]

Even the discovery of diamonds failed to enrich the Griqua. In a grotesque twist of fate, in 1861 Adam Kok III led hundreds of them off to a new home just west of the British colony of Natal. Most were glad to go because they had been cheated of their land titles by such sharp-dealing *Voortrekkers* as the De Beers family, on whose farm the great diamond bonanza was found a few years later. As their precious treaties with the British had all been trashed by Sir Harry Smith, their pleas for justice went unheard.

So, when Selous and Laing set off for Griquatown they were moving into a burnt-over region where beaten and fragmented communities clung precariously to dying ways of life. Fred regretted that his breech-loading double-barrelled Reilly rifle had been stolen at the diamond fields, but the truth was he was unlikely to meet anything worth shooting on this trip.

Turning a Profit

The choice of Griqualand and the Orange River as a destination was probably influenced by the guide Laing had engaged. W.J. Crossley had once held an important position as Secretary to Adam Kok's government at Philippolis. For whatever reason he had chosen not to join the great migration and had subsequently fallen on hard times. Selous found him full of good sense and information when sober, but otherwise a hopeless drunk. Without his services as guide and interpreter, they had little chance of turning a profit.

As he tells in his book, Selous had his first encounter with an African chief on the banks of the Vaal River on the 2 November 1871. The influential chief 'Manchuran'[10] rode up with about twenty of his followers and invited himself to dinner. The novice traders were shocked to hear the chief beg them for gifts of sugar, tea and coffee. Knowing nothing of his troubled history, or the traditions of hospitality in the region, Selous merely put it down to ill-breeding and bad manners. 'A Kafir', he wrote, 'will seldom miss a thing for want of asking for it.' The comment could well have been an afterthought inserted when he was preparing his book for publication. Either way it shows how easily the young Selous fell into the settler's habit of making generalizations about racial character based on a few personal experiences. The next day the boys reached a Tlhaping village and spread their wares out for sale before a discerning crowd of consumers who 'looked at everything and talked a great deal before they would buy anything'. Nonetheless, at the end of the day Fred and Arthur counted up 'about £4.16 into the till, making a profit of about a hundred per cent on what we sold'. The next page in his book purports to describe the dwellings of the villagers: 'Very clean, nice, and comfortable. They are divided into two compartments, whilst outside there is a sort of verandah and round the front of the house a yard very neatly enclosed, and plastered with cow dung.'

Comparing the book with his original journal reveals that this passage is actually lifted from an account of houses in a Tswana village he visited three months later.[11] It may very well be that the houses in

both places were built in a similar fashion, but the passage is significant for showing us the cut-and-paste method Selous would employ
when translating material from his journals into books. Though we
have nothing to go on after March of 1872 it seems fair to assume that
he took the same loose approach to the use of his notebook jottings
in later years. He treated the journal as a quarry of material, cutting
out bits which he later rearranged to suit his literary ends. He was not
punctilious about chronology or factual detail, except when it came to
recording specimens shot and collected.

At Campbell's-dorp and Griquatown the boys saw the tragic
history of the old LMS missions spread out before them: 'deserted
gardens and ruined cottages'. Once again Selous jumped to conclusions based on first impressions, blaming the poverty of the people on
their laziness. Only a handful of the remaining villagers hung on to
houses 'quite as comfortable as those of the lower class of Transvaal
Boers'.

On the fledgling traders tramped from farm to farm, buying stock
and ostrich feathers. As for hunting, 'one might almost as well look
for game in Hyde Park as in Griqualand'. Fred and Arthur celebrated
Christmas on the banks of the Orange River with a 'decent old Kafir,
Hendrick Kievet'. It was a moment both poignant and comical. For
the last seven weeks these young gentlemen had been masquerading
as simple peddlers of beads, blankets, pots and pans to a battered,
impoverished people. Neither Selous nor Laing had previously worked
for money. Their knowledge of local cultures was confined to racial
stereotypes picked up in casual conversations with white men they
had met. However, their very inexperience moved them to ignore the
conventions of a complex racial order they had barely begun to master,
and to share Christmas with Hendrick the farmer. Their festive
pudding was concocted from flour and eggs, topped by an improvised
sauce of chocolate, honey and milk. Hendrick 'was enchanted with the
pudding, declaring he had never tasted anything like it, and, judging
from the amount he stowed away, evidently thinking he never would
again'.

A few days later Selous marked his twentieth birthday (New Year's
Eve) on the north bank of the Orange. A little further west he saw the
devastation South African summer storms can wreak when lightning
struck a Koranna hut, killing two of the seven inhabitants. From that

moment he treated thunderstorms with the same respect he later showed to wounded lions and buffalo.

Having exhausted the trading possibilities on this stretch of the Orange, the young men turned their steps north toward Tswana villages in the Lange Berg range, the last stretch of inhabited territory before the springs of the Highveld gave way to the sands of the Kalahari. Thankfully, summer rains had spread a luxuriant carpet of grass across the hills. Once again Selous grabbed his gun and set out in search of antelope – and once again he came back empty-handed. The problem, as he saw it, was that 'the Kafirs having hunted everything into the far interior, [there was now] more game within five miles of Cape Town than here where we were, more than six hundred miles up country'.[12]

He might have guessed as much from his reading of Cornwallis Harris's *Wild Sports of Southern Africa*. Game had been scarce in these regions thirty-five years earlier. Ever-growing demand for African hides, horns and feathers had since pushed some species close to extinction. Every trade done by Selous and Laing put another nail in the coffin of the South African wild animal business.

While Selous scoured the desert sands for elusive game, Laing fell seriously ill, probably from dysentery. At the end of February 1872 they decided to wind up their affairs and head back to the diamond fields. To their considerable amazement, when all was totted up they had a clear profit of about £100, gained from trading with some of the most wretched people of South Africa. Sick of digging, sick of trading, and just plain sick, Laing headed back to England. Crossley headed for the tavern while Selous set out to find some real hunting. In five months he had bagged a total of one bushbuck ram, one duiker, one springbok, one klipspringer and eight roebucks. Not an encouraging start to his chosen career.

3

Lost on the Missionaries' Road

Back at the Kimberley diamond diggings, Fred set about preparing for a hunting expedition to the northern interior. He had already purchased oxen, a wagon and some horses when he happened to run into George Dorehill, a young man he had met on the ship to South Africa. Dorehill enthusiastically offered to join him, provided he could take another friend, T.V. Sadlier, a veteran of the recent American Civil War. The three knew how to shoot and ride, but next to nothing about lions, elephants or Matabeleland, their intended destination. The way, however, was easy enough to find. Historians know it as the Missionaries' Road because the route connected a chain of London Missionary Society posts running from the Orange River up into present-day Zimbabwe. Traders and hunters followed, including one of Fred Selous's heroes, William Cotton Oswell, who accompanied David Livingstone on his first substantial expedition of exploration to fabled Lake Ngami in 1849.

In April 1872, less than two months after his return from his apprentice trading journey, Selous was on the road west to Kuruman, the famous mission developed by Livingstone's father-in-law, Robert Moffat. Though it should have been a short journey, Fred's inexperience in African travel delayed his arrival because he let his horses run away and spent more than two weeks rounding them up. Kuruman was, he declared, 'by far the prettiest spot' he had yet seen in Africa. There he met an experienced hunter and trader named William Williams who gave the young men a great deal of information about Matabeleland and its rulers. Mzilikazi had not died after his defeat by the grand alliance of Boers, Griqua and Tswana at Mosega in 1837. He had gradually made his way north of the Limpopo River and established a new capital at Bulawayo, where Moffat renewed his friendship with the king in 1854 and secured permission to plant mission stations in his country. Soon the Missionaries' Road ran all the way to Victoria Falls on the Zambezi.

If Selous wished to hunt in Matabeleland he would need permission from the current ruler, Mzilikazi's son Lobengula, who had cemented his hold on the kingship by defeating the army of a rival claimant in 1870. The young king's power rested on the prowess of his warriors whom he used, like his father, to extract tribute and raid cattle from villages scattered over a wide swath of territory. Elephant hunting brought firearms to Matabeleland, adding a deadly new dimension to African warfare. By charging traders and hunters for the right to enter his territory Lobengula was gradually accumulating the firepower needed to ensure his success in future conflicts.

One reason why the Missionaries' Road took its course through the territory of Tswana chiefs was that the Boer republic of the Transvaal had been attempting for years to blockade the sale of firearms to Africans beyond its borders. The Boers believed, with some reason, that LMS missionaries condoned the arms trade. By travelling west of the Transvaal border on the Vaal and Limpopo Rivers, hunters and traders evaded the embargo. Not that the ban was ever very effective. Since the discovery of diamonds African workers at the mines had been using their wages to buy guns which no government could effectively prevent from reaching their chiefs.

Williams also gave Selous some useful advice on guns. As far as Williams was concerned the weapon of choice for Boer and African hunters was a smooth bore, muzzle-loading gun weighing a little over twelve pounds. The secret to its success was the size of its bore, which took a huge four-ounce ball driven by a ferocious charge of gunpowder. When he examined the model he bought from Williams for £6, Selous found it was 'a duck gun of the very commonest description' made by the English firm of Isaac Hollis in Birmingham. Before long he learnt that it had its drawbacks, but there was no doubting its capacity to bring down the biggest of big game.

44

Into Bechuanaland

Pushing the wagons forward on the sandy road from Kuruman proved hard going, but the countryside grew progressively more attractive – similar, thought Selous, to an English park. Twenty days on they arrived at the town of a prosperous Tswana chief, Montsua, who greeted them like any respectable Christian in European clothing, including top hat, collar and necktie. Another day's travel brought them to the town of Sechele, a chief whose influence extended all the way to Matabeleland, and whose fame had spread beyond Africa through the writings of David Livingstone. Detractors often comment disparagingly that this chief was Livingstone's 'only convert'. This reflects a profound misunderstanding about the way Christianity spread in southern Africa. Nowhere did the first European missionaries convert people *en masse*, or even in sizeable numbers. Typically they might preach for years before converting anyone other than their household servants. It was only when African evangelists began spreading the word in the language and idioms of their people that the groundwork was laid for large-scale adoption of the new religion. Livingstone's baptism of Sechele in 1848 was therefore a rare and hugely significant event. Robert Moffat witnessed the impact first-hand on his 1854 visit to Lobengula at Bulawayo, where he found black headmen conducting Sunday services and singing hymns.[1] It was not any European missionary but Sechele who had brought this about. Moffat did not think much of their Christian orthodoxy but had to acknowledge the power of the chief's teaching and example. Selous was impressed with his physical presence at the age of about fifty-five:

> to me, a stranger, he appeared to be a very pleasant old fellow. He was living in a large well-built house, over the dining-room table of which stood a handsome good-sized mirror; above the doorway was a large clock, while in the bedroom I caught a glimpse of a fine iron bedstead. We had tea with him, and I was surprised to see it served in a silver tea-pot and a handsome set of china tea-things. ... [He] appeared to me to be the most completely civilized Kafir that I had yet seen. I have since heard that although a most diligent student of the Old Testament (for he can read the Sechuana translation), he is not thought, by those who consider themselves capable of judging,

to be a particularly good and sound Christian. He was very anxious about Queen Victoria's health, and seemed much concerned to hear of the recent illness of the Prince of Wales.[2]

Sechele was a central figure in the development of the country that eventually became Botswana. His proselytizing and marriage into the family of Khama III helped make Protestant Christianity virtually the state religion. This in turn solidified an alliance with the British that protected his people from the designs of the Transvaal Boers, the Ndebele and Cecil Rhodes. Otherwise the country may have been absorbed into South Africa and suffered all the trials of the apartheid regime. Sechele was also a shrewd trader and diplomat. When Selous met him, he was nearly at the apogee of his influence.

By the end of June Selous and his friends had moved on to the town he called Bamangwato, better known in later years as Shoshong. The town and the surrounding region had been suffering huge upheavals during a three-way tussle for supreme power among the Ngwato branch of the Tswana people. Long-time chief Sekgoma had fallen out with his son Khama over the issue of Christianity, to which the old chief remained resolutely opposed. More recently a rival claimant to the paramount chieftaincy had emerged in the person of Matsheng, Sekgoma's uncle, who had grown up among Mzilikazi's people as a full-fledged Ndebele warrior. He was regarded by many as a stalking horse for Lobengula. Matsheng was temporarily in the ascendant when Selous made his first visit, but not for long. Khama outlasted and outmanoeuvred his relatives, emerging unchallenged as Khama III in 1875. Thanks to his leadership his line would reign as kings of all the territory the British called Bechuanaland and we now know as Botswana.

With upwards of 30,000 people Shoshong was by far the largest African town Selous had so far encountered. The Tswana people of the region prided themselves on their prowess as hunters. Archaeological and linguistic evidence confirms that hunting had been a favoured pursuit of Tswana men for centuries.[3] By the time Gordon Cumming came to hunt in the early 1840s, there was a well-established trade in ivory, skins, feathers and other high-value animal products. Like other early European ivory hunters, Cumming got far more ivory by trade than by his gun. In return the Tswana acquired wagons, tools, and firearms. Like Lobengula, Khama profited from the trade by requiring all hunters to seek his permission before trying their fortunes in his country; certain regions he reserved entirely for his compatriots.

By the time Selous arrived, Shoshong had become the main gathering place for European adventurers operating beyond colonial frontiers. There could be found congregated the most varied collection of white traders and hunters imaginable. Among their ranks, according to a visiting British major, might be found: an Oxford man and another from Cambridge 'drinking himself to death', wanted men from the Cape Colony, deserters from the British military, 'ruined gangsters from the diamond fields', and any number of habitual drunkards who only sobered up when hunting.[4]

Lost

By the time his party left Bamangwato in August 1872 Selous had gained a valuable addition, an experienced South African hunter named Frank Mandy. It was just as well, for at every turn the man who would one day be hailed as Africa's greatest hunter showed his inexperience and poor judgement. Back at the diamond fields he had lost an expensive rifle. On the way to Kuruman he lost his horses. A little later he lost his eyebrows and a good deal of skin while loading cartridges from a bag full of gunpowder. (George Dorehill leaned over to have a look and some embers from his pipe fell into the powder, which promptly exploded. Both were badly burned round the eyes, face and neck. Had Sadlier not remembered the Civil War soldier's trick of rubbing oil and salt on the wounds, both might have suffered permanent scars.) Then, a little way out of Bamangwato, Selous lost himself.

Frank Mandy had impressed upon him the importance of getting a 'salted horse', that is, one immunized against the pulmonary horse disease endemic to all but the highest altitudes of southern Africa. As all of his five horses were 'unsalted' and likely to die in the lowlands of Matabeleland, Fred had bought one at Bamangwato through a series of trades. Once again he failed to secure his horse properly and African trackers spent a week retrieving the errant beast. Meanwhile he and his friends looked for something to hunt. Five months on the Missionaries' Road and the intrepid hunters had little to show for their effort beside assorted antelope. No wonder they got over-excited by a troop of giraffes, the first that either Selous or Dorehill had seen in the wild. They spurred their horses with no thought for anything but the chase. Considering the near catastrophic consequences, what stood out most in Fred's memory was the beauty and grace of the giraffes in full flight:

> The giraffes, about twenty in number, came up wind, looking splendid, with their tails twisted up over their backs like corkscrews, and we at once galloped obliquely towards them, and managed to make up a good deal of ground. They have a most peculiar gait – a sort of gallop, their hind legs being straddled out at each step and coming (one on each side) in front of the fore legs. If you only look at their bodies and necks from behind, they appear to be sailing or gliding along without making any movement at all.[5]

With three riders in pursuit the fleeing giraffes hived off in several directions. Before long Selous found himself alone riding furiously through a scrubby forest. An instant later he had collided with a tree trunk and lay writhing on the ground with a badly injured leg.

The situation was not good. Giraffes gone; friends nowhere to be seen; location extremely uncertain. What was worse, equipment minimal. He, Dorehill and Mandy had left Sadlier in charge of the wagons and had ridden off after a hastily gulped cup of coffee. He carried no food, no water and no blanket to shield him from the bitter cold of a wintry night in desolate country. On one of his popular television series, *Escape from Hell*, modern-day adventurer Bear Grylls reckons there is scant likelihood of surviving four nights in such a situation, even for experienced outdoorsmen. Selous had little more to fall back on than his 'strong constitution' and indomitable spirit.

He also had a gun and six cartridges. He fired off one cartridge and heard a shot in reply. Riding in the direction of the sound brought no results, so he fired another shot, and a third. This time there was no response. His next thought was to find the main wagon track, which surely could not be far away. With the setting sun as his guide he rode steadily in what he hoped was the right direction and continued on by moonlight, until his faltering horse could go no further. A fire would help him through the night. Having no matches, he improvised a spark by rubbing some powder from a cartridge into a bit of torn shirt and pushed it into the gun barrel. Then he used the remaining powder to charge a shot. As he hoped the cloth ignited, but try as he would he could not coax a heap of dry grass and twigs into a flame. Repeating the experiment merely wasted his remaining cartridges. Now, he had no hope of shooting something to eat.

After a shivery night he remounted his poor horse and resumed his search for the wagon road. In an effort to get a better idea of the country he climbed a small hill and surveyed the wide horizon. On all sides lay a vast and undifferentiated ocean of forest, with no particular landmark to guide his steps. A momentary wisp of smoke suggested human habitation but it had disappeared by the time he reached the place he imagined a fire had burnt. He became increasingly preoccupied by the thought that he had failed to see the wagon track in the moonlight and had inadvertently crossed it. In that case he had better retrace his steps. The rest of the day was spent going backwards. Changing course again, he turned his horse toward the setting sun until night fell. Hoping the animal might find some relief from thirst by grazing, Fred did not tie him to a tree. Instead he devised a hobble that would allow the beast a little movement while he slept on a hastily devised bed of dry grass. Again he passed a night of bitter cold. When he awoke his horse had gone, having dragged the hobble in a frantic search for water. To his unpractised eye the spoor was too faint to follow. Besides, who could say how long the horse had been on the move?

Having hung his saddle on a tree, he shouldered his gun and made for a distant line of hills he fancied might be the range above the town of Bamangwato. His face burned from the sun and his parched throat ached beyond endurance. Mechanically placing one foot before the other, he trudged the whole day until he gained the summit. Instead of the maize fields of Bamangwato nothing met his eye but succeeding low stony ranges stretching out as far as he could see. Gazing at the stars from his bed of rocks he reflected that if he was going to die, as it seemed he surely would, he did not want to die 'like a rat in a hole'.

Next morning he again scanned the horizon. This time something caught his eye. A small detached hill – or, as the Boers would say, *kopje* – could faintly be seen in the middle distance. From its position relative to other hills, he felt sure it was one he had marked out as a distinctive feature of the landscape a few days earlier. If he was right he would find water there. Towards this new goal he now directed his weary feet. A little before sundown he stumbled upon two Tswana hunters and followed them to their cattle *kraal*. He knew too little of their language to send a message to his friends but by gestures succeeded in trading a knife for a calabash of goat's milk and a little meat. That night he lay down gratefully by a large fire. Another twenty-five miles' march brought him once again into the company of his friends. They of course had practically given him up for dead. The Bushmen they had employed to follow his track had returned with a cock-and-bull story about finding the hoof marks of his horse headed in the direction of Bamangwato.

Would he have made it through another night without water? Maybe, maybe not. 'Africa's greatest hunter' could quite easily have died before his career had even begun. As it was, Selous took away some crucial lessons about survival in Africa. Don't ride off without the supplies you will need to pass a night in the open. Keep track of your position, your animals and your companions. The most valuable commodity beyond the frontiers of civilization is African knowledge about the country. Learn the local languages or engage good interpreters. Expect to pay for African knowledge; like any other valuable commodity in the country it has a price. As for himself, Selous had been tested like never before in his richly cossetted life in England. His greatest gift, he reflected, was his rugged constitution; his most conspicuous talent, tenacity in the face of adversity.

4

In the Kingdom of the Great Black Elephant

Over the next few days Selous saw his first lions in the open. A shot in the direction of two females roused an impressively maned male who stood staring for a few seconds while Fred struggled to reload. Before he could get off a shot, all three had trotted away. A promising pursuit of giraffe ended abruptly when Frank Mandy fell from his horse. Determined to avoid a repetition of the last giraffe hunt, Selous gave up the chase. Only ten or possibly twelve weeks remained before the end of the hunting season and he had nothing to show for his time, effort or money.

A few more days on the road north brought them to the Tati gold fields near what is now the modern city of Francistown, Botswana. The discovery of gold here in 1865 provoked the nearest thing to a rush yet seen in southern Africa. More precisely, it was the *re*discovery of gold in a region where Africans had mined for centuries. At Tati prospectors dislodged a large rock and found it had been used in times past to block the entrance to a shaft cut a hundred feet or so down into gold-bearing quartz. For a thousand years and more, African miners had been extracting small amounts of gold from similar mines across the Zimbabwe plateau and trading it down to the East African coast for goods made as far away as India and China. Faced with the evidence of the old shaft, Selous made the correct deduction that the ancestors of local Africans had sunk this mine. In later years a great deal of mental energy was spent trying to prove that a lost race of white people were responsible. Perhaps these were the mines that made the Bible's King Solomon rich. Selous hypothesized that it was the Shona people who dug at Tati: 'a wonderful work for the Mashuna, but there is no one else to whom to attribute it'.[1] A little later he found more evidence for his theory at the site of an African furnace used to smelt ore from quartz rocks.

White miners were not making much headway at Tati. Getting gold from quartzite reefs required heavy equipment to crush and treat the ore. With the nearest railway more than a thousand miles away, machinery had to be dragged in by ox wagons. Another problem was that the reef did not appear to run very far in any direction. A syndicate formed to exploit the mine struggled on for a few more years and then collapsed. Nonetheless, there was now something more than ivory to excite the lust of European adventurers. Every year there were more missionaries, traders, hunters and prospectors. Mzilikazi had led his people to a place so deeply buried in central Africa that his safety was assured for the next thirty years. Now his son and heir, Lobengula, found the kingdom once more exposed to marauders. His response to the threat was to make sure all the roads to the interior ran through his well-fortified capital Bulawayo. Without his permission no one could safely hunt, trade or search for gold within his sphere of influence.

After leaving Tati at the end of August 1872 the young men passed through country which, Selous reflected ruefully, had until 'very recently' been 'one of the best hunting-grounds for elephants in South Africa'. Now they had all moved away to the distant low-lying country where hunters seldom ventured. Fred seemed destined to be always just a little too late. After sending messengers ahead at the Matabele outpost of Minyama's *kraal*, he and his friends rode on to Bulawayo. The further he advanced into Lobengula's realm the more Selous was struck by the beauty of the young women:

> The Matabele girls we saw were very pleasant to the eye, having most good-tempered-looking faces, and fine, upright, well-developed, dark chocolate-coloured figures, the naked beauty of which was but little hidden by their very scanty attire, which in some cases consisted of a small flap of goat or antelope skin in front and another behind, and in others of a little fringe of 'umbentla' (a soft fibre extracted from a kind of grass) in front, and nothing at all behind.[2]

Among the hunters he met was George 'Elephant' Phillips, a giant of a man who would become a lifelong friend. After eight years in the country, he spoke the language well and offered his services as interpreter for Selous's memorable first interview with Lobengula. It must have been a tense moment for Fred, standing before an African king whose prowess had already been tested in the battles for succession and the name of whose capital meant 'place of slaughter'. Unfortunately, no photographic portraits survive. Accounts of Lobengula's age vary, likewise his stature. He was anywhere between the ages of thirty-five and forty-five at this time, and stood something between 5 ft 10 in and 6 ft 4 in.[3] All agree that he carried his considerable girth with royal dignity.

Lobengula sauntered down to the hunter's wagon dressed in a greasy shirt and dirty trousers. On being told that Selous wished to hunt for elephants, the king burst out laughing, 'Why you're only a boy.' He would be better advised to chase after steinbucks and other such small game. After a few more remarks in the same vein Lobengula moved away, followed by his admiring retinue. 'How, how' they cried approvingly, 'oh thou prince of princes, thou black elephant.'.

When Selous renewed his request, Lobengula sarcastically asked whether he had ever seen an elephant. No? Then he would most likely be chased out of the country. And where might he hunt? 'Oh, you may go wherever you like; you are only a boy.'

The country lay open before him, but where to hunt and with whom? His friend Dorehill had gone off on a trading expedition with a former official of the Transvaal, so he was out. Selous and Sadlier were on the verge of trying their luck alone when they ran into an African hunting legend. As a youth Jan Viljoen had joined the great Boer trek out of the Cape Colony and in 1848 fought the British at the Battle of Boomplaats. Later, when the game abounded, he had carved out a career as an elephant hunter. Now over sixty, he was still a marvel of spry toughness. After the Boer fashion his family followed a semi-nomadic existence, living out of their ox wagons and moving with the seasons. An invitation to hunt with Jan and his sons was not a chance to be missed.

With his now accustomed bad luck, Selous did miss it. The day before the party was to set off from the Viljoen encampment at Gwenia Fred cut his foot so badly as to make walking impossible for at least a week. That would not matter so much had he been hunting on horseback, but Viljoen planned to hunt on foot in 'the fly', i.e. country infested by the tsetse fly, the bite of which was fatal to horses and oxen.

Selous's career in Africa revolved around disease, both human and animal. Endemic sickness in horses, as we have seen, precluded their use below a certain altitude in southern Africa. They, and almost all other domesticated animals introduced to Africa during the last three millennia, could not survive in regions infested by the tsetse fly. Malaria and other mosquito-borne diseases existed in virulent forms that killed a large percentage of newcomers who, like Selous, had not acquired resistance in childhood. The precise causes of these diseases remained a mystery until the turn of the twentieth century. David Livingstone guessed that oxen died from the bite of the tsetse, but not until 1895 did researchers identify the deadly trypanosome carried by the flies. Quinine had been used as a prophylactic against malaria since the eighteenth century, but its use did not become common among European travellers in Africa until after the Niger Expedition of 1854 and Livingstone's personal experiments proved the efficacy of various quinine compounds. Even then the role of the mosquito in the transmission of the disease was not scientifically confirmed until the decisive laboratory work of Ronald Ross in 1897. Previously, the fevers were attributed, as the name malaria implies, to 'bad air' or miasma rising from swamps. Personally, Selous inclined to the theory that a 'strong constitution' warded off or delayed the onset of disease. He observed that some oxen only died after several bites and he assumed they must be the stronger ones. Donkeys he thought less susceptible to trypanosomiasis than either horses or oxen. And when put to the test himself, he attributed survival to his own strong constitution (toughened by Rugby School) and a healthy lifestyle.

Of course, trial and error found ways of dealing with these threats. Africans chose fly-free places to graze their cattle. European hunters avoided swampy terrain and moved to higher ground during the rainy season. Elephants and other large mammals with inherited resistance to trypanosomiasis moved to low-lying wetlands which humans avoided. Thus, by the time Selous arrived on the scene, there were few elephants on the high ground but plenty in the malarial tsetse-ridden regions. Jan Viljoen and Sadlier went on foot because neither horses nor oxen could travel safely where they were headed. Because it was near the end of the cool, dry season mosquitoes were less prevalent.

Meanwhile, Selous made himself useful by driving a wagon to a distant village to purchase supplies of sorghum and rice. On the way he chanced upon another celebrated Boer hunter, Piet Jacobs, who had 'probably shot more lions than any man who ever lived'. Eight days earlier, his luck had run out. In an attempt to kill a lion that was threatening his horses, 'this old Nimrod' got horribly mauled and his life hung in the balance. Amazingly, he survived to hunt another day. More amazing was the way Selous related the story, which he heard second-hand in the Afrikaans language. Though he had yet to tangle with a lion of any description, he wrote as though he witnessed the whole drama. Old Piet was reclining in the shade of his wagon when his daughter-in-law noticed a pig down by the water. 'That's no pig, my child; it's a lion stalking the horses.' He 'seized his rifle and, followed by three splendid dogs, ran down to drive the marauder away'. He fired one shot, missed, and hurried to reload. In the meantime the dogs held the lion at bay atop a low stone outcrop. There 'the tawny monster' lay, 'flat and motionless on top of a great stone, its head couched on its outstretched paws, whilst the dogs were barking furiously below, and endeavouring to jump on to the rock. As soon as the lion saw its new adversary, it sprang from the stone and, hotly pursued by the dogs, charged straight for him at full speed.' Piet had just enough time to get off another shot, which 'must have missed, for the furious brute, with open mouth and glaring eyes, rushed upon him and, seizing him by the thigh, threw him to the ground'.

As it was not his habit to make verbatim notes of conversations in his journal, Selous must have concocted all of this out of his own memory of the wounded man's ravings and a large dose of his own imagination. Readers praised him for his powers of observation and plain speaking, yet he put his first hunting tale together like an accomplished novelist. It should be borne in mind that, up to this point, he had seen a total of three lions, and those only for a few moments. Somehow, from his reading of novelists like Dickens and Thackeray, and travellers such as Gordon Cumming and Livingstone, Selous acquired the knack of spinning an exciting yarn.

He was not yet a big game hunter, but he already knew how to be a big game writer.

Into 'the Fly' with Cigar

On his return trip with a wagonload of supplies Selous stopped briefly at an encampment of Griqua wagons where he met a most engaging character known in hunting circles as Cigar the Hottentot. More racially prejudiced white men knew him as Cigar the 'half-caste scoundrel'. By this time the words 'Griqua' and 'Hottentot' had lost whatever specific ethnic and historical meaning they had possessed in the eighteenth and early nineteenth century. They were used in casual conversation to denote Afrikaans-speaking mixed-race people from the Cape Colony. Before taking up elephant hunting Cigar had been a racehorse jockey in the city of Grahamstown, a job for which his short, wiry frame eminently suited him. He was disappointed to hear that Fred planned to shoot with Viljoen, for he would have loved to introduce him to the business. For his part Fred marvelled at Cigar's endless fund of colourful hunting stories. When the Viljoen party failed to show up at Gwenia on the appointed day, Fred straightaway let Cigar know he would be delighted to venture under his guidance into 'the fly'.

Selous's maps and writings do not pinpoint the location of their hunt, but it cannot have been far from the modern town of Kwekwe. From here they travelled north to where the Sebakwe River valley drops down among plentiful forests. Going into the tsetse-infested region on foot meant travelling light. Cigar was accompanied by two specialist marksmen and three other Africans who carried blankets, powder and food supplies of sorghum meal and meat. Fred left two of his 'boys' behind to look after his horses and oxen, taking only a single porter who carried his blankets and spare ammunition. He carried his own elephant gun and a pouch holding twenty of the required four-ounce balls.

Success came quickly. They shot and dined upon a big eland bull the first night out and next morning pushed into country recently ravished by elephants. Among the broken trees and trampled ground they picked up a fresh spoor which Cigar recognized as that of an old bull. To his evident delight Fred spotted him first, his huge head towering above the thick bush, while his ears flapped gently to and fro. He was clearly unaware of their presence, which gave them time to prepare for a chase. They slipped off their trousers and ventured out clad only in long flannel shirts, underwear and boots. They advanced to within fifty yards before the bull, sensing the threat, wheeled to face them. Cigar gallantly whispered to Fred to take the first shot, which he directed at the shoulder. With a roar the elephant plunged into the thickets. Fearing that he might lose the trail, Selous ran after him without even taking time to reload. When Cigar managed another hit, the great beast turned upon them, just as Fred was recharging his muzzle-loader. His second shot to the shoulder brought the bull crashing down. Cigar administered the *coup de grace.*

Selous's first elephant was a whopper, with tusks weighing a total of more than 118 lb. Because Cigar had given him the first shot and he had brought it down, the hunters' code decreed the ivory was his. That night he helped slice and roast the enormous heart – 22 lb or so – which he henceforth esteemed as the 'greatest delicacy an African hunter is likely to enjoy'.

Their luck held next day when they came upon a big herd after a long trek under a blazing sun. Once again Cigar allowed his young apprentice to take the first shot, which pierced the heart of a young bull. After killing another and wounding a third, Fred lay panting on the ground while the more experienced shooters continued the slaughter. By day's end Cigar had felled four elephants, and his assistants, two more.

Wednesday, Thursday, Friday, Saturday, Sunday – the hunt continued with such success that they reached the limit of the ivory they could carry back to the wagons. Selous had learned a great deal. In 'the fly', game was as plentiful as it was scarce in the rest of the country. His naturalist's eye drank in teeming wildlife of all description: antelope, zebras, buffalo, hippos and rhinoceros. One of his party, evidently not him, came away with a horn of the increasingly rare white rhinoceros. Whatever the risks, Selous would head to 'the fly' in future hunts. He now had a pretty good idea of the requirements. Fitness mattered first and foremost in chasing down elephants on foot. He would have to trudge long distances to find them and then be prepared to run hard in pursuit of wounded beasts. Cooperation and congenial companions mattered too; the more eyes on the lookout, the better. Cigar's party of six was probably the bare minimum. There was no point getting more ivory than the porters could carry. Lacking the wealth of Cornwallis Harris, Selous could not afford to shoot for sport and leave the tusks to rot. Mutual trust was essential. Behaving like racist white farmers could be fatal on a hunt in 'the fly'. Cigar gave Fred the benefit of his knowledge and allowed him the first shot at a standing elephant because Fred treated him with respect. Servants could not be abused or they might make off at night with the ivory. However hot and bloody the work, elephant hunting carried Fred to a height of exhilaration he had never known. When he found the main Griqua camp had run out of ammunition and other essentials he drove his oxen day and night to restock in Bulawayo. Ten days later he was back and itching to go.

He found his friend Sadlier totally disenchanted with Jan Viljoen's hunt. The Boers, he said, had unfairly claimed as their own elephants which *he* had hit with the first shot. So disgusted was he that he vowed not to hunt again and left the country. Doubly pleased with his own choice, on 2 November 1872 Fred walked back into 'the fly' with Cigar.

Luck seemed to follow the little man wherever he went. On their first afternoon on the trail they struck a herd of ten bulls, two of which fell to Fred. More followed, so after another trip back to the wagons, Cigar and Selous decided to venture once more into 'the fly'. This time they stayed out for a month, a somewhat dubious decision because the rainy season set in with a vengeance. Dry creeks became rivers; dry pans became lakes. Insect life awoke and Selous spent most nights soaking wet under a makeshift shelter. Worse, the game became scarce. Late in December he and Cigar conceded defeat, hauled their load of tusks back to the wagon and started on the long road back to Bulawayo. Before his twenty-first birthday on New Year's Eve he had cleared his debts and made a profit of £300. In addition to 450 lb of ivory from elephants killed by his gun, he disposed of another 1,200 lb acquired by trading. The relative figures give some idea of the social composition of the ivory business. As an Englishman he had access to credit, wagons and oxen. These enabled him to bargain for ivory with the Africans, who were doing most of the killing but lacked the where-withal to get their tusks to market.

Selous presented his only surviving horse to Lobengula as the fee for hunting in Matabele country. Not only, he said, had he not been driven out of the country by elephants, he killed quite a few of them. 'Well then', the king replied, 'now you are a man'. That part of the story Selous would go on recounting in lectures and interviews for decades to come. However, the rest of the conversation appears only in the first edition of his book, *A Hunter's Wanderings*: "'Why, you're a man; when are you going to take a wife?' Upon my telling him that if he would give me one I would take her at once, he said, "Oh! you must *combeesa*[4] [court one] yourself; there are lots of them."'

That fact had not failed to register with the boy just come to manhood.

5

Elephants Galore

Before finally breaking camp with Cigar, Selous had the luck to run into another veteran hunter/trader, George Wood. He was about the only one of the old coterie of British hunters left in the region. Others had given up the ivory business or moved north when the big game moved into 'the fly', mainly because they lacked either the will or stamina to hunt on foot. Wood had just returned from an expedition with Fred's friend Frank Mandy and pulled up his wagons only a few miles from the main Griqua encampment. Among the curiosities they brought from Mashonaland were a few quills of alluvial gold panned from a sandy northern river.

A quill of gold was just that; a measure of gold dust carried in a hollow quill cut from the feather of a large bird. Spanish traders had employed it since the days of Cortez and it was still in use in Portuguese Mozambique.[1] Unlike the quartzite reef at Tati, this kind of gold might be worked cheaply by individual prospectors. Where there was dust there might be nuggets, and where there were nuggets there might be a mother lode. Such speculation could easily set off something like the Californian rush of 1849 or the Australian rush of 1854. Selous and Cigar learnt about the gold when Wood joined them for dinner at their camp. And although Selous does not mention it, that little get-together threw Bulawayo into a panic.

As told to an English traveller in 1875, Cigar informed Lobengula of Wood's find, commenting that now that the English knew where to get gold, 'an army of white men would soon come and take their country from them'.[2] The king ordered all the resident white traders confined to their wagons, while he investigated the truth of the rumour. When two months passed without the arrival of any army, Lobengula concluded that Cigar had lied, whereupon Cigar promptly cleared out of Matabeleland.

The whites blamed 'the half-caste scoundrel' for spreading wild rumours in the hope of gaining some mineral concession of his own but, viewed from the longer perspective of southern African history, Cigar was justified in raising the alarm. Back in 1832 a man named Jacob Msimbiti had related a similar prophecy to Dingane, King of the Zulu. In his Xhosa homeland on the Eastern frontier of the Cape Colony, Jacob had seen how colonialism nibbled away at African independence. First the English would ask for a grant of land; then they would erect a building on it; a little later they would begin subduing the nation with their witchcraft and firearms. Kings would die and the people would groan under the colonial yoke.[3] Cigar had seen the results himself in Grahamstown, which stood on conquered land. He and his fellow Griqua hunters had seen the same scenario played out when diamonds were discovered. The country once promised to them by treaties with the British Crown meant nothing. An army of diggers arrived and their country was lost to them. In the course of time all the prophecies of conquest came true. Lobengula would lose his country to an army of settlers guided by Frederick Courteney Selous, but only after another twenty years had elapsed.

The gold scare probably accounts for Lobengula's refusal to let Selous hunt with Wood in Mashonaland. Instead they would have to try their luck in 'the fly', i.e. the tsetse-infested country south of Victoria Falls and even then they were not allowed to leave until the middle of June.

The situation of Mashonaland was at that time indeterminate. The Portuguese in Mozambique claimed it on the basis of sixteenth-century expeditions to the interior. The government of the Transvaal expected it might one day fall into their hands, owing to the number of Boer trekkers who had established semi-permanent farms and camps in the country. Selous's enquiries could not discover the derivation of the term 'Mashona'. He believed it to be a word recently coined to describe politically fragmented people with a common language and cultural practices who had dominated the central plateau before the arrival of Mzilikazi. As far as Selous was concerned, Mashonaland comprised

the whole region lying between Matabeleland and the eastern mountains which today form the border of Zimbabwe and Mozambique.
Lobengula frequently conducted raids for cattle and tribute into this
region but did not subject it to the centralized and hierarchical form of
government imposed on his own people. Selous frequently complained
of Matabele atrocities committed on the Shona. On the other hand,
he could not help but admire the ceremonial colour and splendour of
Lobengula's court, as displayed at the annual *inxwala* festival of the
first fruits, which he saw for the first time in 1873.

George Wood had limped into Bulawayo in January, laid low with
malaria: the price he paid for hunting in 'the fly'. After his recovery
he and Selous made the best of the rainy season by dragging their
wagons from village to village, meeting local headmen, trading for
ivory. In February they returned to Bulawayo for the *inxwala*. There
was nothing to compare with it. Four thousand male warriors turned
out in ostrich feather capes and headdresses. They bound round their
waists the skins of leopards, civet cats and monkeys. This costume
Fred thought enough to make even an 'undersized ugly savage look
well', and:

> as the greater part of the Matabele are physically a fine tall race
> of men, they look magnificent, and when standing in a semicircle
> round their king, with their large ox-hide shields in front of them,
> must present, I should think, as imposing a spectacle as any race of
> savages in the world.[4]

Then there were the maidens, bare-breasted with short calico skirts –
'the prettiest, if not the most imposing, part' of the festival.

The *inxwala* continued for three days in a dance marathon that
tested the endurance of the strongest men. Indeed, for the Matabele,
the Zulu and other southern Bantu kingdoms, dancing was the principal form of fitness training, with competitions held throughout
the year. On the last day they took turns bounding into the central
circle, each showing with spear thrusts, leaps and twirls how they had
despatched enemies to the underworld. Finally the king took the stage.
No greasy shirt and dirty trousers this time, but clad as a warrior
among warriors. As he rushed forward to hurl his *assegai* repeatedly
to the heavens, his men beat their leathern shields with the butt end of

their spears, 'producing a noise literally like thunder'. Fred Selous was no ethnographer, but he came away profoundly moved.

Impatient for the elephant country, he and Wood set out at last in June on the track north-west toward Victoria Falls. They built a strong campsite with fortified cattle enclosures on the margins of the tsetse country, from which they ventured out in periodic tramps into the Gwai River valley, which runs north to the Zambezi. Even in the twenty-first century this remains the realm of 'the fly', which is why elephants are still found in large numbers in Hwange and other national parks of the district.

In the course of the next four months, armed only with his 4-bore muzzle-loading elephant guns, Selous shot forty-two elephants, of which eleven were 'tuskers' – big bulls whose tusks averaged 44 lb apiece. Wood came away with fifty, while their Matabele assistants downed forty more. As in his previous hunts with Cigar, success required a good understanding among all the members of the party. After four months Fred found that he could speak the Matabele language 'tolerably well'.

For two of the four months, Selous and Wood split up, indicating how much Fred had grown in confidence. They also adopted different strategies of hunting. Selous was keen that every elephant at which he had the first shot was credited to his bag. Like the butterfly chaser he had been as a boy, he kept a precise record of what he shot, how big were the tusks, the height of the elephant and every other particular that seemed relevant. Wood, on the other hand, 'who had probably shot more elephants than any man alive', let his Matabele shooters fire at will and at random, caring only for the total amount of ivory he took away.

The procedure for each hunt was the same. They chopped out the tusks with American axes and then buried them deep enough to deter hyenas and other scavengers. The heart and other choice bits of meat were sliced, seasoned with salt and pepper, then roasted over the fire and consumed in enormous quantities. When they had as much ivory as they could carry, they would retrace their steps, dig up the ivory and head back to the wagons. Selous evidently took enough notes to enable him to write up his adventures at some future date, most likely, he imagined, for *The Field*, the magazine for gentleman sportsmen he had been reading since his Rugby days.

He particularly relished the memories of dangerous encounters and disasters. On one blood-chilling occasion, as he and his men rushed in for the kill, one of them missed the elephant and put a four-ounce ball through the chest of his mate, Mendose. Another time Fred ran for what seemed endless miles in pursuit of a beast he could hit but was seemingly unable to kill. After each shot, he threw one of his weapons to Balamoya his gun-carrier and plunged ahead with the other. After one cap misfired the gun was unwittingly given another charge, so that when he eventually got off a shot, he was thrown violently backwards by the recoil caused by the double dose of gunpowder. In the process, the butt of his gun struck him under the cheekbone, inflicting a scar he carried for the rest of his life. Shaken by the recoil of the elephant gun, he resolved to buy a less dangerous weapon when he got the chance.

At the end of November 1873 Selous and Wood yoked their oxen and drove the wagons back to Bulawayo carrying more than 5,000 lb of high-quality ivory. Once again they spent the rainy summer season trading, including an ox wagon trek in March down to Tati in company with two young Scots, James Fairbairn and James Dawson, who carried two cartloads of ivory acquired through trade with Lobengula. This underlines the point that extermination of elephants was an interracial, intertribal, international enterprise. White hunters contributed a very small part of the total human effort expended in delivering piano keys to Victorian drawing rooms.

We can only guess at the nature of Fred's life during his Matabele trading expeditions, for he says virtually nothing about it. For example, from December 1872 until the middle of June 1873 we know nothing of his doings apart from his attendance at the *inxwala*. The same goes for other rainy seasons. It is impossible to say where he and Wood got their trade goods and what profit they made. He implies that they dealt with headmen at various Matabele villages, but says nothing about the negotiations involved. He knew and got on well with the whole community of white trader/hunters whose drunken revels in the offseason were notorious, as were their liaisons with African women. To what extent did he join in the debauchery? In later life he avoided alcohol altogether, but he may have moved gradually toward the temperance habit. His pointed comments on the young Matabele women suggest that he was unlikely to resist temptation. Any relationship would have to be carefully negotiated because patriarchal protectors closely guarded the chastity of both married and unmarried women. An open affair would be treated no differently from marriage, which required a presentation of cattle, usually to the father. But here, too, we can only guess.

At Tati in March 1874 Selous met two gentlemen tourists, J.L. Garden and his soldier brother, who intended to visit Victoria Falls and do some hunting in the vicinity. They gladly agreed to team up with more experienced hands, so it was a sizeable expedition that moved out in early May – five wagons in all plus a large African staff. The established track ran to the west of Matabeleland. After a month on the road they built a fortified base camp at the Deka River, about sixty miles south of the Falls. From here on, they found elephants aplenty. For the first time Selous had engaged Bushmen trackers whom he knew by the colourful names of Arotsy, Hellhound and Hartebeest. In their company he speedily repented of his early opinion that they were the lowest of primitive men. They possessed extraordinary powers of observation and an encyclopaedic knowledge of flora and fauna. These particular Bushmen of Khama's country were known as Masarwa (a term that nowadays has derogatory connotations for people who would rather be called San). So far as Selous could determine, they were the result of intermarriage and intermixing among several different groups.[5] Although their language was closely related to that spoken by the San people of South Africa, their taller stature and close association with the Tswana indicated that some of their ancestors were Tswana who had taken up life in the arid regions as a result of cattle and other hardships.

Selous's thoughts on first viewing Victoria Falls were commonplace: 'How I wish I could give you some idea of their wonderful grandeur and beauty! But the task is far beyond me.'[6] He did much better in writing up the elephant hunting that followed. After a week at the Falls he decided to push westward along the Zambezi with the Garden brothers, while Wood insisted on returning to the scene of the previous year's fabulous hunting on the Gwai. This trip took Selous into the territory that now makes up the Chobe and Okavango national parks of Botswana. Although plagued by tsetse and mosquitoes he found this stretch of the Zambezi River valley perfectly enchanting. Wherever he went villagers welcomed him because of the prospect of fresh meat from the animals he shot. He was glad enough to buy safety, guidance and friendship with his gun in regions where people had not seen a white man since Dr Livingstone.

One among the many hunting stories from this trip which he included in *A Hunter's Wanderings in Africa* (1881) gives an insight into his technique of constructing compelling narratives from the briefest of diary jottings:

> Monday, August 24. Shot two elephant cows
> Tuesday. Went to chop out the tusks of the two elephants but found that one had got up in the night and gone off.

From this slender entry he wrote up at a much later date a story full of colour and adventure. Footprints by the river told him that elephants had come to drink the previous night. Although it was late in the day, he set off with Hellhound and Arotsy to look for fresh spoor. They had barely gone half a mile before they came across four good-sized females along with their infants. 'As I looked at them, trying to pick out the best, a little calf kept endeavouring to insert its head between its mother's forelegs and get at her breasts.' He shattered this scene of domestic tranquillity with a shot to the chest of the finest elephant, who let out a mighty roar, plunged into the forest and ran about a hundred yards before falling dead from a bullet straight through the heart. A second shot brought another cow to the ground, 'with all four legs sprawled out like a spread eagle'. However, she soon picked herself up and sped off, 'head raised and tail carried straight in the air'. Running out sideways I gave her another bullet just behind the ribs, which only seemed to accelerate her pace.' During a long chase through deep sand under a hot sun he managed to hit her twice more in the flanks before administering what should have been the final blow with a side-on shot to the shoulder. Down she crashed, though she continued to struggle. To make sure, Fred put 'the muzzle of the gun between her ears, within six inches of her head, and fired, on which she lay perfectly still'. Arotsy was on the point of cutting off the tail when Hellhound saw that she continued to gulp for air. Taking up the gun again Selous put yet another ball in the back of her skull. 'This time I placed the muzzle within an inch of the skin, and the smoke from the powder came curling out of the hole in a thin blue wreath.' Certain of her death, he doubled back to cut meat for dinner from the first elephant, and went to sleep well satisfied with the day's bag. Returning next morning to the gruesome killing ground, he found to his horror not the 'bulky carcass and long white tusks' he expected but only the impress of the elephant's form on the bloodied sand. 'Though I could scarcely believe my eyes, the fact remained. The elephant, after having received five four-ounce bullets in the body, and two in the back of the head, had got up in the night and gone off! Truth is stranger than fiction, it is said, and certainly this anecdote of mine is very strange, and yet absolutely true in every detail.'

True in every detail? Sceptics – knowing the tricks memory plays – may well raise their eyebrows. Moreover, most modern readers will instinctively recoil from the scene of butchery, made all the more appalling by the self-possessed lucidity with which Selous recounts it. A great deal more in the same vein is served up in the hunter's narrative of this, his first foray to the Zambezi. Another arresting passage describes a literal bloodbath:

> The huge carcass, or rather what remained of it, lay on one side, as it had fallen, with the legs extended. Behind the ribs and just over the belly the Kafirs had peeled off a large slab of skin, about three feet square, and through the trap-door thus formed dragged out the stomach and intestines; they had also cut out the heart, liver, and lungs, so that what was left was merely a hollow shell, in the lower half of which the blood had formed a pool a foot deep. Into this cavity they and the Bushmen now kept entering by twos, disappearing entirely from sight, searching eagerly for small pieces of fat along the backbone and about the kidneys, and bathing in and smearing themselves all over with the blood. This is a common practice amongst all the natives in the interior of Africa whenever large game, such as elephants or rhinoceroses, are killed, particularly if they happen to be the first of the season.[7]

A third example from the Zambezi expedition appears in Selous's first book under the heading, 'A PLUCKY ELEPHANT CALF'. Running hard through the bush, he got close enough to:

> give the best cow I could see a ball on the hip. She at once left the herd, and followed by a good-sized calf, started off at a long swinging

walk, that gave me all my work to keep up with. Another shot from behind, however, slackened her pace considerably, and enabled me to pass her and give her a third shot in the shoulder. This I at once saw was a mortal wound, for the poor beast commenced to throw large quantities of blood from her trunk; after standing under a tree for a short time, her limbs began to tremble, then she made a few steps backwards, and sinking on to her haunches, threw her trunk high in air, and rolled over on her side stone dead.[8]

Selous then describes what happened with the calf:

which was quite large enough to pound one to a jelly, and had teeth protruding six inches beyond the lip, was now beside himself with rage, and with ears extended, and trumpeting loudly, charged viciously at any one who approached within fifty yards of his dead mother. Once I let him come on to close quarters, and then dashing a heavy *assegai* into his face, sprang past him at the same time. This feat, which after all required nothing but a little presence of mind and judgement, seemed greatly to astonish the Kaffirs, who declared that 'to-day have we seen that the white man's heart is hard.'[9]

Most twenty-first century readers would nod assent; a hard heart indeed.

Without apologizing for his profession, Selous freely acknowledged the brutality and sheer wastefulness of the business. Toward the end of this, his third successful season, he reflected that it did seem 'dreadful to slaughter so many of these huge creatures merely for their tusks; for, if there are no Bushmen or other natives about, the carcasses are abandoned to the hyaenas [*sic*] and vultures.'[10] But, in the end, a man had to live. Nothing in this part of Africa apart from ivory repaid the heavy expenses involved in hunting. 'And if you depend on your gun for a living, as was my case, it behoves you to do your best when you get a chance.'[11]

Grateful to have survived another bout of hunting in 'the fly', Selous took his wagons to Wankie's Town where he acquired still more ivory through trade. Then he rejoined George Wood and headed back to Tati, where on the 11 December he found letters from home telling of his father's grave illness. He concluded his business affairs as quickly as possible and took ship for England from Durban in April 1875.

During three hunting seasons he had killed a total of seventy-eight elephants, far more then he would bag in the remainder of his long life, notwithstanding his reputation as Africa's 'mightiest hunter'. It bore no comparison with the huge numbers killed by his predecessors – white and black – who had ridden the first wave of advancing ivory frontier north from the Transvaal to the Zambezi. He owed his success – such as it was – to his willingness to follow Cigar into 'the fly', a strenuous and even foolhardy enterprise that could easily have cost him his life. Stronger men than he had succumbed to malaria and the other deadly fevers endemic to the realm of the tsetse. Much as we may find our sympathies enlisted all on the side of the elephants, hunting them on foot was an extremely dangerous business in which a single misstep could be fatal.

Still, he was determined to return as soon as possible. There were more elephants to bag, more species of antelope to enumerate, more unknown territory to explore. He was only twenty-four, prodigiously fit, and in love with Africa.

6

Hunter Heroes

Back in London Selous found his father badly affected by an unidentified illness. It was sufficiently severe to keep him away from his office but evidently not terminal, for he lived another seventeen years. His affliction could only have been exacerbated by the financial panic that sent global stock markets into a tailspin in October 1873. It was the world's first truly international depression and stifled economic growth in Britain for the next six years.

While catching up with relatives at the family home and country estate, Fred devoted himself to writing articles about his hunting adventures for *The Field*. The full name of this omnibus magazine was *The Field, The Farm, The Garden: The Country Gentleman's Newspaper*. Nothing like it exists today. It carried articles on cricket competitions, chess, archery, mountaineering, school sports, whist and every other conceivable leisure pursuit.

A headline on hunting invariably meant riding to hounds, never running on foot after wounded elephants, so Selous's contributions to *The Field* appeared sometimes under the heading Naturalist, but more often in a section called Travel and Colonization. His vivacious style and exotic subject matter evidently caught the editor's imagination. At first he was identified simply as FCS, but was soon given a proper by-line as Frederick Courteney Selous. Although there was no money in it, Selous was sufficiently flattered to make *The Field* his favoured outlet for the rest of his life. Unlike the more scientific journals, it allowed him to combine thrilling tales of the chase with analytical descriptions of animals and their behaviour. His first piece appeared in three parts during October and November 1875. Unsurprisingly, it covered his first expedition with George Wood from the time of Lobengula's great *inxwala* ceremony down to their triumphant return to Bulawayo with a huge haul of ivory.

The historical and ethnographic detail in the article is impressive, showing, among other things, Fred's linguistic skill. Most people called Lobengula's people by their Tswana name, Matabele. Here Selous uses the more correct Zulu form, Amandebele. He incorporated most of this article in chapters five and six of his first book. Among the parts dropped in the later version was his explanation of why big game was so plentiful in the Gwai River valley. It was not the tsetse fly, he claimed, but Matabele policy that was responsible. Since the days of Mzilikazi the kingdom had maintained a depopulated buffer zone around its territory as a defence against potential enemies. Whenever the Africans they had driven out attempted to re-occupy territory between their grazing lands and the Zambezi, Lobengula's regiments were sent to destroy their huts and villages.

Selous's articles struck a chord with the growing worldwide audience for hunting stories and trophies of the hunt. The French-American naturalist Paul Du Chaillu thrilled readers with accounts of the gorillas he shot in Gabon, but for pure joy in slaughter it was hard to beat William 'Buffalo Bill' Cody, who was already a household name by the time Selous wrote his first articles for *The Field*. Only five years his senior, 'Buffalo Bill' had been a pony express rider, a hunter, army scout, a fighter of Native Americans, and a state legislator. Latterly, he had taken to the stage, playing himself in theatres across America. His autobiography, published in 1879, told how he had killed his first Native American at age eleven and fought bushwhackers with his friend 'Wild Bill' Hickok. In his work for the Kansas Pacific Railroad, Cody hunted Native Americans almost as often as bison, claiming they were all horse thieves. Contractors for the Kansas Pacific Railway Company paid him $500 a month over eighteen months to clear buffalo from the line and supply meat for their workers. It was lavishly wasteful work, as the contractors only wanted 'hams' cut from the hindquarters and humps of the bison. The rest was left to rot on the prairie. By his own count Cody killed 4,280 beasts during his employment. Kansas Pacific was impressed enough to adopt the bison as the railroad's unofficial trademark. The best heads Bill brought in were mounted and displayed in stations and depots all along their line.

Cody delighted in showing off his prowess in chasing down hapless bison. Once a group of cavalry officers hunting 'for pleasure' mistook him for a novice and offered him the meat of all the bison they killed – apart from the tongues and tenderloin they reserved for themselves. Bill, riding bareback and without a bridle, spurred his horse to a gallop at the first sight of buffalo. Raising his rifle, 'Lucretia Borgia', he picked off eleven buffalo with twelve bullets before the astonished officers had time to get off a shot. On another occasion he and Billy Comstock staged a buffalo-shooting competition on the Kansas prairie before an appreciative audience who had come out in coaches from St. Louis. The wager was $500 each side, and the crowd celebrated each round of shooting with cheers and champagne. By the end of the day Cody had killed sixty-nine (bulls, cows and calves), while Comstock's total stood at only forty-six. To the popping of more champagne corks Bill was crowned champion buffalo hunter of the plains.[1] His career helps put Selous's elephant hunting into perspective.

An important part of what is seen here is the democratization of the formerly aristocratic sport of hunting. 'Buffalo Bill' presented himself as an archetypal common man whose feats of derring-do put his social superiors to shame. Without resorting to this kind of inverted snobbery, Selous played down his privileged upbringing in his books and articles, portraying himself as a plain-speaking modest man who happened to earn his living hunting elephants.

Since the time of the Crystal Palace, international exhibitions had devoted increasing space to hunting and taxidermy. America's Centennial Exhibition at Philadelphia in 1876 featured a tableau called 'the Hunters' Camp' including life-sized figures of 'several stalwart fellows – practical hunters – in the buckskin garb of their profession. They lounge on the rough log couch, smoke, dress skins, cook and eat, thereby illustrating their manner of living in the West'.[2]

It was as if these democratic hunters had become mounted specimens akin to the animals they killed. The hunter also made an appearance in verses of the Centennial Song:

> My mates are bold and bearded men,
> My songs the tempest shrill –

The panther screaming in the glen,
The war-whoop on the hill.

My bride my trusty rifle is,
My babe my bowie-knife –
Tis but a copper's toss if this
Be not my last of life.

And yet I sleep with babe and bride
Below God's rounded wall,
As soundly and as satisfied
As if in guarded hall.

The morn may wake to mortal strife,
The day may lay me low;
Yet I shall die with babe and wife –
Good-bye – lift hands – I go!

One of the big commercial hits at Philadelphia was a stuffed grizzly bear holding a tray and labelled 'Dumb Waiter'. British taxidermist Rowland Ward subsequently 'executed an endless number of "dumb waiters" which proved an exceedingly popular feature' at his Piccadilly display rooms.[3] Selous commissioned Ward to mount the skins and heads he brought back from southern Africa, inaugurating a partnership that endured into the twentieth century. Fred's proud parents were more than pleased to have them hanging in their home.

Ward and his taxidermist peers made a lot of money mounting heads and 'dumb waiters' but took most professional pride in their ability to revivify dead animals by arranging them in poses that suggested action in their natural habitat. Anyone who has visited a natural history museum knows that this effort can only go so far. Selous sought the same goal through words: to bring readers into the presence of living, breathing large mammals.

He paid particular attention to their eyes, which seemed to reveal personality traits. This set his writing apart from Bill Cody, who treated bison as mere objects for target practice. The more dangerous the animal, the more malevolence Selous found in its eyes. Through a gap in a thicket 'the head of an elephant, with the immense ears outspread, and the little eyes twinkling wickedly, burst into sight!' Another turned 'suddenly round, with his huge ears extended, his trunk stretched straight out, and his wicked, vicious-looking eyes gazing in our direction … ready to charge, no doubt'. An elephant with a 'fine thick pair of tusks' spread 'his enormous ears' and 'stared hard with his vicious-looking eyes towards where I stood'. Selous found 'nothing majestic or noble' about the lion he held 'at bay, standing with open mouth and glaring eyes'. It was intensely unpleasant to see a pair of lionesses turn 'their villainous greeny-yellow eyes upon me'; it looked as though 'the one with the cubs was coming at me'. He disagreed with hunters who regarded a wounded Cape buffalo as the most dangerous of all big game, but had to move fast to dodge one who, 'after glaring … a few seconds with his sinister-looking, blood-shot eyes, finally made up his mind, and, with a grunt, rushed at me'. He nearly ran into the horns of a female 'before I saw her, and she at the same time seeing me at once charged, with eyes on fire, and her nose stretched straight out, grunting furiously'.[4] He came to believe after a number of close encounters that the eyes of wounded lions and leopards actually changed in colour and quality. 'One who has not seen at close quarters the fierce light that scintillates from the eyes of a wounded lion, or any other of the large Felidae, can hardly imagine its wondrous brilliancy and furious concentration.'

He read quite different character traits in eyes of less dangerous creatures. A giraffe cow he brought down with three bullets 'reared her lofty head once more, and gazed reproachfully at me with her large soft dark eyes. For the instant I wished the shots unfired that had laid low this beautiful and inoffensive creature.' A dying eland looked 'ruefully with his soft brown eyes upon his destroyer'.

Selous often sounds this almost melancholic note of regret, which is entirely absent from Buffalo Bill's autobiography. This is perhaps because he does not cast himself as the harbinger of progress and civilization. On the American frontier, at least from the time of Daniel Boone, the hunter was entrenched in the popular imagination as the advance guard of the Manifest Destiny that would extend the borders of the republic all the way to the Pacific Ocean. Exterminating harmless bison and hostile Native Americans belonged to the same great enterprise as building railways and busting prairie sod. The place of the hunter in southern Africa of the 1870s was far less assured. The elephants may have been retreating but African people were not. Large and well-armed kingdoms like those of Lobengula and Khama did not look like succumbing to the fate of the Sioux, Seminole and Cherokee peoples. Disease remained a big obstacle. White settlers were pushing into new territory, but whether the African interior would be claimed by Boer, British or Portuguese was an open question. No one as yet talked of a railway from Cape to Cairo. Most of the continent still figured in the minds of ordinary Britons as 'Darkest Africa'.

As a naturalist Selous continued to marvel at savannahs teeming with game and did not envisage – certainly not at this point in his career – their replacement by farms and villages. Nor does he picture himself as a path-breaker for civilization. On the contrary, he frequently writes as though he is a dark angel of Fate: Man the Destroyer. Advancing upon two bull elephants he finds them:

> evidently enjoying a little rest, their large ears flapping listlessly against their sides like two enormous fans, and little thinking of the persevering enemy who had followed them like an avenging Fate through all their turnings, and now at last stood so near them as they slept in fancied security.[5]

At a later date he wrote of Man:

> that foe who, whilst immeasurably inferior in physical power to the elephant's giant strength, yet by the subtle power of intellect, which has enabled him to imagine and fashion weapons of deadly power, has ever been that animal's bane and curse, and bids fair to destroy ere long the last of his race in Africa, as in days gone by the savages of Central Europe utterly exterminated his mighty prototype the mammoth, beneath the gloomy forests of Germany, Britain, and of Gaul.[6]

Selous also stood apart from most other hero hunters of his era in the careful attention he paid to the species and varieties of game. Much as he liked to speak of elephant hunting as just his way of earning a living, he shot many other animals and took extensive notes on every one that fell to his gun for the first time. Though he complained of lack of space in his wagon, he always found room for a new type of antelope. This was more than a matter of zoological science, for in every case what counted most to him was the size and length of horns. In this respect he shared the preoccupation with masculinity that is so striking a characteristic of European hunters in this period. The biggest horns were always the better horns, and invariably came from the males. He recorded their measurements for the purpose of comparison with those shot by other hunters. Only when it was a question of meat for dinner would he prefer a female giraffe, rhino, buffalo or antelope. All the handsome plates in his first book are devoted to antelope heads and horns.

In his evaluation of trophy heads Selous did not distinguish between aesthetic appeal, size and taxonomic novelty. An article for *The Field* in 1876 analysed the running and swimming style of lechwe antelope bucks and went on to describe how he had shot 'the finest ram out of a very large herd'. It ranked as the finest because, in the first place the horns 'measured 24½ in. in length, and had a spread of 18 in. from tip to tip'. This and the other heads he brought back from Africa had 'been most excellently set up and mounted by Mr. Rowland Ward, of 158, Piccadilly, and the distinctive characteristics of each species so well retained that competent judges have pronounced them to be the best in that particular they have ever seen'.[7]

By the time this article appeared Selous was already, as he wrote to his mother, out 'on the briney' bound for the Cape. His father, whose health remained a cause for grave concern, had nonetheless dragged himself down to Plymouth to see him off. Though not much of a letter writer, there was no question of his devotion to his eldest son. He had been sufficiently impressed with Fred's success to make a sizeable investment in the ivory business. On his first voyage Selous stepped ashore with £400 of father's money and 300 lb of equipment. This time he brought twenty times as much equipment, plus enough ready cash to buy a wagon and a span of oxen.

Father's financial commitment weighed heavily on his mind. Impatient to get back to elephant country, he took no joy in shipboard life. Bad weather and rough seas dogged the first leg of the voyage to the Canary Islands. By the time the ship reached Saint Helena he had tired of his fellow passengers. There were no young gentlemen like Arthur Laing or George Dorehill to enliven his days. He wrote disparagingly to his mother about a Mrs Newman who 'hasn't got an

"H" in her vocabulary, a deficiency which she shares with several other passengers'. He hoped that father had not suffered another 'attack'.[8]

Anxiety only increased as he totted up the expenses of landing goods and purchasing equipment. Within a few weeks of landing at Algoa Bay he was consumed by the thought that 'Father must be sick and tired to death of the many and long bills, which he has been paying for my outfit.' Perhaps mother could quietly arrange for bills to be paid in a way that would avoid upsetting the old man.[9] If he were to carry out his planned expedition to the upper reaches of the Zambezi, it would be more than a year before ivory sales began to offset expenditure. It would take at least four months to haul the first load of equipment up to Shoshong to be stored while he went down to the diamond fields to get more supplies. By then the rainy season would have set in, so it would probably not be until May the following year 'when my business will commence'. Even that prospect was cast in doubt by the tardy arrival of his latest shipment of goods.

So much had changed since his trip to England. Prices of transport and oxen had risen alarmingly.[10] All this fretting suggests that after an initial rush of elation at his father's support, he was worried sick that he had painted much too a rosy a picture of the rewards he was sure to reap from the vast herds of elephants he would surely find on the happy hunting grounds. In 1871 he had gone to Africa in search of the 'free-and-easy gipsy sort of life' described by hunters like Gordon Cumming and W.C. Baldwin. Now he was as consumed by nail-biting angst as any London stockbroker in the Panic of '73.

7

'Elephants are Now Almost a Thing of the Past'

His timing could have been better. With so much heavy equipment to move, there was little chance of elephant hunting ahead of the rainy season. No list of his cargo survives from 1876, but from its weight it is evident that Selous intended to set up on a scale to rival big hunter-traders like his friend George Wood. He carried many more guns than before, including the latest models of breech-loading express rifles. Much of the rest of his cargo must have been high-quality trading goods, because success would depend more on trading for ivory than his own shooting. The white man with capital and heavy equipment was the end point in the largely African network of elephant killers who were pushing steadily into territories north of the Zambezi. Selous could buy cheaply from people who lacked his ability to get ivory out to the markets where the prices were much, much higher. Provided, of course, that he found ivory to buy.

A Slow Start

He had plenty of time to mull over the possibilities on the four-month trek up to Matabeleland. Although he travelled alongside six Boer wagon drivers as far as Kimberley, he thought no better of them than of his shipmates on the voyage out. In fact, he felt 'more alone in the company of these men with whom I have not one single thought, sentiment or feeling in common, than ever I was when alone with my following of untutored savages on the banks of the Zambezi.'[1] There was more to worry about by the time he reached the Marico River in

July. A letter from his father reported that the discovery of an ivory substitute threatened to drive the price down to a ruinous level. The thought that his enterprise might be doomed before it had even begun filled him with despair, made worse by a rare snowstorm that killed two tame wildebeest he had recently bought in the hope he could sell them to a zoo at a handsome profit.[2] To top it off, the lung sickness that had broken out among his oxen threatened to wipe out the whole team.

Thankfully, at the Tati gold mines, he met his old friend George Dorehill who introduced him to two gentlemen adventurers keen to try their hand at African game shooting: Lt. W.J. Grandy of the Royal Navy and Lewis Horner. Grandy was an experienced traveller, having commanded the expedition of 1872 which attempted to send relief to Dr Livingstone by travelling up the Congo River.[3] Over the next three months Fred made a number of small trips in their company, mainly to hunt giraffe, lions and antelope. In October he and Grandy visited Lobengula, seeking permission to hunt the next year. The following month he met for the first time the most successful ivory trader in all central Africa. From his headquarters at Pandamatenga (now a town in north-western Botswana) George Westbeech operated a trading operation into Barotseland where he had established such a good working relationship with King Sipopa of the Lozi during the years 1871–3 that he took out £12,000 worth of ivory. Over the next few years Westbeech was shipping 20,000–30,000 lb per annum, most of it from Barotseland in what is now west central Zambia.

He was what we would call today a functioning alcoholic, drunk every day, but fully capable of carrying on a thriving business. His spoke perfect Tswana and was by all accounts a charming companion. In a memorable character sketch Selous recalled him pointing to a toothbrush fixed in his hatband. 'That's,' he said, 'the last link between me and civilization, old man.' Later Selous watched George parley with a village headman: 'Westbeech was no longer a white man, but had become to all intents and purposes an African. As I watched the beer pot going round and listened to my host talking to his hosts with the utmost fluency in their own language, every now and then gravely taking snuff with one or another of them, I marvelled at his dual nature.' He had no desire ever to return to England. 'From Kazangula to Lealui, a distance of some 300 miles, I don't think there was a village along the Zambezi in which there was not a least one lady who called him husband.'[4]

Selous coveted the ivory, if not the lifestyle. A full year after his return to South Africa, he had nothing to show but a few skins, heads, horns and a pile of bills. With high hopes he set off in April 1877 for the Okavango and Chobe regions where elephants had been so plentiful three years earlier. He followed the previous plan of establishing the main wagon camp on the Deka River, from which he and his hunting companions made their way up the Zambezi. In addition to Dorehill, Grandy and Horner, Selous had engaged two young men to hunt 'on the half'. That meant that in return for a place in his well-equipped entourage they could keep half of all the ivory they shot.

Today a tourist can pick up a rental car at Francistown near the old Tati gold fields and zip along a major highway to Maun on the Okavango Delta in a little over six hours. Many more skip the tedious journey across the sandy plains by catching directly an international flight. Either way it is possible to be out in a light plane spotting elephants and giraffes the same day. There were no such shortcuts for Selous and his companions, who were pleased if they managed four miles a day. With no established tracks across the endless sands and constant worries about water and grazing, the going was tough.

Once on the Zambezi, the party split up. Dorehill, Horner and Grandy went with Westbeech up to Barotseland while Selous and his young 'hunters on the half' revisited the Chobe River and adjacent territory. In addition to these white companions he had hired several African shooters, for whom he paid all expenses. The object of all this effort was to cover as much ground as possible, but it was all for nothing, as the elephants had vanished. At the end of the season their combined efforts had brought down one cow and two calves with tusks worth a grand total of £2, a result both emotionally and financially crushing for Selous. Writing to his mother on 15 October he declared 'the whole country is in a state of ruin'. Both the ivory trade and elephant hunting had 'collapsed suddenly, and in a manner which no one would have foreseen or did foresee, and consequently unless we can get into another part of Africa we are all ruined'.[5] African hunters had evidently killed or chased out every herd in the Chobe and Okavango.

Meanwhile, Westbeech's friend, King Sipopa of the Lozi, had been assassinated, setting off a power struggle along a vast stretch of the Zambezi that severely disrupted the ivory trade. Everything that could go wrong had, leaving Selous to chew over the might-have-beens in that same letter to his mother (15 October):

> Nothing has gone right with me since I left England nor do I think it ever will again. I was born under an unlucky star, for even if I do not suffer from personal and particular bad fortune I seem (as at present) just to hit off the particular year and the particular part of the country for my speculation, when and where everything has gone to rack and ruin. Had I left England in Oct. '75 instead of in Feb. '76 I should in all human probability have done fairly well, and been able to return to England at the beginning of next year, for last year 40,000 lb weight of ivory were traded at the Zanzibar alone, and every hunter did well. This year owing principally to Sepopa's assassination only 2,500 lb have been traded !!!! and not a hunter has earned his salt!! However it is useless repining if it was not for two or three little 'ifs' I should now be worth £10,000 a year.

In only one respect might things have gone worse. He could have died from malaria like Lt. Grandy, who lingered too long in Barotseland after the rains came on. Dorehill and Horner were also badly afflicted but managed to bury their comrade and struggle back to base camp.

Selous's reference to £10,000 a year strikes a new and somewhat jarring note. Up to this point he appeared to have lived for adventure alone. Now money stands at the top of his agenda. Ten thousand a year was a lot more than he needed to live a 'gipsy-sort-of-life'. It would be enough to live comfortably as a country gentleman. Otherwise he would not have talked about returning to England at the end of a year. An income of £10,000 per annum would have easily put him within the top tenth of the top 1 per cent of the population. This – as well as the conversations he had with his father in 1875 – gives us some idea of the scale of his ambitions. The letter to his mother of 15 October 1877 expresses a hope that father will not feel he has been wilfully misinformed by a spendthrift son. A letter to his father two days later sets out more prosaically the cumulative effects of drought, political instability and the dwindling elephant population.[6]

As he began to see the interrelationship of trade, prices, climate, international affairs, supply and demand – those dreary subjects around which his father's life revolved, and which had always bored him to tears – Selous grasped, possibly for the first time in his life, the importance of politics. Rising tensions in Europe could result in a war with Russia that would depress the market for ivory. Continued turmoil in Barotseland would dry up supply on the Zambezi. Meanwhile, the Transvaal Republic had become embroiled in a disastrous war with Chief Sekukuni's Pedi people and tottered on the edge of bankruptcy. Seizing this opportunity to bring the faltering republic into a broader South African federation, Britain announced the annexation of the Transvaal in April 1877, just about the time Selous set out on his dreadfully disappointing hunt. Would the Transvaal Boers accept the re-imposition of British rule which their fathers had thrown off twice before? What would happen to the old ban on sales of firearms and ammunition?

With so many questions hanging in the air, Selous concluded that there was no time to be lost. His only chance to recoup his losses was to follow the elephants on their retreat northward and get into country 'not yet played out'. He would head across the Zambezi toward Lake Bangweulu where Livingstone had perished of malaria and dysentery in 1873; perhaps he might get as far as Lake Tanganyika.[7] Along the way he could do a little prospecting for minerals. Rather than wait for the next dry season, he would leave at the end of October in the company of a new acquaintance, L.M. Owen, a veteran of South African frontier warfare with a reputation as a first-class horseman. Of course, in 'the fly' it didn't matter what kind of rider he was – no horse could survive a tsetse bite – but Selous was glad of the company. A few years earlier he had taken his chances in 'the fly' with Cigar and come up trumps, thanks to his 'strong constitution'. He shared the common but mistaken belief that donkeys could survive tsetse bites that would kill horses. He took them as pack animals to bring out the anticipated haul of ivory. Fred also carried enough money and trade goods to employ African porters who knew the country. In case malaria struck he had a bottle of Warburg's Fever Tincture. Knowing the dangers, but with high hopes for elephants, he and Owen crossed the Zambezi at Wankie's Town on 30 October. Using a canoe to guide the swimming donkeys they commenced their descent into hell.

Among the Slavers

Their route down the left bank of the Kariba Gorge took them into territory where extremely dangerous men dealt in slaves as well as ivory. For centuries the Zambezi served as Portugal's main highway from their coastal colony of Mozambique to the interior. Now that most other European nations had banned the slave trade and British warships patrolled the Atlantic coast of Africa in search of illegal human cargoes, the focus of slaving had shifted to the Indian Ocean. The result was a final burst of vicious slave raiding that precisely coincided with the mid-Victorian ivory boom. The well-armed raiders doing business on the Zambezi were Africans or part-Africans who commanded armies of so-called Chikundas recruited on the lower reaches of the great river.[8]

After weeks of intense heat and humidity Selous and Owen had their first experience with commerce in human flesh when they ran into an armed detachment of Chikundas commanded by a Portuguese trader named Samoés. This 'small, sallow dried-up looking specimen of humanity' offered to exchange girls for any ivory they might be carrying. Further downstream they saw half-eaten human remains still lying in the open where villages had been recently burnt and plundered. At the island of Kasoko they met another Portuguese, Joachim de Mendonça, sole survivor of a settlement that until the recent collapse of the ivory trade had numbered more than twenty white men. The omens were not good.

Every day the startling brutality of the slave business assaulted their senses: runaway girls recaptured and beaten into bloody submission with rhinoceros-hide *sjamboks*; women with babies on their backs, iron rings on their necks and chains on their feet working in corn-fields until the time came for the forced march to market; slaves held during sleeping hours by pegs that bound their ankles in crude holes cut in a heavy log. Presiding over these and other horrors was the local strongman, Basungo Kanyemba. He held some kind of appointment from the governor down in Tete and turned out for special occasions in full-dress Portuguese military uniform and sword. Chikunda armies of up to six hundred gunmen under his command were sent as required to hunt elephants or slaves. This charming personage had two hippos shot and their severed heads brought up to a banquet held in honour of Owen and Selous. They ate that night off china plates a 'better prepared meal' than either had 'tasted for some time'. Selous was no Joseph Conrad but his reports clearly convey his sense of having arrived at the heart of darkness.

For some reason he and Owen lingered nearly a fortnight at Mendonça's headquarters, even though a smallpox epidemic was killing two or three people a day on the island. It may be that it took time to recruit the Chikunda porters they needed. During that time hyenas took all their donkeys. Having learnt from Mendonça that Kanyemba was preparing a huge elephant hunt, Selous and Owen made a hasty departure from Kasoko on 13 December. Their goal was the high country of Manica, north of the Zambezi. Just about the time they reached the plateau rain began to fall and hardly let up for the next several weeks. Temperatures were more bearable but elephants were nowhere to be seen and their store of provisions was running low. In normal times they could have bought maize and sorghum from villagers, but the last plantings had failed and famine stalked the land. They would have to depend on their guns for food and the game seemed to grow scarcer by the day. On 6 January 1878 they reached the headquarters of Sitanda, the most powerful chief in that part of the world. Here they would restock provisions and head off into unknown territory; at least, that was the plan.

The following day Owen woke with a splitting headache, severe back pain and a raging fever. By 8 January he could not move his arms or legs. Having noticed the clouds of mosquitoes at Sitanda's place, Selous slept that night under a net. His hunt for lechwe antelopes next morning took him knee deep into a marsh. He returned with three ewes and a fever. Even as he broke out the bottle of Warburg's Fever Tincture, Fred acknowledged that there would no big haul of ivory this year. Hunting, prospecting and trading were out of the question for sick men. Nine hundred miles of rough travel lay between them and the nearest mission station back in Matabeleland. The rain kept falling and Sitanda refused to sell them any food. Evidently he expected to seize their goods as soon as fever finished them off. Hope revived briefly when Kanyemba arrived with his force of 200 Chikunda elephant hunters. However, no amount of money would persuade him to help. He would not spare a single man, nor would he send a letter to Mendonça. This was no country for softies.

We know now that the key ingredient in the secret formula for Warburg's Tincture was quinine. Had Selous been taking it regularly it might have warded off malaria, but he treated it as a cure, only to be used after fever struck. It worked its magic slowly. Not until 24 January did he and Owen feel well enough to make a start on the long trek back to safety. The only way to get a porter was to buy one, so Fred traded 350 cartridges for a single slave. Five days later their man escaped with the rest of their cartridges. The only remaining hope was to struggle back to Kasoko Island where Mendonça could be counted on for some help. Speed was of the essence, so Selous left Owen in a makeshift camp and pushed ahead. By 19 February he reached the island and had men despatched to retrieve Owen. Not until the 4 April did they cross the Zambezi and even then Owen had to be carried in a litter. The journey would have been agonizing even for friends, but the two had never 'hit it off'. By the middle of the month it was evident that Selous would once again have to leave Owen behind in a desperate effort to reach Inyati mission station before food ran out. Too weak to hold a rifle, he shot nothing on the entire return journey. On 4 May he stumbled into Inyati, where the veteran missionary William Sykes put him to bed and sent men out to retrieve Owen.

In a letter of 20 July he told his mother his tale of woe. 'Elephants', he declared, 'are now almost a thing of the past'. When next they met she would find him a changed man: 'Continual never-ending misfortunes in small matters, and the failure of every speculation, owing to the country being utterly played out, from a commercial point of view, has changed me from a tolerably light-hearted fellow, into a morose, sad tempered man.'

One Last Shot

By September he had finally shaken off the malaria. His mood brightened further when he got a chance to join his old companion George Wood, who had been enjoying a very successful hunt in Mashonaland. By the time Selous reached their camp, Wood's party had already bagged forty elephants. On 17 September he got a few of his own, when twenty-one more fell out of a herd numbering at least seventy.

His last intended victim nearly did him in. Hunting on horseback for the first time in his life, he got off a couple of shots at a large elephant cow. At this point his exhausted horse could barely manage a walk. When Selous fired off the next bullet, the enraged elephant turned to charge. There was no chance of escape before she hit from behind like a battering ram. The horse lurched to one side just as Selous pitched forward onto the ground. He awoke a moment or two later 'to 'a strong smell of elephant'. Wriggling carefully round, he found the stunned elephant slumped to her knees. Her mighty hind legs towered above him while her head and forelegs rested on the earth. Gingerly, but with all possible speed, he rolled to safety before the elephant could get to her feet. Although bruised, battered and bloodied, he found himself miraculously intact – sound enough to recover his rifle and finish the job. When he took to the lecture circuit in later life, he made this story the climax of every performance.

Resolved to take no further chances in 'the fly', Selous sat out the rainy season and travelled down to the Transvaal to re-equip. The little town of Klerksdorp had by this time become a key point of supply for hunters working north of the Limpopo. A Scot named Thomas Leask, who had given up the hunt when the elephants retreated to' the fly', did a thriving business there which extended well beyond selling supplies. Selous and other hunters trusted him to act as their agent while they were off in the wild.

Elated by his September success in Mashonaland, Fred changed his mind. He would make one last throw of the dice. The plan was to return to the Okavango and to push out into adjacent territory, hunting elephants continuously over two to three years. He must have thought that after the last bout of fever he was the equivalent of a 'salted' horse. Having got the required permission from King Khama, in April 1879 he was on the weary road again, driving heavy ox wagons across the sandy wastes that lay between him and the Okavango. Once again he had taken on two young white companions willing to 'shoot on the half'. They might have expected the summer rains to fill pans and creeks along the way and provide plenty of fresh pasture for the oxen, but the rains had failed. As they drew nearer to their intended base camp on the Mababe River the oxen were plainly faltering. Had they not found water on the last stretch, they would surely have perished. Parched earth stretched to the horizon on every side and there was no game to be seen. More worryingly, Fred had a brief recurrence of fever.

From Mababe they went on horseback up to the Chobe River where they unexpectedly found company to share their misery. Unknown to Selous, his old friends Robert French and Henry Collison had been following their wagon tracks for weeks. (Another friend, Matthew Clarkson, who had been part of George Wood's Mashonaland hunting party the previous year, had started with them but had been killed by a lightning strike.) They told a familiar tale of woe, having lost several oxen along the way. A party of Khama's men sent to collect tribute from the San desert people had no better luck; they too lost many oxen.

At every village starving people implored the hunters to shoot game for them. Selous had no trouble recruiting fifty African helpers with little more than a promise of fresh meat along the trail. That was enough to encourage him to leave the horses and venture on foot into 'the fly'. Early on he shot four elephants, but that was the end of his luck. At least he escaped the dismal end of Robert French who followed a wounded elephant into a marsh, lost his way and perished. By October Selous was ready to throw in the towel. He was feverish again, and so were the young men 'shooting on the half'. There was precious little ivory to share out. Trading had been as hopeless as shooting in a famished land.

Many years later he told the sorry story of the homeward trek in a magazine article ironically titled 'Christmas in an African Desert'.[9] He and Collison had joined Khama's tribute collectors in a caravan of nine wagons and 150 bullocks. At the end of the dry season water and pasture were as scarce as the game. Every few miles wagon wheels stuck in the sandy drifts. The slightest sniff of water drove the oxen into a mad rush toward the source. The inevitable result was that every muddy pan and creek bed got trampled into mush before any of them could drink. Only six miles short of the pools of Mahakabi, when his oxen could pull no more, Selous cut them loose and walked them to the water. Other oxen in the party lost their way and left their bones to bleach on the trackless wastes.

A few weeks later, in the relative comfort of the little *dorp* of Zeerust in the Transvaal, Fred totted up his losses in a letter to his mother. This latest disaster proved beyond question that African hunters had overrun the 'whole district and effectually driven away the elephants'. He would 'give up hunting elephants as it is impossible nowadays to make it pay'. Much as he feared he would never again see his father ('now a very old man' of seventy-eight), he must mount one last expedition to the interior – not to shoot elephants but 'to try and collect some of my debts, sell off various things that are valueless anywhere else, and in fact settle up my affairs altogether'.[10] Incredibly, he planned also to go north of the Zambezi one more time and explore the country up to Lake Bangweulu. His aim this time would be exploration. He hoped to regain some of the money he had lost by writing a book, 'and I think that a journey into a country where no one has ever been before would greatly enhance the value of what I publish'. Selous planned to travel with a rich young gentleman adventurer, James Sligo Jameson, whose father Andrew ran the famous Jameson Whiskey distillery of Dublin. Four years younger than Fred, Jameson had acquired a taste for natural history and hunting during travels to South Asia. With such a wealthy backer, Selous would be able to fit out the Lake Bangweulu expedition on a lavish scale, including a large team of donkeys.

Based on his previous experience it would be reasonable to question his ability to survive another season among the Chikunda slavers and mosquitoes. In fact, he told Jameson that, as he did not want to take responsibility for his life, the young man would have to re-cross the Zambezi before the rains set in.[11] Selous himself, being more acclimatized, would stay on alone.

As it happened, politics intervened to nip his mad scheme in the bud. The British Administrator of the Transvaal, Owen Lanyon, flatly refused to allow Selous to carry any firearms or ammunition beyond the Limpopo. Selous blamed him for bureaucratic obstruction, but there were broader considerations on his mind. Since the annexation of the Transvaal in 1877 the British had been drawn into conflicts with three separate African kingdoms. The Pedi held first the Boers and then the British at bay with an arsenal of weaponry that even included a small cannon. Second, the British High Commissioner for South Africa, Sir Bartle Frere, had provoked a war with the Zulu kingdom for the express purpose of destroying its military capabilities. At the time Selous made his application to Lanyon, a third conflict was in the offing, this time with the Basuto who had been ordered to surrender all their firearms. It was not simply a question of Owen Lanyon's personal judgement. Already there was talk of a possible Boer rebellion. Showing that he meant business in enforcing the old Transvaal

Republic's embargo on the export of firearms might keep public opinion on his side. The neighbouring Cape Colony had just passed a Peace Protection Act in a bid to stem the arms trade. There was a general nervousness about any threat to white supremacy.

Selous was not sure where he stood on these larger political issues. On the one hand he believed there could be no permanent peace in South Africa so long 'as the military power of the Zulus remained unbroken'. On the other hand there was no glory in the way Frere 'manoeuvred so as to bring on a war'. Moreover, one could not 'but admire and pity the Zulus, who made a brave but unavailing resistance to men armed with far superior weapons'. As for the Transvaal Boers:

> I do not admire them; mentally they are, I should think, the most ignorant and stupid of all white races, and they certainly have not one tenth part of the courage of the Zulus. Physically they are immensely big as a rule, and capital shots, but there can be only one end for them to an open rupture with the British authorities, death and confiscation of property, which will leave another legacy of hatred between the Dutch and English inhabitants of this country for many years to come.[12]

With their Zambezi plans quashed, Selous and Jameson decided to combine hunting with exploration in Mashonaland. Their aim was to trace the course of the Umfile (Mupfure) down to its junction with the Mniati (Munyati) River and then follow that river upstream to their camp. Along the way they encountered elephants – the first Selous had seen in a long time – and each was rewarded for the effort by a good pair of tusks. They also shot buffalo, rhinoceros and hippos. Selous contrasted his humane method of despatching hippos with a rifle to the savage Shona method, which was to trap the beasts in a rock pool and slowly starve them to death. The distinction may perhaps be lost on twenty-first-century readers.

Entranced by his first experience with big game, Jameson fully intended to bankroll Selous on future expeditions, and would have done so had he not suffered a mysterious paralytic seizure in 1883.[13] September and October brought no more adventures worth reporting. With the rains coming on, it was time to break camp.

When Selous got back to Bulawayo in December 1880 he learnt

that the Transvaal Boers had risen in rebellion, so he would have to travel down to the Cape via the diamond fields. Having cleared his debts (other than to his father), he considered options for the future. One was to follow a suggestion of Sir Bartle Frere made shortly before his removal as High Commissioner for South Africa. Thomas Leask, the hunting outfitter of Klerksdorp, had recommended Selous to Frere as a source of geographical knowledge about the far interior. Fred offered his services while disclaiming any knowledge of scientific surveying instruments. He also told Frere that he could collect specimens of rare and beautiful animals for government museums. Frere's dismissal ended any chance of immediate employment but the High Commissioner did send the correspondence on to the Royal Geographical Society in London, which published some of it the following year.[14] A second possibility for the future was to take up the proposal of his friend Frank Mandy that he join him in managing ostrich farms for a wealthy farmer at Port Elizabeth. The third, and most immediately enticing, was to make some money by writing a book:

> I know that people have got good sums for writing bad books on Africa, full of lies, though I do not know if a true book will sell well. My book at any rate will command a large sale out here, as I am so well known, and have a reputation for speaking nothing but the truth.[15]

Already he imagined one illustrated by his talented sister Annie.

8

Author, Collector, Explorer

Selous spent just seven months at home in 1881, but managed during that time to finish the manuscript for his book and put it in the hands of a publisher. He also got in touch with the Royal Geographical Society (RGS) and the Natural History Department of the British Museum. The RGS welcomed any material he might supply on unknown territories of central Africa, while the Natural History Museum gave him orders for specimens. He took his animals' skins and heads to Rowland Ward for 'artistic' mounting. All this frantic activity suggests a man in a hurry to redeem himself in the eyes of the father who had lost serious money in their ill-fated ivory venture.

As Father was nearing eighty and had recovered his vitality, he probably gave the prodigal spender a forgiving welcome. Sister Annie threw herself enthusiastically into the work of illustrating his book with whimsical drawings that drew favourable comments from reviewers. His mother Ann would have had much to say to him about difficulties within the family to which she had alluded in letters over the past three years. With only his side of the correspondence to go on it is difficult to say precisely what had gone awry. Back in 1878 Fred wrote that he had 'read with indignation all the information that you gave me of family matters, and shall not forget them'.[1] Not long before his departure from South Africa he wrote ironically that 'the pictures which you draw of our happy home, and the blissful state of peace and love that reigns among the various members of our family present a charming prospect to a man of quiet and subdued habits like myself.'[2] Mother and son would also have had some deep discussions on political affairs. She had deplored the Zulu War on humanitarian grounds while he believed a check to 'the insolence of the Zulus' was necessary to end the frontier warfare that had retarded progress throughout southern Africa for more than a century. A war would show:

> the brutal savages [that] there are more things in Woolwich Arsenal in the shape of Gatling guns, etc. than were dreamt of in their philosophy. If they will only come out into the open, they will be slaughtered by the thousands, and their carcasses given to the hyaenas [sic] and vultures, the only thing they are good for.[3]

Author

Whatever their differences on these questions, Ann was surely impressed by the assurance with which Fred went about writing *A Hunter's Wanderings in Africa*. She had published verses and contributed articles to magazines but had never attempted a book. Fred's method was the same as he had used in his 1876 articles for *The Field*. He drew on his incredible memory and vivid imagination to flesh out the details of scenes sparsely recorded in his journals. In 1880 he told his mother he had 'any amount more journal but I shall not have time to write it out this year'. Thus when he sat down at his desk in London his task was to convert his existing notes into coherent narratives. In addition, he was able to incorporate large sections of his work previously published in *The Field*. He bolstered his credibility as a naturalist by including two papers he had delivered to the Zoological Society in June. His sister's drawings were sent to a woodblock print-maker who reduced them to the required size. A separate set of engraved plates illustrating every species of antelope he found north of the Limpopo River were drawn by a professional artist, using the specimens mounted for Selous by Rowland Ward. When the additional expenses are taken into account, he made very little, if any, money from the book. All 1,000 copies printed sold within a year but his costs exceeded his royalties by £12![4]

More importantly, though he did not see it clearly at the time, he had established himself as a contemporary authority on African big game hunting, zoology and geography. There had been nothing like his book since the same publisher brought out William Charles Baldwin's *African Hunting* in 1863. This meant more opportunities to meet wealthy, influential people like James Jameson. It meant being taken seriously by learned societies. It opened the door for grants and engagements as a celebrity hunting guide. It made retrospective sense of his adolescent African escapade.

Dr Albert Günther enthusiastically welcomed Selous to the Zoology Department of the Natural History Museum at South Kensington. Architect Alfred Waterhouse's magnificent new building had just opened and Günther's staff were still busy moving displays from the old premises. This energetic 50-year-old German-born expert on reptiles had been Head of Zoology since 1875. He pointed out seriously dilapidated specimens that needed replacing and gave Selous orders for a range of African fauna presently missing from the collection.[5] He was confident that he could match the best prices offered by other museums and private collectors. The work of his department maintained close connections with the best London taxidermists, which worked to their mutual benefit. Firms like Rowland Ward offered Günther the pick of their recent work, while the curator could dispose of duplicates through Ward's Piccadilly showroom, 'The Jungle'. Both Ward and Günther depended absolutely on hunters to supply their needs. By teaming up with them Selous became a key figure in a complex network of animal business. He would deliver skins and skeletons to Thomas Leask of Klerksdorp who would then forward them to distant museums and taxidermists. These metropolitan buyers then deposited funds into nominated accounts used to bank profits and pay off debts while the hunter continued on the move in Africa.

No doubt about it, natural history was big business in this first great age of public museums. It differed from the ivory business in that, all along the supply chain, it was conducted by well-to-do, educated white people. Most killing of elephants, on the other hand, was done by unnamed Africans in remote places who then traded tusks on to dealers like George Westbeech or Zanzibar Arabs. Killing and preserving animals for museums required specialized equipment and know-how. The hunter needed to take careful notes of where and when each animal was killed, as well as its biological class, order, family, genus and species. Close observation of the animal's behaviour, habitat and manner of moving helped the taxidermist prepare more compelling and accurate displays. If the skins and skeletons were not properly preserved and packed they were useless and museum curators would refuse them. Only perfect specimens brought top prices.

The Royal Geographical Society's headquarters at 1 Saville Row lay only a stone's throw from Rowland Ward's 'Jungle' on Piccadilly. Selous left maps with them but did not have an opportunity to give a lecture before he was off again to Africa. Since the days of Joseph Banks and Roderick Murchison the Society had been a very gentlemanly, almost aristocratic organization, so an introduction from Sir Bartle Frere carried a lot of weight. When Selous submitted a second paper for publication in the Society's *Proceedings* the editor sent it to Frere to referee. His glowing review cemented Selous's reputation as the kind of explorer the Society liked to support.[6] In 1883 he was given the first of three RGS grants he would receive to aid his expeditions to central Africa. In the eyes of his contemporaries he was now an explorer.

He boarded a ship for Cape Town before the first reviews of his book appeared. However, his publisher had been laying the groundwork for the public reception of *A Hunter's Wanderings* by planting extravagant promotional paragraphs in newspapers that read very much like reviews.

> Mr Frederick Courteney Selous, the most famous hunter in all South Africa, and scarcely less well known for his hospitality and advice to travellers in that region, has written an account of his nine years' 'Wanderings in Africa,' which will be published this autumn by Mssrs. Richard Bentley and Sn. It will include notes of his explorations beyond the Zambeze, on the Chobe, and in the Matabele and Mashuna countries. As might be anticipated, special attention will be given to the natural history of the larger mammals, about which probably no man living knows more than the author. The work will contain twenty-one full-page illustrations and a map.[7]

Quite a leap for Selous. A few months earlier he was lamenting his long run of bad luck. Now he was 'the most famous hunter in all South Africa'.

Genuine reviewers took Selous at face value. The *Morning Post* called *Hunter's Wanderings* 'a book written for sportsmen by a sports-man'. Thankfully it made 'no great pretensions to literary merit, being characterized by the rough-and-ready style of an African hunter rather than the polished manner of an accomplished writer'. One of its many virtues was its 'moderation of tone' compared with the over-blown claims of other hunter-authors who revelled in hair's breadth escapes. 'Mr. Selous', in contrast, 'has a sufficient collection of genuine adventures to recount to render it quite unnecessary for him to draw upon his imagination, even were he disposed to adopt so unsports-manlike a resource in order to give his tales point.'[8] The *Pall Mall Gazette* likewise praised Selous as 'a thoroughly business-like hunter who has written a thoroughly business-like book. He went to Africa not for sport, but for money and he tells us in a clear, simple, straight-forward way what he saw and what he did there.' There was no need to apologize for his literary style; 'it is far better than that of many more pretentious writers who give themselves high airs and graces'. Even the most exciting episodes were 'told so quietly, soberly, and historically that we feel at once we are listening to a perfectly truthful narrator, who merely tells what he has seen without any attempt at exaggeration or theatrical colouring'.[9] The reviewer for the *London Standard* was equally taken in by Selous's impersonation of a simple frontiersman: 'Mr. Selous is just a hunter who shoots elephants for the sake of ivory, and other creatures in order to feed his followers and any natives whom he might wish to keep on friendly terms with him.'[10]

No one picked up the Rugby-educated son of the London Exchange Chairman, the ex-medical student, or the connoisseur of music. Nor did they detect the undercurrents of anxiety, depression and self-pity that swirl through the correspondence with his parents during the years 1876–80. It was as if the book and the letters came from different hands. What is more, everyone accepted his claim to have written the unvarnished truth based on his journal entries – ignoring the amazing feats of memory and imagination involved in turning them into stories. Selous had pulled off the enviable trick of creating a literary persona that everyone took for the real Frederick Courteney Selous. As time went by he seemed increasingly to prefer the persona to the person. He would insist that he, the hunter-naturalist, knew nothing of the machinations of capitalists, politicians or socialites. He could only tell the truth as a plain man saw it.

Finally, the book gives the lie to a belief still current that he gloried in the slaughter of animals and boasted of his 'bag'. In the preface Selous was at pains to explain that his lists of animals shot were not intended:

> to boast but to show where different species may be found. [People who considered those lists] 'a dreadful record of slaughter' should bear in mind that I was often accompanied by a crowd of hungry savages, exclusive of the men in my employ, all of whom were entirely dependent upon me for their daily food, whilst in some of my expeditions my rifle supplied me almost entirely with the means of obtaining from the natives corn, guides, porters, etc. which better-equipped parties would have paid for with calico, beads, or other merchandise.[11]

Never, he claimed with slight exaggeration, had he shot an animal for the sake of sport alone. This helps explain why he saw no contradiction between his early career hunting elephants and his later work on behalf of national parks, game reserves and conservation.

Collector

Right up to the moment of his landfall at Cape Town in November 1881 Selous believed he was on his way to manage an ostrich farm for wealthy Mr Bennett of Port Elizabeth. A letter from Frank Mandy explained that the job had evaporated. After losing his shirt speculating in diamond shares, Bennett had committed suicide. Moreover, the bottom had fallen out of the ostrich feather market.[12] It was another lesson in financial markets for the son of a stockbroker. The whole Cape economy was depressed, so his every effort at finding work failed. Another factor, in Fred's opinion, was that potential employers looked on him as a footloose character unlikely to stick at any job for very long. There was nothing to be done, he decided, but to go up to Klerksdorp and fit out another expedition. This time his object would be collecting specimens for museums and knowledge for the Royal Geographical Society.

He already had orders for animals from Günther at the Natural History Museum and Rowland Ward the taxidermist. At Cape Town he had picked up another set of orders from Roland Trimen, Curator of the South African Museum. Selous also notified Henry Bates at the Royal Geographical Society of his change of plans. At the diamond fields he met his friend H.C. Collison, who had just come back from Matabeleland, leaving his whole crew of hunting assistants at Klerksdorp. When Selous got to Thomas Leask's store he found all of them eager for employment, including a very handy Griqua lad named Laer, who spoke several African languages in addition to his native Afrikaans. He would prove invaluable in unknown territory. Thomas Leask sold Fred the team of oxen he had just bought from Collison, and a roomy wagon.

Selous was no longer the boy who lost his horses, his guns and his way. He went about his business with confidence and efficiency. Heavy rains made the trek from Klerksdorp up to Shoshong more tedious than ever, with frequent stops to free bogged wagon wheels. On the other hand, he enjoyed the companionship of a young Scots missionary, Frederick Arnot, who intended to plant a station somewhere north of the Zambezi. This audacious individual had come out on his own initiative without the backing of any established missionary society. As a member of the fundamentalist Plymouth Brethren, Arnot was the polar opposite of the materialist Selous. What they shared was the thirst to venture into the wilderness without regard to personal safety, and the joy they found in hunting. Missionaries were not much liked in the white settler communities of southern Africa, where they were suspected of spreading the dangerous idea that all men were equal in the eyes of God. Beyond the colonial frontier, however, hunters and missionaries often formed bonds based on mutual interest. They depended on the same distant sources for supplies and news. European hunters like Selous provided rare company for families on lonely mission stations. The missionary, in turn, was often a welcome friend in need. Had there been no station at Inyati, Selous would most likely have perished on his earlier return journey from beyond the Zambezi. Though he was probably an atheist, he never had a bad word to say about missionaries.

Selous parted company with Arnot at Shoshong and moved on to north-eastern Mashonaland, where he established his base camp. Collecting specimens for museums was a less chancy and arduous business than elephant hunting. Most of the specimens he sought could be found in the healthy high country. They generally did not have to be chased very far. There was no competition from African, Griqua or Boer shooters. Most hunting could be done on horseback. However, great care had to be taken at every stage of collecting fragile animals. It did not matter where an elephant was hit, so long as it fell; once the tusks had been cut out, they could be buried for safekeeping until it was time to load the wagon. When Selous went after a fragile antelope he had to think carefully about what kind of rifle to use and where to aim. The wrong kind of bullet could destroy the value of a skin before the animal had gone cold. So could a misdirected shot. Before the hunter bedded down for the night he needed to ensure the specimens were safe from lions and hyenas. Once the skin and bones had been removed they needed to be tightly packed and stored, with all the pieces precisely identified. Fred's correspondence with Albert Günther and Rowland Ward details the many frustrations and anxieties he faced in the field.

Inevitably, Fred's big concern was money. Before setting out from Klerksdorp he despatched a hartebeest skull and a duiker antelope he had shot near Port Elizabeth. He hoped Günther would agree that the skull should be priced at £5 and the duiker at £4. At his end, Günther pencilled in a price for the skull of '£3 no lower'. The arrangement was that upon receipt of specimens in good condition he would have payment made through Fred's London agent, Mr Chittenden, who would then pass the money along to Thomas Leask's agent, who would use it to reduce the large sum of £500 still owed to him.[13]

By August 1882 Selous had collected enough animals to fill his wagon. He had pinned 300 butterflies, but had seen no elephants. The white rhino Günther coveted had likewise proved elusive. Fred was pretty sure he could get one by venturing into 'the fly' on foot, but what would be the point, when he could not get the corpse out on an ox wagon? The big problem with museum specimens was the room they took up. Sale of a full wagonload at good prices would barely meet the costs of the expedition, even if they brought good prices in London or Cape Town.[14]

Günther did his best to encourage Selous in letters that were slow arriving. One, for example, had been carried to William Sykes' mission station at Inyati by Matabele runners. From there it was handed to a Shona hunter who eventually caught up with Selous in his camp on the Umsengaisi River. Günther reiterated his desire for the white rhino:

> The skin with horns well above two feet long in their central axis should fetch £200. If the horn be considerable longer than 2½ feet, I may feel justified in recommending the purchase of the Trustees at a higher figure; but I do not think that we should pay more than £250; and in either case the skin must be fit for mounting and perfect in all respects.
>
> The skeleton would be worth from £80 to £120 according to size and age of the animal, and if complete.
>
> Thus, in the best case you may expect from these two sources £370; and for an inferior specimen £280; in both cases minus carriage and freight.[15]

In a word of warning he added that Selous would:

> have to consider that the skin may possibly be injured, or that bones may be lost during transmission, and that in this case you would get nothing like those sums.
>
> In fact, there is considerable risk in the undertaking, and you would have to make up your mind to be paid by the result. But I must leave it to your judgment whether you will engage in the matter.
>
> If you do, and are successful in killing an animal worth preserving, be particularly careful in skinning the head and feet; you must pare away the flesh from the sole and toes, until you are sure that no decomposition can set in those parts, and perhaps spoil the whole specimen. On the other hand, it would be, of course, grand if you succeeded in getting home 1 or 2 skins and skeletons and 1 or 2 calves living.[16]

As a herpetologist, Günther also encouraged Selous to collect lizards in out-of-the-way places by 'shooting them with dust' but 'they must not be too much lacerated'.[17]

Selous fully appreciated the need for scientific care and exactitude. At the same time he struggled to meet these strict conditions in the wild. A string of small disasters plagued him. Lions killed his best dog and carried off two fine, freshly killed sable antelope skins, one of which he had already treated with arsenic soap. He lost a donkey to hyenas. He got a lovely oribi antelope but his shot with a hollow bullet inadvertently struck the head, rendering the specimen useless. A misdirected shot that shattered a bone was just as bad. Once the meat was stripped out, heads and skins were preserved and packed. The next step was to clean the skeletons worth preserving. Having lost many small bones in the process of boiling down skeletons, he commissioned the blacksmith at the Tati mines to make him an iron cauldron big enough to hold the stripped carcasses of most animals.[18] Taking account of the large number of animals he shot in the 1880s, he must have spent many hours of every day during the hunting season in very demanding physical labour. He frequently complained that he seldom had time to write letters or make journal entries.

The logistical problems involved in maintaining his camp, getting shipments out and arranging payment would have taxed the minds of a whole team of skilled collectors; he was working alone with an untrained African crew. The meat from the animals he shot was used to feed his crew and the perpetually hungry Africans who clustered around him. Keeping them satisfied was the best strategy for maintaining personal safety. He had to drive his wagon hundreds of miles down to Klerksdorp every time he had a full load. Consignments had then to be separated into goods destined for Cape Town and specimens shipped to England. He could not be sure what specimens Günther would accept. Rejects in pristine condition went to Rowland Ward's sales rooms for exhibit and purchase. Leftovers went to the taxidermy firm of Gerrard in Camden Town, North London. A few were retained for Fred's personal collection.

In addition to his primary business of supplying public museums, Selous hunted animals favoured by private collectors. Few people had the floor space to accommodate the whole body of an antelope, let alone a giraffe. The big demand was for mounted heads to decorate walls, not just in private homes but also in clubs, hotels, restaurants and waiting rooms. Splayed skins of big cats – cheetahs, leopards, lions – joined oriental carpets as fashionable floor coverings. Selous was constantly on the lookout for male lions with big manes, although females also brought good prices. Heads of zebras, buffaloes and large antelopes such as eland, hartebeest and 'koodoo' (i.e. *kudu*) also found a market. There had never been and probably never would again be such a vogue for displaying dead animals. The consumers of Europe and North America were ultimately responsible for their slaughter. Selous was merely the man at the sharp end of the business.

As purveyor of dead animals to the aristocracy and upper middle class, Rowland Ward of Piccadilly stood at the top of his profession. For the public at large his showroom, 'The Jungle', functioned as the Madame Tussaud's of exotic fauna. Ward valued his association with Selous for a number of reasons. The specimens arrived in excellent condition and came with detailed notes of their provenance. That made them more valuable. Fred's accounts of animal behaviour in his book and articles for *The Field* helped Ward make his exhibits more lifelike and authentic. It was also in his financial interest to popularize Selous as a celebrity hunter. Beginning in the 1880s he became his unofficial PR representative, writing letters to the papers informing readers of the mighty hunter's whereabouts and escapes from tight situations. He also featured animals shot by Selous in the major exhibitions he held from time to time to promote his business. Because shooting big game in Africa and India cost so much, Ward encouraged rich men to take up hunting.[19] Anyone interested in an expedition to central Africa was encouraged to contact Selous.

Fred, who was by no means a rich man, complained constantly in letters to Günther about the costs involved in collecting. By 1886 he had no idea how he was ever to pay his debts. It was not just that he had failed to make money, he had actually lost the £400 he had brought out in 1882. 'The fact is that the time and outlay involved nowadays in getting specimens of South African mammalia (or rather South Central African) is so great, that they have altogether cost me more than I get for them.'[20]

Explorer

There was practically no money to be made from exploring, but Selous found it feasible to combine geographical observations with collecting. Almost all of his exploring work in the 1880s was conducted in the north-eastern part of Zimbabwe, east of the river he called the Umniati, which we now know as the Munyati. This country, which contains the capital Harare, had only been vaguely mapped a decade earlier by the intrepid artist/explorer Thomas Baines. Using Baines' map as his guide, Selous took compass bearings from natural landmarks, which he plotted on scraps of paper.

Quite a few of these little sketch maps survive in the archives of the Royal Geographical Society (RGS), where they are filed with the original manuscripts of articles Selous submitted for publication. They are done with extraordinary care and often include valuable auxiliary information about his activities, lists of trading goods and equipment. The council of the society was sufficiently impressed to award him its Cuthbert Peek Grant in 1883 and the Back Grant in 1889 in recognition of his explorations in Mashonaland.

From the sketches Selous compiled a number of larger maps showing in reasonable detail the routes he followed on his expeditions between 1872 and 1892. They enable the biographer to find most of the locations mentioned in his correspondence and publications. His exploring journeys took him through some of the most ruggedly beautiful but fearfully difficult topography in eastern Zimbabwe. I have found many of the deep-cut valleys and sheer granite mountains impossible for the best of all-terrain vehicles. He clearly deserved the accolades of the RGS.

9

Neither Monk nor Saint

During his first ten years in Africa Selous kept journals, from which he wrote a more or less chronological account of his doings. Since there are no other sources for that period besides letters to his parents, there is an overwhelming temptation to let him write his own biography. That strategy will not work for the 1880s. By the time his second book came out in 1893 Selous had emerged as a prominent propagandist for the British South Africa Company, which laid claim to the whole of the territory called Rhodesia. *Travel and Adventure in South-East Africa* vilifies the Matabele and their deposed King Lobengula. It touts the new colony as a paradise for rosy-cheeked English settlers. Selous tells some good hunting stories – and recycles some from the 1870s – but there are a great many other stories that are not told. There are huge gaps and some deliberate omissions. He is rarely candid about the reasons why he undertook particular expeditions. Comprehensively bamboozled by the lack of a clear chronological thread, his first biographers pass quickly over the years 1881–8. Why the gaps and what can be done to fill them?

It may be that Selous kept less careful track of his life in daily journal entries. However, his meticulous record of every butterfly, every reptile, every bird and beast collected argues otherwise. He could have filled in the missing autobiographical detail, but chose not to. Fortunately, there are other sources that help us reconstruct his movements. After the success of his first book any report of Selous was considered newsworthy in British and South African papers. Articles he wrote for *The Field* and the *Proceedings of the Royal Geographical Society* help to flesh out the chronology of some years. His correspondence with the RGS and the Natural History Museum supplies important details about health and money matters. *A Hunter's Wanderings* and Rowland Ward's promotional efforts made Selous a celebrity African hunter. Other travellers sought him out and told of their encounters in their books. Missionaries of various stripes reported favourably on the assistance they got from the man who interpreted all life and death in terms of a Darwinian struggle for existence. And there is a single precious paragraph in the papers of another hunter, James Dawson, that shines a light into an obscure corner of his domestic arrangements. In March 1888 Maurice Heany, late of the US Cavalry, told Dawson:

> Selous got into Shoshong on the 27th inst. He brought his woman down with him and means to get rid of her. She did not care to go into Zambesi and he did not press her. He keeps the children. While at Shoshong he messed [dined] with Borrow and I, and he saw much of him. He is a grand fellow in every respect.[1]

A grand fellow he continued to be, but when he wrote *Travel and Adventure* in 1893, Selous was engaged to be married to an English vicar's 19-year-old daughter. He had pressing reasons to leave big gaps in the record of the 1880s.

Was 'his woman' tall, short or medium? Young and pretty? We can't say. Was she Shona, Ndebele or Tswana? We don't know. Despite the 'known unknowns', Stephen Taylor, who spotted Heany's letter in the National Archives of Zimbabwe, felt justified in making some assumptions and deductions. She was probably African because otherwise she would not have been called 'his woman'. There must have been at least two offspring to justify the reference to children. The youngest must have been well beyond the age of breast-feeding, otherwise Selous could not have contemplated keeping the child. Nor would he have taken an interest in children he had not fathered.

Going further, we can calculate the gap between the births of the children as ten months at the very least. That means the relationship must date back to 1884 or earlier. On the other hand, it almost certainly commenced after his return from England in 1881. No way could he have settled an African family in Port Elizabeth in plain sight of racist white settlers. However, the ostrich farm was on his agenda right up to December 1881. Selous was alone when Frederick Arnot offered to join him on the trip to Shoshong, so it is reasonable to conclude that the relationship with the mother of these children commenced sometime between May 1882 and 1884.

Taylor reasons that she was probably a Tswana woman, because Heany learnt of Selous's intention to discard her at the Tswana king's capital. That does not necessarily settle the question; Shoshong was a cosmopolitan place harbouring displaced people from distant regions. Nor can we say for certain that Selous carried out his intention there. What was meant by Heany's statement, 'he keeps the children'? Does it mean he intended to keep them with him, in which case they almost certainly would have perished on his expedition to the Zambezi a few months later, when he very nearly lost his own life. Or does it mean merely that he would keep them in the sense of providing for their well-being? Taylor wonders whether the John or Jan Selous referred to elsewhere as 'my boy John' was one of the children thus provided for. We know from other sources, however , that John Selous was a completely different person. In *African Nature Notes and Reminiscences*, Selous tells how 'his boy John' – still alive in 1908 – was born into the Koranna community of Klas Lucas about 1850. In 1871 he ran away from his Griqua master and remained with Selous for many years.[2] In 1884 Walter Montagu Kerr described him as 'Koranna John', an elephant hunter who served his apprenticeship with Selous. At this point we hit a wall.

Although no more can be said about Fred's African family, knowledge of the relationship helps make sense of many gaps and silences in his accounts of the period 1882–8. Among the white hunting community, where concubinage was the rule rather than the exception, everyone would have known – including, for example, George 'Elephant' Phillips, who would be best man at his wedding in 1894. Selous implied as much when he cited H.T. Buckle's *History of Civilization in England* in defence of the hunters and traders of central Africa:

By bringing a better class of guns, powder, and every other species of trading goods into the country, the Englishman beat his competitors out of the market, and thus did more to put an end to the slave trade carried on along the central Zambesi by Portuguese subjects, and to raise the name of Englishmen amongst the natives, than all the pamphlets of the stay-at-home aborigines protectionists, who, comfortably seated in the depths of their arm-chairs before a blazing fire, are continually thundering forth denunciations against the rapacious British colonists, and the 'low immoral trader', who exerts such a baneful influence upon the chase and guileless savages of the interior. I speak feelingly, as I am proud to rank myself as one of that little body of English and Scotch men, who, as traders and elephant-hunters in Central South Africa, have certainly, whatever may be their failings in other respects, kept up the name of Englishmen amongst the natives for all that is upright and honest. In the words of Buckle, *we are neither monks nor saints, but only men*.[3]

The Missing Years

Bearing that in mind, let us see what can be done to plot the outlines of Selous's life from the time he parted company from missionary Frederick Arnot in May 1882. By the beginning of the next month he had planted a fortified hunting camp on the Bili River, about 100 kilometres to the south-west of present-day Harare. At Chief Lo Magondi's village he stocked up on maize, attracting in the process the usual crowd of about fifty people hoping for the customary bounty of fresh meat. Over the next six weeks he shot and preserved enough antelope specimens to fill his capacious wagon. He also had the unexpected pleasure of meeting George Dorehill, still hunting eleven years after their first expedition together in 1871. This time George had brought along his English wife and two young children, an indication of the relative safety they enjoyed in the wilds of Mashonaland. As it was still too early in the season to count on good grazing for his team of eight oxen on the road south, Selous left a few of his crew to guard his horse and wagon, while he set off on an exploratory trip across the unknown territory that lay between his camp and Portuguese posts on the Zambezi.

His party included his right-hand man and chief interpreter, Laer, two Matabele youths, three Shonas, two of Khama's people from Bamangwato, along with a donkey as the only pack animal. As he told the story in *Travel and Adventure*, he met village after village of Shona people who lived in terror of Matabele raids. However, his 1883 report to the Royal Geographical Society fails to mention the climate of fear. It may be that he retrospectively exaggerated its extent in 1893 when the British South Africa Company justified war against Lobengula on the grounds of alleged atrocities committed on the Shona.

Not long after plunging into unknown territory his donkey was killed by hyenas and from there on the going was tough. A letter to Günther at the Natural History Museum spoke vividly of the troubles that beset him practically every step of the way:

A day or two after writing to you in the beginning of August last, finding that I had as many specimens as I could load onto my wagon, and that it would be useless preserving any more large mammals this year, I made up my mind to try and make my way from the Hanyame (Manyame) river up to the Portuguese settlements on the Zambesi, as the intervening country is quite unknown, and a perfect blank upon all the maps. I hoped too, to fall in with Lichtenstein's Hartebeest on the road, and took a pack donkey with me to carry the skins in case I got any specimens. On the 6th August I crossed the Hanyame [Manyame] with seven kafirs and a young Griqua, and struck northeast. On the second night a hyena killed my donkey, biting it between the thighs and tearing out its entrails. I originally intended to have visited Tete, but got foul of a frightful chain of mountains which edged us away too much to the north, and at last after 15 days very hard walking through a dreadfully rough hilly country, very sparsely populated and almost destitute of game, I reached the Zambesi at a place called by the Portuguese 'Chabonga' and by the natives Chimbuna.

I then travelled along the southern bank of the Zambesi to the eastwards and on the fifth day crossed the river to Zumbo at the mouth of the fine river Loangwa. Here there were five white men, Portuguese, a miserable lot to look at. One, from the effect of constant attacks of fever was the mere wreck of a man, with a fearfully swollen liver; the second was suffering from dysentery and the other three from syphilis! Senhor Gourinho, the gentleman with the swollen liver, treated me, however, with the greatest hospitality, during my stay with him.[4]

The visit to Zumbo inspired other feelings apart from pity and disgust.

It moved him to an uncharacteristic soliloquy on the transience of human endeavours. Here Jesuit missionaries had built a flourishing station three hundred years earlier. All that remained of their labours were a few vine-covered ruins.

> Little dreamt the priests in those bygone days, as they performed the solemn rites of their church, and thought with human pride of the many converts they had made amongst the native population, that in less than two hundred years' time the only relic of their pious work that would still remain to tell the passing traveller that they had ever been there, would be a few stone walls fast crumbling to decay.[5]

Unfortunately, he let his melancholy contemplations run on too long:

> On the fifth day I started southwards again. For three days we travelled through dreary, parched up Mapani forests, having to walk very hard for water and the heat of the sun most intense. The third night we slept without water, just at the foot of the mountains. The next morning early, however, we got water in a spring on the summit of the first range. This was a very trying day, climbing up and down successive ranges of rugged stone mountains under a very hot sun. Whilst in the Zambesi valley we had been 'struck' by millions of Tse-tse fly and were, I think, very thin and weak in consequence. That evening two of my kafirs and I myself got a bad attack of fever.
>
> We were now in a bad plight for we were in the midst of an uninhabitable country surrounded by rugged hills, in which there was no game whatever, and had only a little rice and a few ground nuts sufficient for one day, and worse than all I had not a grain of medicine of any kind with me. Things being so we were forced to continue our journey in spite of the fever, and the next afternoon reached the first Mashuna town. After this I got on another three days, but was then done for as were the two sick kafirs. Here I remained for seven days, and I never thought I should see the wagon again, as I had the very poorest of food and no medicine. Being, however, now well out of the 'fly' country I sent for my horses, and ultimately reached the wagon in the middle of Sept last near the river Umfile [Mupfure], the two kafirs who had first got sick and whom I had to leave behind,

not getting there till the end of the month. Three more of my kafirs, and the young Griqua boy fell ill immediately they reached the wagon.[6]

Günther could only wonder what Selous thought he was doing going into the Zambezi valley without quinine.[7] 'If you had not a constitution as tough as a Rhinoceros skin,' he wrote, 'you would probably have never seen Matabele Land again.' The modern reader will also wonder what on earth he was doing. The pursuit of Lichtenstein's hartebeest could hardly justify the expense. Once Selous saw the Zambezi, his exploring of new territory was done and he could have turned back. Some other motive pulled him back to the devil's domain where he had suffered so fearfully in 1878. Whatever it was, it seems very unlikely that he was travelling with a woman or children.

Having got this far in the story, he goes suddenly mute, saying only that he reached the Matabele country in late October and then trekked down to Klerksdorp with his specimens for despatch to Cape Town and England. The next we know it is May 1883 and he has again made camp in Mashonaland.[8] On a manuscript map he sent to the Royal Geographical Society, Selous indicates that he set up camp at the same spot on the Hanyame [Manyame] River in 1883, 1885 and 1887.[9] He then jumps to 11 July 1883. Having recovered from a broken collarbone suffered in a fall from his horse, he resumed his pursuit of Lichtenstein's hartebeest and the white rhinoceros.[10] His fruitless six-week hunt is described in some detail, but the next we hear of his movements is the break-up of his camp in early November. He remarks pointedly that:

> I had not seen a white man since leaving the Matabili country in the previous April; but I knew that two hunters, an Englishman and a Boer, were camped near the River Zweswi, three days' journey from me, and so resolved to make for their camp and spend a few days with them and enjoy the pleasure of speaking my own language once more.[11]

At this point in his book he interposes a chapter on a Matabele raid on people living near Lake Ngami, before describing a lion hunt on his journey back to Bulawayo, which he reached in November. That means that all told he has accounted for a total of about six weeks out the previous fifty-two.

Most likely he had met 'his woman'.

It was often said that Lobengula regarded Selous as a special friend, but evidence of any close relationship is lacking.[12] Of course, he had to ask permission to hunt, but otherwise Selous tells us very little about their interactions. One incident that particularly riled him happened during his brief stay in Bulawayo in December 1883. Owing to a prevailing belief that drought would follow the killing of large numbers of hippos, Lobengula had extended his protection to these lumbering beasts. A white trader had tried to evade the prohibition in the hope of cashing in on the demand for *sjamboks* made of hippo skins, but was detected. To his considerable surprise Selous and several other white trader/hunters were accused of the same crime. He was highly indignant when Lobengula imposed a fine in cows worth about £60 for something he had not done. Whatever trust there may previously have been between them was wearing thin.

Thanks to an unexpected encounter we know much more about Selous's next expedition. Walter Montagu Kerr, son of a Scots aristocrat, Lord Charles Kerr, had gone to South Africa hoping to travel into unknown parts. Having read *A Hunter's Wanderings* he concluded that Selous would be the ideal guide. After fruitless enquiries at the Cape, Kerr pitched up at Klerksdorp and put the question to Thomas Leask. 'My dear sir,' said Leask, 'Mr. Selous is in my house at this very moment. Look there are his wagons! He arrived out last night with two wagonloads of ivory, hides and horns, and a lot of other hunting trophies.'[13] Clearly, Selous had been doing much more trading than he cared to mention in letters and articles. Selous told Kerr that his proposed expedition to the north-east of Matabeleland was quite feasible, provided he secured permission from Lobengula. He described in somewhat harrowing detail the recent row over the hippos and the expulsion of some Americans who had been engaged in clandestine prospecting for gold. There was no time to be lost if Kerr were to cross the Zambezi ahead of the rains. Selous would be glad to accompany him as far as Matabeleland.

On 5 March 1884 they were off, their two wagons piled high with trading goods, firearms and equipment. Teams of sixteen oxen pulled each wagon, while dogs, 'salted' horses, sheep and cattle trotted behind. Around the campfire Selous kept his new friend entertained with stories of his exploits. During the day he pointed to the desolation of a country where elephants and buffalo once abounded – all owing to the unrestrained trade in ivory and hides. In April the party reached Bulawayo, where an epidemic of malaria had broken out. Soon Selous was down with the fever, causing Kerr to marvel at how the fever could reduce the strongest man to a shivering wreck. Bulawayo was not quite the savage capital Kerr imagined. Homes of traders were rising on all sides and an English bricklayer was busy on the king's new residence. Kerr was fortunate to have a number of meetings with Lobengula, who proved to be a surprisingly shrewd and entertaining conversationalist. He called Selous 'the young lion'. So far as religion was concerned, he considered missionaries entitled to their beliefs, but, the king added, they were paid to say so. He explained some of the customs of his household and told Kerr that, strictly speaking, his people should be known as the Zulu. Ndebele and Matabele were terms applied to them by the BaSotho. Kerr's keen observations make us wish that Selous had devoted more time to ethnography.

By the middle of May it was time to be off on an adventure from which Selous believed Kerr would never return. As it happened, he did reach Lake Nyasa and the east coast and lived to write a two-volume book that made his name as an explorer.[14]

Had it not been for Kerr there would be almost nothing to tell about Selous's activities in 1884. Even an expedition to Victoria Falls by his younger brother Edmund did not rate a mention.[15] Günther heard a rumour that Selous was 'detained by some rascally chief who treated you well in the matter of food, but wanted you to shoot elephants for him'.[16] As Selous does not mention any such incident, there is no reason to think it happened. In *Travel and Adventure* he wrote that, after looking over his journals for 1884, he found they contained 'but little of any special interest'. He does not explain why he had spent two months in Bulawayo, nor why he chose to return to the Okavango for the hunting season. Nor does he explain why he travelled directly west from Matabeleland to a place shown on his map as Sode Gara. As this was unknown country, Selous hired guides from a village on the Gwai River.

Strange to say, he did not write up this journey for the Royal Geographical Society, nor did he plot it on the charts he made for them. It is hard to say what he did at the Okavango, only that 'there was not much there I wanted', so he turned his wagon back to Sode Gara where he 'remained for some time hunting gemsbucks, and hartebeests, and ostriches'. Then he headed down to Tati, remarking that for the previous six months he 'had never seen a white man, or spoken a word of English'. After a brief stay in Tati he moved on to Bulawayo where he was again laid low by malaria. That is all he has to say: May to December covered in six paragraphs.

For some undisclosed reason Selous spent the rainy season in Matabeleland, sending his museum specimens down to Klerksdorp in another trader's wagon.

In February 1885 he re-established base camp at his favourite spot on the Hanyame (Manyame) River in Mashonaland (about 90 kilometres due west of present-day Harare). On the way up from Bulawayo he encountered the largest herd of elephants he had ever seen, in fact, the only elephants he had seen since 1881. By the end of the day he had shot six of them and believed that, on a better horse, he would have got more. A month later he got another big bull. Clearly, he had lost none of his zest for the chase, for his account is as packed with detail as any in his first book. And with that his account screams to a halt:

> As to give any detailed account of my various journeys in search of game during the remaining months of 1885 would ... prove tedious ... I will content myself by saying that in the course of the season I again made a journey to the River Sabi in search of Lichtenstein's hartebeests, and on this occasion succeeded in shooting and preserving five fine specimens of those animals.[17]

At the beginning of the next chapter he remarks that having 'brought my narrative down to the end of 1885' he would 'pass briefly over the next two years'. That he does – in two paragraphs – which means that from late 1883 to March 1888 his second book tells us practically nothing of his daily life apart from his routes and a few hunting stories.

Since it was precisely March 1888 when Selous told Heany he intended to get rid of 'his woman', it seems reasonable to conclude that his evasiveness about the years 1883–8 is connected with the suppression of this relationship. By the time Selous wrote up his

Travel and Adventure in 1893, another five years had gone by and he stood at the pinnacle of fame – seemingly on the brink of wealth undreamt of during the years of hardship and isolation. He was also engaged to be married to an Englishwoman. The manners and mores of Matabeleland were very different from those prevailing in England in 1893. He had good reason to be evasive. So we must put *Travel and Adventure* aside and turn to other sources to reconstruct his movements and motivations from the end of 1885 to March 1888. Also, we must take account of big changes in politics and economics, movements of which he would have followed closely on his periodic journeys down to the Transvaal.

Visions of Eldorado

By January 1886 Selous told Günther he had sunk to a very low ebb:

> I am now getting so deeply into debt that I do not know how I am to extricate myself. During the last four years, I have led a very hard life and certainly a very frugal one, yet instead of making anything by my collecting, I have lost the £400 I brought from England with me four years ago.[18]

This may have exaggerated his situation, because it excludes any mention of his trading ventures. A letter to his mother written in April 1884 said that he had cleared many of his debts to Leask and that he owned wagons, stock and equipment to the value of about £2,000, which he would have difficulty selling, because of 'the depressed state of the country'.[19]

Everything changed in March 1886 when a huge gold reef was found in the central Transvaal. Within months, a camp of diggers had sprung up at the place they called Johannesburg. While this was going on Selous made a trading expedition to Matabeleland during which he says he did 'little shooting or collecting', then in August he did what he called a 'quick run home to England' where he spent six weeks before racing back to South Africa. If he had wished to sell his stock and equipment then, he could have made a handsome profit because demand was high. It was the diamond fields all over again, but on a far grander scale. A tsunami of capital was about to engulf the country.

By a quirk of fate, Britain handed the Transvaal back to the Boers just before the great gold rush. What is worse, it occurred at a time when other nations had been staking out claims to African territory. For centuries disease and African resistance had barred the Europeans from the continental interior. Quinine and machine-guns swung the balance of power the other way. In 1877 Henry Morton Stanley traced the course of the Congo River from East Africa to the Atlantic, showing that vast stretches of the mighty river could be opened to steam navigation. Soon the French were competing with King Leopold of Belgium to sign treaties with chiefs on either side of the Congo. In 1882 the British occupied Egypt and not long afterwards the French commenced a drive to connect their West African coastal colonies via the Niger River to their North African colony of Algeria. Between 1884 and 1885 Germany laid claim to Togo and Kamerun (Cameroon) in West Africa, Tanganyika in East Africa and South West Africa (Namibia). An international conference in Berlin grappled with the complex issues raised by these hasty grabs for territory. It was generally agreed that navigation should be free on African rivers and that no land claim would be recognized unless there had been 'effective occupation'. Whatever that might mean, it required something more than lines on maps and flags planted on mountain tops. The Berlin Conference of 1884–5 also acknowledged the existence of Leopold's Congo Free State as an independent sovereign entity after Belgium refused their monarch's offer to assign it as a colony.

Leopold had embarked on a kind of private enterprise imperialism. He planned to make his Free State pay by selling the right to exploit mineral and agricultural resources. If he could do it, others might do the same. The British dusted off the seventeenth-century concept of the Chartered Company and used it to extend the protection of its flag to privately owned businesses operating with Royal Charters in Nigeria and East Africa. Germany used a version of the same instrument in the initial phases of its operations in South West and East Africa.

Who knew what might ensue south of the Congo River basin? British Prime Minister William Gladstone, who had cheerfully given up the Transvaal in 1882, now faced the prospect of Germany connecting their east and south-west colonies with yet another annexation. The Transvaal, heir to a long tradition of Boer expansion, might use the wealth of the Witwatersrand gold to expand north toward the Zambezi or west to German South West Africa. Boer freebooters, with clandestine backing of the Transvaal, embarked on brief experiments with expansion westwards into Tswana territory on the Missionaries' Road and south-east through the old Zulu kingdom to the Indian Ocean. To check these alarming moves the British annexed the whole of Zululand and proclaimed a protectorate over Bechuanaland.

The big question remaining when Selous made his brief trip back to England in the summer of 1886 was what would happen to the territory he had been criss-crossing for the last fourteen years. There was nothing to stop the Transvaal Boers challenging Lobengula in Matabeleland as they had challenged his father Mzilikazi forty years earlier. Portugal was making noises about ancient claims to territory along the Zambezi from Mozambique right across to their Atlantic colony of Angola.

Above all, if gold had lain unnoticed under the feet of Transvaal farmers for half a century, surely there must be lots more north of Tati, where Africans had been mining it with primitive equipment for hundreds, if not thousands, of years.

Selous had not previously shown himself adept at politics or international relations, but he had a firm grasp on the local situation. He had seen at first hand the fragile and limited nature of Portugal's hold on the Zambezi. He knew Khama well and had never had problems getting through his country. He knew Lobengula equally well and, aside from the difficulty about the hippos, had never had a serious altercation. More important from a personal point of view, there was probably no Englishman who had a better working knowledge of the territorial limits to each monarch's effective power. While he was no mineralogist, he had seen ancient gold diggings and Africans panning for gold. On his ill-fated journey north of the Zambezi in 1878 he had hoped to do a little prospecting, so he had some idea of what to look for.

There can be no doubt these matters were the subject of deep conversations with his father when he got back to London in August 1886.

10

Maholie Lies

During Selous's brief stay in London, Rowland Ward put a proposition to him. In line with his practice of encouraging rich men to hunt big game, Ward had persuaded three wealthy enthusiasts to try their luck in central Africa. The party would consist of John A. Jameson, another scion of the Irish whiskey family; Mr Frank Cooper; and Mr A.C. Fontaine of Norfolk. Cooper and Jameson were already well known in hunting circles for their exploits with grizzlies and mountain sheep in North America, Fountaine was better known as Master of Hounds to His Royal Highness Albert Edward, Prince of Wales and the future Edward VII. It took Selous about half a second to agree to be their guide. Though there is no receipt among his papers, he would have been handsomely remunerated. Things were looking up.

As a reader of popular novels, Selous could not help but have noticed that the literary sensation of the moment was Rider Haggard's *King Solomon's Mines*. It tells of a seasoned South African hunter, Allan Quatermain, who guides two well-born English gentlemen on a quest for treasure lying somewhere beyond 'Sitanda's kraal': the very place where Selous caught the fever that ended his expedition in 1878. Haggard had read his book! Now came a real-life invitation to guide three wealthy hunters; a coincidence, of course, but the timing was uncanny. In January 1887 Ward announced that:

> one of the most completely equipped expeditions that has been ever organised for the African fields is just about commencing operations. During Mr. Selous's short visit to this country in ... 1886, I was

enabled to complete the organising of the expedition which I induced him to share. In the late months of that year Mr. Selous left for Africa to fit the wagons (of which there will be seven), and to prepare all necessaries in Africa, by the light of his exceptional experience. This has now been done, the members of the party will soon start for Matabele Land, where all good sportsmen at home will wish them success on those fields where yet the romance of sport may be tasted.[1]

Selous maintained a discreet silence about this grand expedition in *Travel and Adventure*, remarking merely that 'space will not permit of my giving any detailed account of our various peregrinations during this year'. Other sources help us reconstruct some of what went on. Selous had travelled to Bulawayo early in the year to make the required request for permission to hunt. The British High Commissioner wrote a separate letter to the king, explaining that Selous's companions were well-respected men of substance who should be given special protection. Lobengula obliged by saying 'the way was open'.[2]

By the end of May the party and their seven wagons had made their way to Fred's favourite base camp on the Hanyame (Manyame) River, from which they made extensive forays into the surrounding countryside. The large extent of territory they covered is shown on the extremely useful map which Selous sent to the Royal Geographical Society to illustrate a short article published in its *Proceedings* in May of the following year. The map shows not only the route taken in 1887, but all of his journeys east of Victoria Falls dating back to 1872. Some of the country was previously unknown to Selous, so exploration and hunting would have kept the men fully occupied until they broke camp in November. An account of lion hunting in another chapter of *Travel and Adventure* tells us that at the end of October they were hunting wildebeests near the source of the Sebakwi River, which places them in the vicinity of the modern town of Chivu, more than a 150 kilometres south-east of their main camp. They subsequently got a number of lions, thanks to their large pack of hounds. Lions, Selous remarked, stood no chance against anyone who could muster fifty dogs.[3] The passage on lion hunting also reveals that Jameson, Cooper and Fountaine brought English valets along who participated in the hunt.

His article for the RGS *Proceedings* also tells how Selous and Fountaine climbed Mount Wedza and ventured beyond the Save River toward Chimanimani on the Mozambique border. A third foray took the party back to the confluence of the Mniati (Munyati) and Umfile where Selous had found elephants with Jameson's brother in 1880. On another side trip they discovered the Sinoia (Chinhoya) caves, now one of Zimbabwe's national parks. They also trekked beyond Mount Hampden, north of modern Harare, which Selous had named in 1880. On his manuscript map a crescent-shaped region east of the mountain is coloured gold and marked 'Alluvial Gold Fields'.[4]

The reference to gold helps explain a worrying episode that threatened to bring the expedition to a premature end in August 1887. The hunters travelled with a large entourage of African helpers, perhaps a hundred or more. Like Africans recruited by Selous for earlier trips, they are likely to have included Tswana, Matabele and Shona. On 31 August Selous despatched a furious letter to Lobengula complaining that an armed contingent of the king's men had come to drive their 'boys' away:

> Three days ago, just as we were on the point of starting a journey to look for buffaloes and rhinoceros, the news came over to our camp that Umcheso and the people you have sent in to drive away our boys, were at Umfule. All our boys at once ran away, and slept in the veldt.[5]

The root cause of the incident was the anxiety felt in Bulawayo about the consequences of the gold fever ignited by the Witwatersrand discoveries of the previous year.

Since becoming king, Lobengula had lived in fear of a white invasion spearheaded by prospectors and miners. In 1870 he had granted a concession to Thomas Baines to search for minerals. That was never revoked, but the king's attitude shifted after he witnessed the British annexation of the formerly Griqua diamond fields. In 1875, as we saw in Chapter Five, Selous's friend Cigar set off a panic after seeing the quills of gold George Wood had brought out of Mashonaland. In 1886 Lobengula heard rumours that the English were set to annex the Transvaal again, because of the gold discoveries.[6] He feared the defeated Boers would push him out of his country across the Zambezi. He also kept a close eye on his neighbour and rival, King Khama, who had granted extensive mining concessions, some of which encroached on land he regarded as his. With Khama's acquiescence the British had proclaimed a protectorate over southern Bechuanaland. The first colonial administrator Sidney Shippard advocated pre-emptive annexation of a swath of territory reaching all the way to the Congo. In a report to the South African High Commissioner dated 21 May 1887 he stated his opinion that owing to its rich gold deposits 'Mashunaland is beyond comparison the most valuable country South of the Zambezi'.

By the time Selous's big hunting party left Bulawayo several sets of concession hunters were competing for Lobengula's favour. Two syndicates backed by politicians and speculators from the Cape Colony obtained permission to travel into Mashonaland: one headed by J.G. Wood, a member of the Legislative Assembly, the other backed by influential citizens of Cape Town. The latter group, known as the Northern Goldfields Exploration Syndicate, recruited several troopers from the Bechuana and Border Police to lead their expedition. The leader was 21-year-old Frank Johnson. These developments would have been well known to Selous through his network of trader and hunter acquaintances. In fact, another of the gold-seeking hopefuls, who claimed to have succeeded to ownership of Thomas Baines's 1870 concession, was a syndicate formed by his close friends George Westbeech and Thomas Leask.

Though Selous does not say so, it is entirely reasonable to surmise that Lobengula sent a contingent to his camp in August because of reports that they, too, were seeking gold. His letter to the king complained:

We have only been in here three months, when you send in people to drive away all our boys; and why? Because I hear that some Maholie has told you lies about me. When I come to Bulawayo, I want that Maholie to come before you, with me, and Malabamba, and say before my face what he has told you behind my back, and if I can show that he lies, you ought to make him pay for his lies with his head.

But it seems to me that you want to kill me with lies, and that is why you are ready to believe any lies your accursed God forgotten, Hell begotten, slaves choose to tell you.[7]

When Selous talks of 'Maholie lies', he uses a slang form of the word *amahole,* meaning 'lowly, worthless persons, no better than slaves'. Malabamba was evidently someone important from Lobengula's court who had accompanied Selous's expedition. The letter goes on to say that Malabamba had been to see the king's emissary, the *induna*, Mchesa, who chased away his 'boys' and succeeded in convincing him that lies had been told about their doings. A temporary arrangement had been worked out to get the men back to work. However, Selous feared:

> it is now too late. The mischief has been done. I do not think that our boys will remain, and expect they will all leave us. And then what are we to do? Messrs Jameson, Fontaine and Cooper are so disgusted with you and your people, that they would like to come out at once and leave your country as quickly as possible. But they cannot as the oxen are now so poor [through lack of grazing] that they will not be able to trek until the rains begin to fall. There is one more thing that I must tell you. Before leaving the Matabele country, we made arrangements with Mr. Carnegie to have our post sent us. The letters were brought in, and we all (Messrs Jameson, Collison, Fontaine and Cooper, and their servants) answered them and wrote out to our friends. Now Mcheso [*sic*] and his boys have rumba'd [probably a slang form of *ththumba*, meaning 'to rob'] the boys who were carrying these letters, and also taken a gun from them belonging to me.[8]

Although Selous addressed the king as 'most truthful amiable and friendly of my black brothers', the letter carried a veiled threat of British intervention. He wrote, he said, not on his own account but on behalf of:

> my friends Mssrs Jameson, Fountaine and Cooper. I ask you to remember that they are men of consideration in their own country and not dogs to be barked at and annoyed, by any Maholie who chooses to go and tell you lies about them. ... I must tell you that the hearts of my friends Messrs. Fontaine, Jameson and Cooper, are very black and they say they are very sorry that they ever came to your country.[9]

The Massacre

The letter must have done its work, for we hear no more about troubles with staff and find the party still happily hunting right through

October. There was, however, a sequel which threatened the reputations of all concerned. In mid-November a story appeared in South African newspapers, purporting to describe a massacre of Matabele men at Selous's camp. Within a month it was being widely circulated in the British press. Its gory detail and political attitudes merit quotation in full:

> Fred Selous, the celebrated hunter, with three friends recently from England (true British sportsmen) were away in Mashonaland after big game, accompanied by a bodyguard of one hundred and fifty Matabele warriors under an induna. The duties of these men, ostensibly acting as guides, bearers, beaters, and servants generally, were to keep a sharp look out on the doings of the white hunters, to prevent their leaving the actual hunting districts, and above all, to thwart their slightest attempt to prospect in the gold-bearing regions, or to meddle with the natural surface of the ground. Lobengula always insists on providing the hunter with a number of these men, under the pretext that he is performing a great service, of which it is moreover customary to make the king a suitable present, not as a mercenary *quid pro quo* but rather as a token of respect, admiration and gratitude all combined. On the present occasion Lobengula furnished an unusually large native retinue to the adventurous Britons, as he shrewdly perceived that they were persons of note and considerable worldly possessions. Selous, himself, is a great favourite with his corpulent majesty, and of the other three, Jameson was a *persona grata* who had won the king's good will on previous hunting tours. The remaining huntsmen, Capt. Fountain [*sic*], Master of the Prince of Wales's foxhounds and another, whose name has slipped my memory, were on their visit to Lobengula's territory, but their introduction was unimpeachable. The inordinate hankering after gold in its native state proved too great a temptation to the newcomers at least, if not to Selous and Jameson, both of whom should certainly have shown a little more wisdom: and after a good spell of hunting, the whole party divided from their proper course, and proceeded toward the northern gold fields, discovered by Thomas Baines, the explorer. There they imprudently set to work prospecting the country they passed through, turning over every likely looking rock or stone, and frequently doing a little business

121

like panning, with, it is said, dazzling results. It was the duty of the induna in charge to have put a stop to this sort of thing at once, and indeed, to have frustrated all attempts to leave the hunting grounds. By acting contrary to the king's orders, he and his party courted the implacable vengeance of the all but ominipotent monarch. One of the Matabele, fearful of the consequences which upon discovery would surely attend their rash proceedings, sneaked away to Gubulawayo [Bulawayo], and reported the facts to Lobengula, who instantly ordered out one of his regiments to administer the inevitable punishment for disobeying the king's commands. In due time, the regiment singled out to do the deed overtook the hunting party, all unconscious of their terrible fate. The king's messenger summoned the guilty induna, and acquainted him with the object of his sudden appearance. On his part the unlucky induna called his one hundred and fifty warriors together, and made known to them the king's unalterable decree. Without more ado the fearful slaughter commenced close to Selous's wagons. Not a single man of the transgressing party uttered a cry, but accepted his fate unmurmuringly, with stoic calmness. Two spear thrusts in the body and a blow on the head from a Kerrie, and all was over. In this manner one hundred and fifty Matabele subjects of splendid physique received their quietus, and crossed the Stygian ferry to that happy hunting ground, which, like the Indian of the far west, they believe is the future of every brave man of their nation who dies unflinchingly either in battle or by order of the king. It can be imagined that the white hunters were, as far as they knew to the contrary, in a nice quandary, although assured by Selous that no harm would come to them personally. They had, however, to witness the cold blooded butchery of their late dark-skinned hunting companions, a sickening sight, which they were only too glad to track away from, leaving seven score and ten bodies to be devoured by the wild beasts and carrion [scavenger] abounding in the neighbourhood. The hunters were then escorted back into the heart of the territory assigned to them for the exercise of their sporting proclivities, and warned to be more careful for the future how they offended savage royalty. After their late experience, it is improbable that they will ever again seek out the Mashonaland gold-bearing reefs so long, at any rate, as such a proceeding is contrary to the express orders of the reigning king.

So much for the last great massacre-extraordinary in Matabeleland. Those of an ordinary nature are so regular in their occurrence that no heed is any long paid to them.[10]

Stephen Taylor, who takes the story at face value, speculates that it was Fountaine and Cooper who collected gold samples, but Selous should have known enough to stop them before it was too late. 'Selous's judgment had been poor throughout the affair, and he knew it reflected no credit on him. He never mentioned it, and in his subsequent writings almost entirely glossed over the hunting trip of 1887.'[11]

In the case of this particular report, however, Selous took immediate steps to deny the story as soon as he read it in a paper at Shoshong. He was even more shocked to find this farrago of lies reprinted in his favourite magazine, *The Field*, where it was sure to be seen by all the friends and associates of Jameson, Fountaine and Cooper. The supposed massacre, he insisted was:

> a most impudent and mischievous lie, emanating from the brain of a drunken newspaper correspondent, probably at the time suffering from an incipient attack of delirium tremens, I hope that you will at once publish a refutation of the statement. I ask this in justice to Lo Bengula, and also to myself and the three gentlemen who were with me, and through whose indiscretion the alleged massacre is said to have taken place.[12]

Apart from his own denial, there are plenty of good reasons to side with Selous on the question of the massacre. The newspaper report gets key details wrong, failing to name Cooper, misspelling Fountaine and confusing John Jameson, who was in Africa for the first time, with his brother James who had previously accompanied Selous on hunting trips. The idea that wealthy men of high social positions known for their prowess in hunting would be diverted into prospecting for gold is risible. They stood to gain nothing by finding deposits, however rich. Only a mineral concession granted by a recognized chief would have any prospect of realization, and then only after the injection of substantial capital. Most of Selous's discretionary silence on the great expedition of 1887 can be explained in social terms. His wealthy clients were not the kind of men keen to get their names print, unless in the pages of *Debrett's Peerage*.

Had Fountaine, Cooper and Jameson been blinded by the lure of gold they would not have been hunting lions. The massacre report is, furthermore, conspicuously lacking in details of date, time and place. The 150 Matabele warriors of splendid physique comprise a suspiciously round number. By November, when the massacre rumour first began to circulate, Selous's party was on its way back to the Cape.

The story moreover played into the hands of all those hoping to discredit Lobengula as a prelude to grabbing his country. A better explanation for the whole business is that reports of Selous's troubles in late August got muddled up with entirely different problems afflicting competing teams of concession hunters in November. Lobengula had indeed sent a detachment to investigate Selous's activities after hearing 'the maholie's lies'. Far from bravely going to their deaths as unflinching Matabele warriors, the frightened 'boys' hid in the bush.

A couple of months later, in mid-November, both the Johnson and Wood parties of concession-seekers were called to account by Lobengula. According to Johnson, it was Wood who got them all into trouble by searching 'for gold when supposed to be hunting'. In a general atmosphere of panic over the real motives of the concession seekers, both got a tongue-lashing from the king. Johnson was fined £100 and sent away with no concession. Wood received a small concession, but it applied only to a small section of country already promised to Johnson by Khama.

Evidently the rumour mills of southern Africa ran the two stories together and spiced them up with the salsa of a massacre, which is confirmed by no other source, black or white. That said, it is necessary to add that Selous told the Royal Geographical Society in January 1888 that 'the map I am now sending you is one of a country which is bound to be of great importance in the near future, for there is an alluvial gold-field of a large extent and wonderful richness'. He could 'speak with some authority, as it has this year been roughly tested with really extraordinary results – backed by a country of great fertility, and watered most plentifully'. He doesn't say he did the prospecting and testing, but somebody did. In 1886 the most he had to say about Mashonaland was that it would be grand place for a Christian mission.[13] His sights were now evidently set higher.

11

Escaped Alone with His Life

B y the beginning of January 1888, Selous had reached the town of Zeerust in the north-eastern Transvaal, where he sent off a report of his recent discoveries to the Royal Geographical Society.[1] He had, he said, tired of the region south of the Zambezi. In the New Year he would take his wagons through the Okavango up into Barotseland where he would spend 'a couple of years in the wilds, hunting and collecting. I shall then, I think, return to England.' This means his wealthy hunting companions had paid him enough to sustain another big expedition. Every time he had gone north of the Zambezi in the last ten years he had been lucky to get back alive. What lured him back to a region where he had known nothing but heartbreak? If previous experience was not enough to deter him from this expedition, he got a spooky warning from beyond the grave.

Zeerust was the home of Caroline Kirkham, daughter of the veteran Matabeleland missionary T.M. Thomas. Two years earlier her brother David had been murdered on the Zambezi where he had been struggling to establish a new mission station. Disconsolate, Caroline had turned to spiritualism in the hope of contacting her lost sibling. She convinced a highly sceptical Selous to join her in a seance of 'automatic writing'. As he told the story a few years later, he held a pencil while she laid her fingers on the back of his hand. Immediately, the pencil began to move:

'David Thomas. Selous, go out of the country.' After reading this Mr. Selous asked why? His hand wrote 'you will be murdered'. Then it stopped. Presently it began again and wrote, 'Because you will be murdered by the natives.' Mr. Selous still kept his hand upon the table, and the message was repeated two or three times. As it was evident that his hand was going to keep on writing 'Selous, go out of the country, because you will be murdered by the natives,' Mr. Selous laid down the pencil and got up. Mrs. K-- took up the pencil and, laying her hand upon the paper, waited to see if the same mysterious force would use her hand. Her hand began to move, as Mr. Selous's had done, and wrote exactly the same message.[2]

Selous had discussed spiritualism with his mother in a letter where he expressed his doubts about the whole business, so was unlikely to have paid much heed.[3] Besides, like all oracles, the spirit had been vague about the circumstances. What country was he supposed to 'go out of'?

By the end of January he was in Cape Town, sending off specimens and more reports. With a railway running up to Kimberley, travel was faster. Selous got his equipment together at Klerksdorp and by March 1888 was back in Shoshong, where he dropped the news to Heany and Borrow that he would be getting rid of his woman. They had even bigger news for him. Cecil Rhodes had sent an agent named Rudd to trump the concession hunters who had been swarming over Matabeleland. He was 'said to have a grand scheme on with regard to Loben's country – some view of purchasing the whole box of tricks and a big thing generally.'[4]

Rhodes could do this because he had just this month put the last piece in place in the jigsaw puzzle of the Kimberley diamond claims he had been accumulating over the last decade. His great rival, Barney Barnato, had capitulated. A single company with Rhodes at its head, De Beers, now controlled the entire supply of South African diamonds. The company's trust deed allowed it to 'acquire any asset of any kind' including 'tracts of country'.[5] While the consolidation of the De Beers monopoly had distracted him from doing anything big on the Witwatersrand, Rhodes believed there were other, richer gold fields to be found north of the Limpopo. If, as Baines and Selous had written, Africans had been mining there since time immemorial, imagine what could be done with big money and machines.

It says volumes about Fred's deepest aspirations that he turned his back on all this in 1888, just as he had turned his back on the diamond diggings in 1871. With his connections in Matabeleland and his knowledge of Mashonaland, he could have been a player. He could have pitched a proposition to Rhodes. Instead, he went methodically about preparing his expedition to Barotseland. Adventure and exploration still mattered more to him than political scheming and rocks in the ground.

His first stop was George Westbeech's headquarters at Pandamatenga. No white man knew more about the Barotse kingdom. Thanks to adroit diplomacy over many years, most of the ivory coming out of Barotseland had been funnelled through his trading post. Although hard living and hard drinking had taken their toll – in a few months he would be dead – he still had his finger on the pulse of central African intelligence networks. He told Selous that his proposed expedition had no chance of success. A rival claimant to the kingship had challenged Barotse ruler Lewanika and the whole country was in an uproar. Instead of going westward along the Zambezi, Westbeech suggested striking directly north to the Garanganzi country west of Lake Bangweulu, where Frederick Arnot had succeeded in establishing a mission. Since 1882, when Selous introduced the aspiring evangelist to central Africa, the young man had travelled widely in lands unknown. He had, according to Westbeech, written quite recently to say he would welcome a visit from Selous 'in a fine country with a powerful chief' where elephants roamed in 'astonishing numbers'. Selous had tried twice before to get into that very territory. If Arnot got there, surely he could? Third time lucky!

On the spot he changed his plan. Barotseland could wait. He would leave his wagons and horses at Pandamatenga, pack sixteen donkeys with a year's worth of provisions, cross the Zambezi at Wankie's Town and trek north through Mashukulumbwe country.

He and Westbeech would certainly have talked of other matters, including the implications of Rhodes' intervention in Matabeleland. Selous knew that Westbeech and Thomas Leask had been pushing their own 'Baines Concession', though what chance they would have against Rhodes remained to be seen. North of the Zambezi was a different story. What gold and minerals that little-known country held had yet to be uncovered. A good hunter kept his eyes open for all contingencies. By the fifth of June Selous was ready to move out.

Along the Zambezi

It would be wrong to assume that only white men grasped the broader picture of prospecting and concession-hunting in this phase of the scramble for Africa. All the important kingdoms – Lewanika's Barotse, Lobengula's Matabele, Khama's Tswana – had spies at work. Big men like Kanyemba on the Zambezi kept the Portuguese informed. The trouble that kept Selous out of Barotseland was consequential rather than coincidental. Any ruler intending to hold his position needed to maintain supplies of arms and ammunition. That meant increased trading, raiding and looting. Rivalries among Africans spurred the hunt for elephants as much as European demand for piano keyboards.

The turmoil and misery created by the ivory and slave trades that Selous had witnessed on the lower Zambezi a decade earlier had spread steadily upstream. From the moment he crossed the river at Wankie's Town, he noticed the changes. He began to doubt the wisdom of his plan to travel east along the river before turning inland. When he last visited this region, he met people who had not seen a white man since Livingstone. Now everyone wanted money, guns and goods. At any moment raiders might appear from Kanyemba's territory down river, from the Barotse or the Matabele. The pervasive atmosphere of greed and fear meant that every little chief along the river demanded that Selous pay something for the right to pass through his territory. He despaired at the long hours spent negotiating with a chief named Shampondo, which ended in his making over goods worth £10 for the privilege of proceeding another mile or two on his way. As far as Selous was concerned this was extortion pure and simple. Though his heart was 'almost bursting with rage and indignation', he had no choice but 'to preserve an outward appearance of equanimity, talk, argue, and pay calmly'.

Rather than face an endless repetition of his experience with Shampondo, he decided to head inland at the first opportunity. At the next village he recruited guides to take him directly north onto the high plateau. The donkeys would have to pick their way through incredibly difficult terrain, but at least he would be free of harassment. Or so he thought.

His party at this stage included the minimum necessary for his

A simple marker in the Selous Game Reserve of Tanzania marks the spot where Selous was buried after being killed on 4 January 1917 by a sniper's bullet during the British campaign in German East Africa.

A memorial committee formed soon after his death commissioned a stone and bronze memorial which today stands on the right-hand side of the statue of Charles Darwin, on the grand staircase of the Natural History Museum, South Kensington, London.

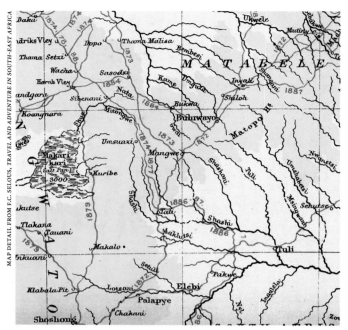

Path (marked '1872') taken by Selous on his hunting journeys in 1872, covering parts of modern Botswana and Zimbabwe.

The line marked '1887' shows the path taken by Selous and his party of gentlemen hunters covering an extensive territory in the eastern regions of modern-day Zimbabwe. The town shown here as Salisbury is today's Harare.

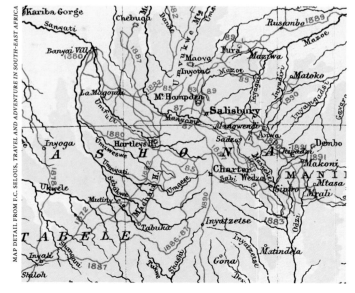

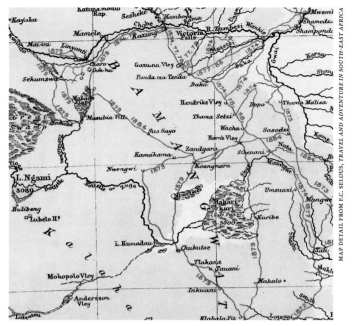

The region south and east of Victoria Falls where Selous had the most successful elephant hunts of his career, during the years 1873–4.

Showing the path taken by Selous in 1877 on his almost disastrous expedition into the Zambezi Valley and up to Sitanda's town.

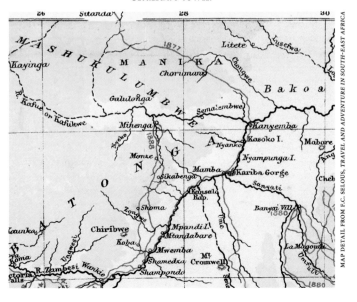

Oil painting by Henry C. Selous, 'Opening of the Crystal Palace Exhibition by Queen Victoria and Prince Albert' (1851).

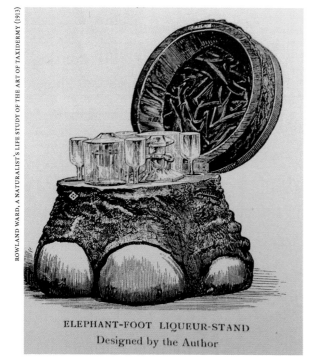

ELEPHANT-FOOT LIQUEUR-STAND
Designed by the Author

Famed London taxidermist Rowland Ward found many ingenious ways to install elephant remains in Victorian salons and drawing rooms.

Sentinel Island at Bukoba Harbour on Lake Victoria, Tanzania, where German searchlights forced a change of plan in the British assault of June 1915.

Ruins of the German wireless transmission tower destroyed during the British assault on Bukoba, Lake Victoria, 22–4 June 1915.

This studio portrait of Selous, taken at the time of his engagement to Gladys Maddy in 1893, is notable for the absence of his trademark rifle and slouch hat. His right cheek still bears the scar caused by an exploding elephant gun.

Selous required elaborate equipment for his expeditions in search of specimens for the Natural History Museum at South Kensington. This rare, slightly damaged, photograph shows him with his collecting wagons.

Captain Frederick Courteney Selous, D.S.O., in uniform – the last photograph taken before his death in action.

GEOGRAPHICAL JOURNAL (MARCH 1917)

In addition to their city home on Regent's Park Road, London, the Selous family acquired this country estate, Barrymore House, on the Thames at Wargrave.

ANTIQUE POSTCARD PROVIDED BY DAVID MONKS, CHELTENHAM

Selous in his characteristic studio pose, legs spread, guns across his lap, slouch hat on his head – every inch the big game hunter at ease.

purposes. There was a Griqua named Daniel who had driven one of the wagons up from Shoshong. A young fellow called Charley had been recruited at Pandamatenga; he was not only an excellent inter-preter but also a good shot. At Wankie's Town Selous picked up a Zulu named Paul who had been living there for several years, and could handle a rifle. Two Tswana men from Khama's capital completed his team of shooters. As general servants he brought four Mashonas who, he said, 'belonged' to him: two young men and two boys. Another fifteen men had been hired as porters at Pandamatenga. So there were twenty-four altogether under his command. As was to be expected, others joined in along the way, hoping for fresh meat from the hunt. Overall firepower was modest. Charley and Selous each carried a 450-bore Medford rifle made by George Gibbs of Bristol. Khama's men had double-barrelled 10-bore rifles, while Paul the Zulu shoul-dered a single-barrelled 10-bore. They had guns enough to deal with every kind of game, but these would hardly count as heavy artillery in a showdown with hostile men.

Ambushed among the Mashukulumbwe

So far the game had been scarce. By the time Selous turned his caravan north to the mountains, he was 200 miles out of Pandamatenga and had fired a total of four shots. His meagre bag so far comprised two antelopes and a zebra. For the next two days the donkeys clambered up and over some of the roughest and most convoluted rocky ground he had ever seen. Fortunately, by the fourth day he reached high country where the air was cool and the game abundant. Selous could shoot what he chose. His immediate objective was the headquarters of a chief named Monze whom Dr Livingstone had met at a place called Kesi-Kesi in 1853.

Political power in this area was highly fragmented. There were many petty chiefs but no paramount ruler exercising the authority of a Lobengula or Lewanika. The people who now call themselves Ila were then known to their neighbours as the Mashukulumbwe. Among their distinguishing cultural traits was the towering conical hairstyle favoured by adult males that in some cases extended more than three feet above the skull. As guns were still a rarity, each man relied on a bundle of wooden throwing spears for protection.

When Selous got to Kesi-Kesi (Chisekesi on today's map) he found that chief Monze was still alive, but had moved several miles north to a place still called by his name. Although old and wizened, he had a lively memory of Livingstone. He was also able to give Selous some disturbing information on the current state of the region. It turned out that the turmoil generated by the power struggle in Barotseland had spread east. At this very moment the man who hoped to displace Lewanika had retreated to a stronghold about fifteen miles to the south-west of Monze. This young warrior was a man of many names. His followers called him Marancinyan or Makunguru. Monze and the Mashukulumbwe people knew him as Sikabenga.

Selous was understandably disgruntled. He had changed his plans to avoid Barotseland, only to find that the civil war had followed him to Mashukulumbwe country. The best thing, he thought, was to push on north as quickly as possible.

Alas, two nights after leaving Monze's place, he woke to find his camp surrounded by gun-toting Barotse and a strong force of spear-carrying Mashukulumbwe. They disclaimed any hostile intentions. What they wanted was to trade ivory for ammunition. They refused to believe that he carried only enough for his expedition, and implored him to return with them to Sikabenga. If Selous refused, they told him he would most probably be murdered by the local Mashukulumbwe.

By now Selous must have been mulling over the warning scrawled by the moving pencil of Zeerust. He knew that the Czech naturalist and explorer Emil Holub had been attacked in this very country five years earlier. The threat was very real. On the other hand, there was no particular reason to trust Sikabenga and run the risk of losing his ammunition. He sent the deputation off with some presents for their chief and moved further north to the Magoye River. There he received a cordial welcome from a chief called Minenga, who told him it would be best to set up camp on the outskirts of his village. Lacking poles and branches, Selous rigged up a shelter made of cornstalks and secured his donkeys.

That evening round the beer pot Minenga was the soul of hospitality. His men would gladly direct the hunters to the elands and zebras that roamed the area and would be grateful for a share of what they shot. On the following day the chief's sons would guide Selous to the wide Kafue River where he kept canoes big enough to carry their donkeys. Confident that he would soon be well on the way to Arnot's mission in elephant country, Selous turned in for the night, while his men joined in some dancing with Minenga's friendly people.

The following day's hunting hardly counted as sport. Selous walked right up to a herd of zebras and brought two down with two shots at a distance of 150 yards. A hartebeest completed the day's haul and he was soon back at the village where crowds of curious people milled round his party. Minenga and his wife professed to be profusely grateful for the meat and other presents.

That night, however, there was no beer, music or dancing. The hunters dined alone as an eerie silence descended on the village. Not one of the strangers remained at Selous's camp, where, one by one, his men dropped off to sleep on the moonless, starlit night of 8 July 1888.

About nine o'clock one of the guides from Monze's town appeared at their cornstalk shelter and shook Paul by the leg. Something was wrong, he whispered. All the women had left the village. When Selous got the translation, he instantly extinguished the fires. Pulling on their shoes, he and his men sat waiting, rifles in hand. Just as Selous was reaching for more cartridges, shots rang out from guns poked through the cornstalks. Fortunately, none of the party was hit. 'Into the grass', Fred shouted in Afrikaans, and they ran for their lives. There was no time to work out a counterattack, or even to name a meeting place. As the large mob of Mashukulumbwe warriors set about pillaging the camp, the hunters scattered. Soon Selous was far out in the long grass, utterly alone. He had a rifle, four cartridges and the light clothes he was wearing.

The obvious thing was to make for the Zambezi more than sixty miles due south. Without an interpreter, he had no way to communicate with anyone he might meet on the way. Under the circumstances it seemed best to avoid people altogether, skirting villages and avoiding well-worn paths. He could only hope that those of his party who survived the attack would do the same, in which case they might eventually meet up. Fixing his eyes on the constellation of the Southern Cross, he set off walking at a steady pace in the direction of the Zambezi.

His Last Gun

On he trudged through the night and most of the next day, growing increasingly hungry. Animals were plentiful but he dared not risk giving away his position by firing his rifle. Towards evening the temptation presented by a wildebeest was too much. He brought it down with a single shot and roasted enough meat to last for three days. At dusk he was off again, hoping he might get beyond the last of the Mashukulumbwe villages before daybreak. As the night grew chill his determination wavered. A little past midnight he came to the last village, where he saw a fire burning. By his calculations he was no more than a couple of hours away from Monze's place. Judging from the old man's previous welcome, he might get some help there. Surely it would not hurt to sit awhile by the fire. He made a few fruitless efforts to make himself understood, which only aroused suspicion. From a nearby hut he heard the unmistakable click of a gun being loaded. With his own rifle clutched tightly between his thighs he felt safe enough. Gradually the cumulative effect of exertion and exhaustion got the better of him and he dropped off to sleep. When he awoke he found two men crouched beside him. Laying his gun to one side he tried once more to explain his situation with fragmented words and gestures. Too late he saw his mistake. A man had sneaked up behind him and snatched the rifle. At that very moment another man threw some dry grass at the fire, making it flare up. Across the clearing Selous's eye caught the glint of a rifle pointing at his chest. With one hand he snatched a piece of his roasted wildebeest, rolled to one side and sprang into the long grass.

Thankfully, no one attempted pursuit. He was alive, but with no means of defending himself or getting food.

As dawn broke he arrived at Monze's village, where at last he could make himself understood. However, he got no words of comfort. The chief told him that if stayed another instant he was a dead man. His only chance was to run, which he did.

Now another thought struck him. If he could get to the camp of the dissident Barotse, he might ask for protection, invoking the name of George Westbeech. Another forty-eight hours of hard walking brought him to Sikabenga's encampment. The young rebel expressed a wish to stay on the right side of Westbeech and other white men, but was evasive when Selous asked for help in recovering his lost property. After much prevarication Sikabenga offered three men to take him to a village where he would find help in getting back to Pandamatenga. There he heard for the first time that several of his men had been sighted on the path to Shankopi's town on the Zambezi. Five days later he and the ten survivors met and exchanged stories. Twelve of the original party of twenty-five had died the night of the attack and another six had been wounded. Paul the Zulu, Charley and one of Khama's men had escaped but managed to hold on to just one of the rifles. Selous does not say whether the two Mashona boys who 'belonged to him' had made it back, so any speculation about their precise relationship to him has to end there.

One more significant detail emerged a few weeks later after a Matabele war party killed Sikabenga and most of his Barotse forces in a surprise attack. A survivor disclosed that it had been Sikabenga himself who organized the attack on Selous's party, planning to seize the ammunition he needed to carry on his struggle. He hoped to hurry the hunter out of the country before he caught sight of any of the goods looted from his camp. Incredible as it may seem, the Matabele regiment returned to Bulawayo with the donkeys and some of the stores taken from Selous.[6] Whether any of these goods were returned to him remains unknown.

Into Barotseland

In any case, he had lost so much vital equipment that he could not contemplate spending the summer out in the field without restocking at Klerksdorp. He did, however, have enough time left ahead of the rainy season to make a brief visit to Barotseland. With the rebellion chopped off at the head, Lewanika faced no imminent threats and could resume his normal business of controlling the ivory trade out of his country. Large sections of his domain were reserved for hunting by his subjects, which guaranteed him a healthy cut of the profits when tusks were sold on through Westbeech. Trade rather than the collection of specimens motivated this expedition. At Pandamatenga Selous sent off orders for essential items lost north of the Zambezi and bought a number of elephant tusks on sale there.[7]

Selous took Charley, Paul and three 'salted' horses, which he

133

planned to exchange for ivory at Lewanika's capital, Lealui. The trip, which lasted just two months, took him through country he found profoundly monotonous. And where it was not tedious – on the rivers – tsetse flies and mosquitoes abounded. He looked with a mixture of pity and admiration upon the French Protestant missionaries, Jeanmairet and Coillard, who had recently settled their families on lonely stations in a charmless land.

Lewanika appeared well on the way to becoming a second Khama. He dressed as a European and had given up beer in favour of Selous's preferred beverage, tea. He received Selous with kingly dignity and assigned him a hut within the royal enclosure. After a formal exchange of presents, the sale of the horses was concluded. Selous left with a fine load of ivory and the king's promise of canoes to carry down-river. As he feared, the country turned out to be as unhealthy as it was unlovely. He, Paul, Charley and several of their porters came down with malaria on the eve of their departure. They were glad to be on their way through grassland that promised good hunting. Just as the animals were becoming plentiful, a hippopotamus sank the canoe carrying the cartridges, thus bringing to an end what proved to be Selous's last-ever expedition as a hunter and collector in southern Africa.

By January 1889 he was back in Shoshong, where Frank Johnson brought him up to date on the vultures circling Lobengula's kingdom. There was a lot to tell. Johnson thought Selous might be interested in a scheme he had in mind for getting the gold of Mashonaland out through the back door.

12

Working for the Colossus

Historians have burnt much midnight oil working out how Cecil Rhodes outmanoeuvred his many rivals to secure possession of all Matabeleland and Mashonaland. None of this mattered much to Selous. What he learnt from Frank Johnson in January 1889 was that Rhodes had carried out the scheme hatched in March of the previous year to purchase 'the whole box of tricks'. Rhodes's agent, Charles Dunnell Rudd, had secured a new concession from Lobengula granting exclusive rights to exploit the minerals of the country. On that basis Rhodes had formed the British South Africa Company in October as a vehicle for managing the operation. He was currently negotiating with the British government for the grant of a Royal Charter that would place the BSA Company and its people under the protection of the Crown, preventing the Germans, the Portuguese, the Transvaal or any other power laying claim to the territory. The deal was that the BSA Company would carry out most of the normal functions of government – policing, road building, taxation, etc. – while Britain looked after external relations and defence. People living under BSA Company rule would be treated as British subjects.

Many questions hung over the Rudd Concession. Why should it trump all the other concessions Lobengula had granted over the years? What exactly had the king agreed to? (He protested too late that all he said was that Rhodes could dig *one hole*.) What were the geographical boundaries of the territory covered by the concession? Rhodes won out despite these uncertainties because of the apparently limitless resources at his disposal. None of the competing syndicates apart from the Transvaal Government could hope to do anything more than form mining companies. The British Government was determined to confine the Transvaal to its existing boundaries, so there was no chance of that bid succeeding. Rhodes dealt with other rivals by buying them out. His treasure chest, De Beers Consolidated Mines, permitted him to outspend anyone. That is not to say there were no risks. Rhodes gambled that a gold reef bigger and richer than the Witwatersrand would be found very soon and justify every penny spent by De Beers. He turned out to be wrong, but no one knew that in 1889.

When Frank Johnson sat down with Selous at Shoshong the territorial question was uppermost in his mind. The concession Lobengula granted to Johnson's Northern Goldfields Exploration Syndicate in 1887 covered territory lying to the west of Matabeleland. What about the east? A few Shona chiefs lived formally under Lobengula's protection, so their country could be fairly reckoned as part of his kingdom. The case was different in more distant territories subject to periodic Matabele raids. It required a stretch of the imagination as well as jurisprudence to argue that the Rudd Concession applied there. Selous could attest from his own experience that parts of Mashonaland had never seen a Matabele war party. And yet, it was there that the most promising gold samples had been found, between Matabeleland and Portuguese Mozambique. Clearly, Mashonaland was bounded on the south by the Limpopo and on the north by the Zambezi, but no lines as yet marked the western and eastern frontiers.

Johnson's idea was that he and his financial backers would build a position in Mashonaland that did not depend on access through the Matabele kingdom. He therefore proposed that Selous should guide a team of prospectors from Quelimane in Mozambique to Mashonaland via the Zambezi. This would simultaneously discover the limits of Portugal's effective occupation and lay the groundwork for a concession granted by Shona chiefs not subject to Lobengula.

Selous accepted on the spot. After the previous year's heavy losses he was in no position to mount another big expedition. Johnson offered cash on the barrelhead.

Mightiest of African Hunters

Knowing how deadly the Zambezi could be in the rainy season, Selous planned to start in June. That gave him an opportunity to make a short trip to England. His book *Travel and Adventure* says nothing about his voyage on the ss *Moor*, which is surprising because he had as fellow passengers two of Lobengula's principal *indunas*, Mshete and Babayane. They were on their way to tell Queen Victoria what Lobengula thought about the bickering over his country. The idea of the delegation had originated with Edward Maund, who had been acting as the agent of a London syndicate backed by George Cawston, Lord Gifford and the financier Nathan Rothschild. Maund planned to torpedo Cecil Rhodes by casting doubt on the Rudd Concession. By December 1888, however, his backers had changed tack. They now proposed to amalgamate their company with Rhodes, with the result that they became part of the British South Africa Company.[1]

Frank Johnson undoubtedly knew about the Matabele deputation and may have heard rumours about the company amalgamation. That would explain why Selous raced down to Cape Town in time to board the ss *Moor*, which sailed on the sixth of February. Selous was unlikely to have passed up the opportunity to speak with Lobengula's *indunas* on the three-week voyage. The only conceivable reason for failing to mention them in *Travel and Adventure* was that he subsequently went to work for Cecil Rhodes and had committed himself to say nothing about the background to the grant of a Royal Charter to the British South Africa Company. That would also explain why, a day after his ship landed on 28 May, Selous was called to the Colonial Office to serve as the interpreter for a interview between the Colonial Secretary and Lobengula's envoys.

For the first time in his life Selous found himself the object of media attention. The *Nottingham Post* gave him celebrity billing:

The mightiest of African hunters, Mr. F.C. Selous, arrived in London yesterday direct from the Zambesi. He has, says London correspondent, arrived in London after a most adventurous journey. What he has to tell of Matabeleland, so recently brought within the British sphere of influence, is especially valuable at the present time. Taken all in all, this is probably the richest country in Africa. The extensive plateau, known as Mashonaland, is a paradise for the agriculturist. Every ridge sends forth its stream, and, unlike other parts of South Africa, these streams run all the year. The vegetation is of the most luxuriant character, and the plateau, 2,000 to 5,000 feet high, is practicable for any kind of vehicle. The whole of Matabeleland is an excellent wheat country, but on the Mashona plateau wheat and any other grain can grow luxuriantly, and European vegetables and fruits of all kinds. At present it is uninhabited, for Lobengula's people, here as elsewhere, have driven away or exterminated the inhabitants, so that they themselves need not complain if they are driven out by newcomers.[2]

Clearly Johnson's backers had already prepared a media campaign on behalf of the Mashonaland venture. Selous was their centrepiece. A week later the *Pall Mall Gazette* reported that the Rudd Concession had fallen through and the whole country was up for grabs. It went on to say that 'an English company has been formed for the purpose of exploring with a view to its ultimate exploitation, the stretch of country on the east of Matabeleland, and to the west of the ill-defined limits of Portuguese territory.' An exploring party would leave within weeks, led by:

> Mr. F.C. Selous, the well-known hunter, who knows the Zambesi region better than any other white man. Mr. Selous's duties will be confined to leading the expedition by the most expeditious route to its destination, which is described as a great tableland, with a healthy climate even for Europeans, a fertile soil and great mineral wealth.[3]

There could be no doubt that Johnson's syndicate had more in mind than gold mines. This was a full-blown scheme for colonization.

Selous was no mere puppet in the business. That became clear when an extended interview he granted to an unnamed reporter appeared on 9 March. This journalist claimed to have spent a good deal of time with Selous since his return. 'I may say,' he remarked, 'that Mr Selous is well known as one of the most precisely truthful, as well as observant, travellers, modest in the extreme, and thoroughly fair-minded.'[4] For the first time in his life Selous laid out an expansive geopolitical analysis of southern African affairs. It was inevitable, he told the reporter, that the Boers of the Transvaal would soon be outnumbered by immigrants attracted to the gold fields, who would insist on taking over the government. When that happened many of the Boers would probably do as their forefathers had done, and trek north to some new territory. Shifting into prophetic mode he declared that a federation of territories south of the Zambezi was inevitable. It would not, however, be under the aegis of the Cape Colony, which was the poorest region of all South Africa. The future centre of the population and of influence:

> ... will not be at the Cape, but on the Mashonaland plateau in Matabeleland, a region quite as large as France, lying at a height of about 2000 to 5000 feet, with of a multitude of perennial streams, of exuberant richness, capable of giving every temperature and South European product in abundance, and admirably adapted for European colonisation. It is, indeed – take it all in all – the richest region in Africa, and Matabeleland, though at a lower level, is not far behind it.[5]

Next Selous launched into a strident denunciation of Lobengula and the whole Matabele nation:

> Mr Selous is of opinion that Lobengula and his people must go. They themselves are intruders and ravagers who took the country from its inhabitants, then almost depopulated it. They are a lot of sanguinary scoundrels, and if they do not show themselves amenable to reason we need have no compunction in wresting from them a region which does not belong to them.[6]

Up to this moment Selous had never spoken of Africa beyond the Limpopo as a field for European colonization or settlement. A year earlier he had told the Royal Geographical Society that Mashonaland was a well-watered, fertile plateau with proven resources of alluvial gold. Now he painted a far grander vision: a country destined to be richer than the Transvaal and home to a larger population of white settlers than the Cape Colony. No doubt he saw his expedition for Frank Johnson as just a first step in the implementation of this vision. He wrote under his own name an article for the *Fortnightly Review*, denying in the strongest possible terms that Lobengula had any claim to a territory the king had never seen and which paid him no tribute.[7]

During his few weeks in England Selous visited the Royal Geographical Society and secured their backing for his coming expedition.[8] He would also have seen Rowland Ward and discussed his plans to write a new book covering the whole of his African career.[9] Beyond this he would barely have had time to catch up with relatives before he shipped out to Cape Town at the end of the third week of April.[10]

Short as it was, his seven weeks in England marked a turning point in his career. The public had taken notice. He was 'mightiest of hunters', 'the famous South African hunter and explorer', 'the well-known hunter', 'the most famous big game hunter in the world'.[11] One reporter compared his account of the escape from Mashukulumbwe country to 'Mr. Rider Haggard's novels'. As noted above, at the same time he was hailed as 'well known as one of the most precisely truthful, as well as observant, travellers, modest in the extreme, and thoroughly fair-minded.'[12] By the end of the year these two storylines converged and the press began to speak of him as 'really the original of Mr. Rider Haggard's hero – Allan Quatermain'.[13]

By dint of repetition this supposition came to be accepted as fact. Neither Haggard nor Selous ever repudiated it, which helped the legend grow. It probably suited them both to remain silent. Haggard liked the idea that the public accepted his character as a reasonable facsimile of a real-life African hunter. Selous could see that the comparison with Quatermain boosted his profile and helped sell books. It was true that Haggard had drawn on Selous's first book for its wealth of detail on the business of hunting elephants in central Africa. On the other hand, he could not possibly have modelled Quatermain on Selous's physique or personality. Allan Quatermain is described as a shortish, wiry man in early middle age with a grown-up son who was training to be a London physician. As Haggard's narrator in *King Solomon's Mines* and *Allan Quatermain*, he discloses a deep and introspective mentality. Selous tells us very little about his interior life in any of his books. The studio photograph that illustrates *A Hunter's Wanderings* shows him as he then was, a very young, very powerfully built man of above middle height.

Was he truly 'the mightiest of hunters'? Most of the large, dangerous animals he killed were shot during his first decade in South Africa: 78 elephants, over 100 buffaloes and something like 20 rhinoceros. Over the next decade he added 20 elephants, a few rhinos, several hippos and more buffaloes. In 1908 he reckoned that over his lifetime he had killed 31 lions. Most of the rest of the animals he shot were giraffes and zebras shot for their meat, and a large number of antelopes collected as specimens to be mounted. Taken together, these were modest totals. Older professional hunters like George Wood, Piet Jacobs and Cornelis Van Rooyen had much, much larger bags of elephants. We cannot begin to count the numbers felled by Griqua and other African hunters. Where Selous outclassed his contemporaries was in *writing* about the business. He made the animals and the chase come alive for readers in an age that valorized hunting and hunters. His connections with the Natural History Museum and the Royal Geographical Society gave him an additional scientific cachet that few hunters could match. The taxidermy firms of Ward and Gerrard promoted his fame because it was good for their business. In the cut-throat world of the African freebooters and concessionaires, the reputation of 'honest, modest Selous' promised to confer a mantle of romance and adventure on what was at bottom a dirty business of cheating indigenous people out of their land.

Mr Rhodes

A few weeks before Selous sailed for Cape Town, Cecil Rhodes had arrived in London. He intended to do whatever it took to secure a Royal Charter for his British South Africa Company. The linchpin of his argument was that the Rudd Concession entitled the company to conduct business throughout all the territory subject to Lobengula. Rhodes included under this rubric any territory from which the king drew tribute – which in his eyes included all of Mashonaland. Selous, who was on record as saying that most of that territory was held by independent chiefs, directly threatened Rhodes' claim to everything between King Khama's territory and the Portuguese in Mozambique. Selous's current plan to make his way into Mashonaland via Portuguese territory would reinforce his credibility on the question of sovereignty.

For the moment, however, Rhodes was free to press his case with the political and financial masters of the Empire, using all the vast resources at his disposal. Lord Salisbury's government was inclined to listen. It had already declared the whole territory as lying within the

British sphere of influence. Here was Rhodes offering to take over all the functions of government without any cost to the British taxpayer. There were moral and legal objections, but every passing month brought Rhodes closer to the coveted Royal Charter.

Selous had not told his parents much about his plans. A letter told of his arrival in Cape Town after a voyage distinguished mainly by the dismal female company:

> We left England with five elderly women; two much bejewelled and very vulgar jewesses, and three other very uninteresting christians, and not one of the five ever laid her hand on the piano the whole voyage. At Madeira we took in a Mrs and Miss Hall; the latter a good tempered silly young woman, feebly musical and by no means pretty. At St Helena we were joined by a Miss Richardson who was going to join her brother at the Cape. She was a very nice girl, though no longer young, and had travelled a great deal in the north of Norway and Lapland. Altogether I must say that the fair sex had very little indeed to do with making the voyage pleasant.[14]

His emphasis on the young unmarried women suggests that mother had been hinting it was high time he found a bride. The snobbish tone gives us a rare glimpse of the man behind the mask of plain, modest hunter Selous. As far as his coming expedition was concerned he said only, 'I do not yet know exactly what I am going to do, but think I shall be employed to lead a prospecting party up the Zambesi. We shall go nowhere near the Matabele, so you need be under no apprehension on that score.' As he had already said a great deal more about the expedition in interviews with the press, he was evidently not keeping his family fully in the picture.

Preparations for the expedition must have been under way long before he arrived in Cape Town. His companions would be Edward Burnett, whom he had met in Mashonaland two years earlier, and an old sailor named Thomas who had left the sea to become a miner on the Australian gold fields. More recently he had been working a shaft at Tati. Selous drank in the pleasures of his new celebrity status at Cape Town. Within a few days he had been the subject of a feature article in the *Cape Argus* and drew a large audience, including the Acting Governor, to his lecture for the Philosophical Society, where

he was commended for his 'flow of language and distinct enunci-
ation'.[15] A week later, on 10 June, he boarded the ss *Courland* with
thirty-seven packing cases of equipment, bound for Quelimane on the
Mozambique coast.

The lower Zambezi was new to Selous but old in the annals of
European colonization. Vasco da Gama had dropped anchor at
Quelimane in 1498. As early as 1531 the Portuguese had established a
settlement at Tete, 260 miles upriver. Selous presented his credentials
to the provincial governor at that town, including a letter of introduction from the Portuguese Consul at Cape Town approving the
staking of claims for any gold they might find in Portuguese territory.
At every town along the way Selous found authorities hospitable, but
justifiably apprehensive about British designs on their neighbourhood.
Apparently, a detachment of troops was on its way to extract pledges
of loyalty from Shona chiefs.

Selous did not, of course, confirm that their suspicions were correct
– it was very much part of his mission to demonstrate the flimsiness of
the Portuguese claims to any part of Mashonaland. The lower Zambezi
held no charm for him. Fever and squalor pervaded this 'very miserable spot on the earth's surface'.[16] He turned inland at the Muta River,
upstream of Tete, and set about finding the Mazowe River near the
alluvial gold field he had marked on the map he made for the Royal
Geographical Society in 1887. From this point on he operated in his
accustomed fashion, mixing exploration and prospecting with hunting
and collecting. On his way he encountered the usual difficulties with
recalcitrant porters and 'extortionate' chiefs. Rather than give into the
demands made by Chief Maziwa, Selous set fire to a pile of trading
goods and moved on while his antagonist watched in impotent fury.

He had the satisfaction of charting territory previously unknown
to cartographers and naming prominent features for some of his
favourite authors. One he named Mount Darwin: 'after that illustrious
Englishman whose far-reaching theories – logical conclusions based
upon an enormous mass of incontrovertible facts – have revolution-
ized modern thought, and destroyed for ever many old beliefs that had
held men's minds in thrall for centuries'.[17]

Selous thoroughly appreciated the irony of Europeans assigning
names to places that already had them. With inspired humour he
changed the name of the hill known to the Shona as Tchakari to

Thackeray: 'as a tribute to the memory of the immortal novelist, whose genius has so often enabled me to escape, for the time being, from my surroundings; to forget the filthy, soulless, sordid, mean, and vermin-swarming savages amongst whom I actually was, and to live again, in spirit at least, amongst the dwellers in Vanity Fair'.[18]

His enquiries showed that Portuguese emissaries had been active among the Shona chiefs, distributing flags and eliciting pledges of allegiance. As a counter he got two chiefs, Mapondera and Temaringa, to put their marks upon a paper he produced, which gave him a mining concession for their territory and stated that 'they were entirely independent and had never paid tribute either directly to the Portuguese Government' or any of its subordinate agents.

This scrap of paper would mean more for his personal fortune than all the game he shot over a lifetime of hunting. On his return to Tete in October he posted a letter to the 'Selous Syndicate' in Cape Town, sending news of his concession and recommending that an expedition establish the basis for a colony in Mashonaland by cutting a road directly east from Khama's country along the Limpopo to a place beyond the limits of Matabele authority, from which it would strike north up to the Mazowe.[19]

The letter does not survive in any archive, so we must rely on Selous's word that he wrote and sent it. The Selous Syndicate to which he referred was a financial device of Johnson and his Cape Town backers, who previous called themselves the Northern Gold Fields Exploration Company.[20] One sentence in Selous's letter was particularly arresting:

Should Mr. Rhodes have got the charter, then this is his true policy: to open up a southern route from the British [Bechuanaland] Protectorate to Mashunaland (which only requires to be made, and which will be quite as good a road as the northern one passing through Matabililand), and then first to develop the eastern slopes of Mashunaland, and not only to exploit and work the gold there, but to send in emigrants and settle up and occupy the country.[21]

Selous did not know it then, but Rhodes had got his Royal Charter. His quick, practical mind had already grasped a fatal flaw in Selous's logic. The Charter and the Rudd Concession that underpinned it were based on the premise that all Mashonaland was a tributary dependency of the Matabele kingdom. Selous's published observations on the effective independence of most of Mashonaland, and the mineral concession he carried, gave the lie to the assumption of Shona subjection, in which case the Royal Charter would not apply to their territory. That in turn would mean that Rhodes could claim no more than Matabeleland proper and the gold of Mashonaland would be out of reach. Portuguese officials were already disputing Rhodes's claim to the territory, citing the article Selous had written for the *Fortnightly Review* the previous May.[22] They were equally perturbed by the concession Selous claimed to have secured from a chief under their jurisdiction.

At every post along the way, Portuguese officials expressed their annoyance at his impertinent meddling. They had heard that he carried a paper purporting to declare the independence of certain Shona chiefs and demanded he hand it over. Fearing the loss of his precious concession, Selous called on a Jesuit missionary to witness a copy he made, which he then surrendered. Despite their hostility the officials made no effort to detain him and he reached the Atlantic coast without incident. (A report about this time in English papers wrongly stated that his goods had been seized and destroyed on Portuguese orders; it was most likely a garbled version of a theft perpetrated by black soldiers on an agent of the African Lakes Company travelling up via the Shire River to Lake Nyasa.)[23] His small boat pulled alongside the steamer *Courland* hours before it sailed from Quelimane on the 15 November.

As soon as he reached Cape Town, Fred got the train up to Kimberley for what was, it seems, his first meeting with the man the whole of the Empire was now calling the Colossus. He explained that occupation of Mashonaland from the Zambezi would be impossible, because the river was in many places too shallow for the large craft that would be required. Then he presented his alternative plan. Rhodes heard him out, but would not at first accept the idea of circumventing Lobengula's kingdom with a new road to Mashonaland.[24] What Selous did not know was that Rhodes had been talking with Frank Johnson and Maurice Heany about a direct invasion. By this time Johnson's company had collapsed, outfoxed by the amalgamation of rivals into the British South Africa Company.[25] He and Heany now proposed to work for Rhodes and march to Bulawayo with a picked force of fighting men. Either Lobengula would let them through or they would destroy his regiments and proclaim the accession of the territory to the British South Africa Company by right of conquest.[26]

Selous scoffed at the idea of overcoming the Matabele with so small a force. Thousands, not hundreds, of soldiers would be needed to guarantee success. What swayed Rhodes in the end was that his right-hand man, Dr Leander Starr Jameson, agreed with Selous. Why take a chance when a peaceful occupation of Mashonaland could be managed by the alternative road? As for Selous's inconvenient views on Shona independence and his concession, they could be dealt with in the classic Rhodes way. On 22 December 1889 Selous wrote to tell his mother that Rhodes had purchased his concession (and his silence) for £2,000. He had entered the BSA Company service on a monthly retainer and would 'get more when the Mashuna country is opened up.'[27] As Rhodes liked to put it, he had been 'squared'.

13

Rhodesia

A year earlier, Selous had walked out of the long grass at Shankopi's village, alone, with only the clothes on his back. Now he was the salaried employee of one of the richest men on earth. He had more money in the bank than he had ever seen. The deal included shares in the De Beers company and a large grant of land when the mission was completed.[1] Selous stood at a crossroads. Behind him lay the tough but glamorous years of hunting and collecting. For most of the previous decade he had been his own boss, wandering where he pleased with his handpicked, multi-ethnic, multilingual crew. By preference he carried no tent, bedding down each night under the wide African sky. Ahead of him lay the possibility of great wealth: farms, shares, a proper marriage, maybe a country house in England. Was this the crossroads where he consigned his soul to the devil in a midnight contract signed with blood?

Certainly Cecil Rhodes makes a plausible devil. He was engaged in daylight robbery on an audacious scale. In exchange for an insignificant consideration he proposed to take control of a country two-thirds the size of France, to carve it into farms and mines, and to sell these off to European interlopers – all without reference to the existing African population. If the Matabele resisted, Rhodes would gun them down. Looked at another way, Rhodes was one more in a long line of conquistadores operating according to a formula that dated at least as far back as Cortés and earlier. Take land from the existing inhabitants, divide it into parcels, distribute some to loyal followers and sell the rest. Cost of land: negligible. Rate of profit after deducting expenses of conquest:

enormous. Texas, Australia, Natal, Canada, Algeria and many other newly settled countries followed the same script. In the American Midwest land seized from Native Americans was sold to white settlers, with the proceeds used to build transcontinental railroads.

In the late-Victorian era conquerors and settlers offered myriad pretexts and justifications for their actions. At the highest philosophical level they argued that they were making more productive use of the land than the natives ever had. The religious claimed God's mandate to take land from the heathens and Canaanites. Others spoke of Nature's inexorable laws and the survival of the fittest. In the particular case of Matabeleland and Mashonaland, the argument was a little more refined. The land on which Lobengula's kingdom stood had been seized by force from the original inhabitants. Lobengula's claim to legitimacy dated no further back than 1840 when Mzilikazi and his ruthless regiments had stormed in from the south. During subsequent decades Matabele raids had depopulated the territory to the north and east of them, killing many of the Shona and driving the rest into hiding. White settlers would build their farms on the uninhabited, depopulated lands. The Shona should be grateful to the settlers for putting a stop to Matabele attacks. And anyway, if Rhodes had not occupied the land on behalf of Britain, it would have fallen to the Germans, the Portuguese or the Transvaal Boers.

These arguments are rarely heard today. It is taken for granted that Rhodes stole the land and distributed it to his gang of thieves. The Shona, whose descendants form the most numerous part of the population of Zimbabwe, do not celebrate liberation from Matabele oppression. On the contrary, they honour the 'war veterans' who re-occupied white settler farms that they considered were rightfully theirs. At the University of Cape Town in 2015 students assaulted a statue of their institution's founder, proclaiming 'Rhodes must fall'. For the most part he had fallen long beforehand. Were it not for the Oxford University Rhodes Scholars, his name would by now have sunk into obscurity.

Selous accepted the commonly held view of his contemporaries that Rhodes was a far-seeing statesman and that Mashonaland was the most suitable region in Africa for white settlement. The only important point on which he dissented from Rhodes was in his well-publicized opinion that most of the Shona had never been subject to Lobengula.

As a newly employed agent of the British South Africa Company he fell silent on that issue.

In Selous's favour it must be said that his proposal to lead settlers into Mashonaland via a newly cut road skirting Lobengula's kingdom delayed, even if it did not prevent, the war with the Matabele that Frank Johnson and Maurice Heany wanted to provoke. Many years later Johnson claimed in his extremely unreliable memoirs that it was he who had come up with the plan for a road around Matabeleland. Selous, he said, knew nothing about the territory to the south-east of Bulawayo and was merely employed to manage the road gang.[2] Johnson must have known his account was a lie that was bound to be exposed by historians sifting through the archives. However, the desire to share the glory due to the pioneers of Rhodesia was too much for him. Nowadays, of course, no one thinks there was anything very glorious about the long march of the Pioneer Column.

Cutting the Road

Johnson had encouraged Rhodes to think that a relatively small, well-equipped force of fighting men could repel any Matabele assault. The British High Commissioner for southern Africa, Sir Henry Loch, fearful of the slightest setback, insisted on a force of at least 400. Rhodes, always a man in a hurry, complied, recruiting 500 officers and men to his newly formed private army: the British South Africa Police. Johnson took charge of an additional body of armed and uniformed 'Pioneers', each of whom was promised a large grant of land at the end of the trek to northern Mashonaland. Their armoury included machine-guns, cannon, rocket launchers and mines. They carried a steam-powered naval searchlight to light up the battlefield at night. As a privately funded experiment in military colonization nothing like this had been seen south of the equator.

Selous had not only to find a route for this lumbering convoy of 117 wagons, but also to cut the road as they marched. For help he turned to King Khama at Shoshong, who played an unrecognized but indispensable role in the enterprise. He offered Tswana labourers for road work along with one of his principal headmen, Makamana, who knew the country to the east along the Limpopo. On every preceding hunting expedition Selous had taken the road through Bulawayo. He had done no hunting or exploration in the country lying to the south and east of Lobengula's capital: it was all unknown territory for him. The real guide for the first half of the Pioneer Column's march was Makamana.

To understand why a black king and his people lent a willing hand to the creation of a neighbouring colony destined for occupation by white settlers, it is necessary to step back and look at the bigger picture. Over the previous forty years hunting and trading had transformed African societies. The traditional source of power had been command of labour. Lobengula's father, Mzilikazi, had relied on the mobilized strength of young men to control territory, raid for cattle and extract tribute. When those faltered in battles against the guns of Boers and Griquas, he moved his kingdom north. But in the longer term there was no escaping the need for firearms. Each of the regional powers that emerged in this period – Lewanika's Barotse, Lobengula's Matabele and Khama's BaTswana – adopted a similar strategy, which was to control access through their territory. The 'gifts' they received from hunters like Selous enabled them to build up their stock of weaponry and secure the loyalty of their subjects. Their organized manpower could also be deployed to extract trade and tribute from their neighbours. Selous had witnessed Khama's men collecting tribute from the impoverished 'Masarwa Bushmen' on the edges of the Kalahari.

The difference between Lobengula and his neighbours was more a matter of style than fundamental political economy. Lewanika and Khama adopted European dress and befriended missionaries. Lobengula held to the old ways, tolerating missionaries but keeping them at a distance. Missionaries proved especially useful to Khama in the 1880s. They were his eyes and ears in Cape Town and London. Thanks to them he held off the Boer freebooters who tried to steal his country. Without the missionaries Khama and his successors would not have continued to rule under the mantle of a British protectorate. He would have preferred independence, but a protectorate was the next-best thing. Khama still enjoys a reputation as the beau idéal of a peace-loving, benevolent African Christian ruler (for example, in the *No. 1 Ladies' Detective Agency* novels of Alexander McCall Smith). Khama's great-grandson Ian was elected to a second term as President of Botswana in 2014.

Khama supported Selous in 1890 not because he was Christian, but because it was very much in his interest to remove a formidable neighbour who laid claim to a large slice of his territory. Through cunning diplomacy and ostentatious support for the BSA Company's 'Pioneers', Khama ensured that Rhodes would not dare to grab any of his kingdom. Selous paid fulsome tribute to Khama, who had 'not only rendered inestimable services to the British South Africa Company, but earned the gratitude of all Englishmen who are interested in British expansion in South Africa'.[3] When a rumoured Matabele attack caused most of the porters and servants to run away, Khama came to Selous's aid with a contingent commanded by one of his brothers.

Prior to setting off, Selous had been told that Lobengula would also send some men to help. When they failed to appear, Selous suspected something was amiss and rode to Bulawayo to find out what had gone wrong. The king reiterated that there was only one road to Mashonaland and that ran through his capital. If Rhodes had other ideas, let the 'big white chief' come and discuss them, man to man. Selous turned his horse and road hard down to Kimberley where he delivered the message. Rhodes could not come himself, but would send Dr Jameson, his right-hand man, to parlay. By the time Jameson arrived in Bulawayo it was the end of April and the main force of BSA police had already begun to roll their wagons out of Kimberley. Lobengula would promise neither war or compliance, so the expedition would have to proceed on the assumption that they might be attacked at any point along the road.

Forewarned and forearmed, Makamana and Selous spent most of May mapping out the first part of the route. The lesson Selous had learnt early in his career once again stood him in good stead: your best guide is always a knowledgeable African.

Soon after the Pioneer army moved out in late June, along the first section of the road a whisper ran round among the servants and porters: the Matabele were coming. Before the rumour could be quashed, most of the 'boys' deserted. Once again Khama came to the rescue, despatching a force of two hundred men under the command of his brother. Fifty-five of them carried breech-loading rifles and thirty-seven came on horseback. Selous divided the mounted contingent into five parties who maintained a continuous patrol over a zone extending twenty miles in front and behind the Pioneer convoy. A correspondent for the London *Daily News* described how 'F.C. Selous, the mightiest of African Nimrods, steered the way with his trusty henchman Jan, one of Adam Kok's Griquas' (the one known as Jan or John Selous). Jan 'picked out the road while Selous, with a graceful wave of his hand, politely pointed the trees he wished chopped. As soon as a tree was doomed it fell, and on swarmed the Pioneers and Khama's Manguatos.'[4]

Frank Johnson, self-importantly keen to claim credit for everything, says nothing in his memoirs about Khama's contribution and he deprecates Selous's role as a road-maker. Johnson's observations are nonetheless interesting precisely because they run so counter to the near-universal praise for Selous as the best and most amiable of companions. Only he amongst the white hunters of central Africa:

> always hunted alone: the others were in parties of twos and threes or even fours, on the grounds that difficulties were best overcome jointly instead of on one's own. Not so Selous, who I found – and this was the experience of others – rather self-willed. He could not be bothered with having to consult and argue with a companion who might advocate action or movement contrary to his own views. He had, in fact, great difficulty in seeing eye to eye with others on any matter and was a supreme individualist. In other words, I believe that both from his life and character he was averse from receiving anything in the nature of orders from anyone, let alone terse military orders.[5]

Selous, he reckoned, had opposed the Rudd Concession because it threatened to 'interfere seriously with his lonely elephant-hunting, and might even end it'. Out on veldt 'he was not amenable to discipline', and he 'wasted a good deal of time uselessly' observing wildlife and taking compass bearings.

Allowing for factual errors, omissions and personal animus, an important truth about Selous's character shines through Johnson's dark portrait. Behind the evident charm, humour and perfect manners that endeared him to practically everyone, he was still at heart the boy poacher of Rugby and Wiesbaden days, defiant of authority when it thwarted him. He also possessed – and here he differed profoundly from the devil-may-care, rambunctious hunters and traders among whom he had lived for twenty years – a spine of steel. He had developed habits of self-discipline, self-reliance and self-belief that preserved him in situations where others would have perished. The phony military ranks and titles assigned to officers in Rhodes' mercenary army would not have overawed or even impressed him. And nothing would have stopped Fred from netting a butterfly or making sketch maps along the way. It was on this road-making mission that he shot the finest 'koodoo' [*kudu*] he had ever seen, one he rated 'the gem of gems' among all his hunting trophies. Measuring forty-five and three-eighth inches in length, this pair of horns featured in Rowland Ward's *Horn Measurements and Weights of the Great Game of the World* (1892) as the largest known to exist.[6] Was Selous likely to pass this up just because he had signed on as Rhodes' Chief Intelligence Officer? Certainly not.

Nor did he slow the progress of the Pioneer Column. By the first of August the convoy had reached the southern side of the range that ran along the southern edge of Mashonaland plateau. Lobengula held his regiments in check. The only difficulty was finding a route through a rock-strewn and difficult terrain. Makamana and the Tswana were no help this far from their own country. After a couple of days' scouting Selous found the opening dubbed Providential Pass. From here on he was in country he knew well. On 11 September 1890 the column halted at the place they called Fort Salisbury (after the British Prime Minister) and raised the Union Jack.

Securing the Eastern Flank

To his parents, Fred confided that to him, the successful occupation of Mashonaland seemed 'like a dream; and I have played a not unimportant part in it all, I am proud to be able to say. The road to Mashunaland is now being called the "Selous' Road", and I hope the name will endure, though I don't suppose it will.'[7]

His head swam with visions of wealth unbounded:

If all continues to go well with the Chartered Company I may make quite a good deal of money in the next year or two, and I want to know how much money will be necessary to buy Barrymore House outright at my Father's death. ... If I buy Barrymore House I shall have to make a sum of money over and above the amount necessary for that purpose, that will give me a sufficient income to live on. ... I am engaged to the Company for a year from Sept 1st last. I get a retaining fee of £50 a month and all expenses and other advantages that may turn out much more valuable and for the sake of a few months it will not do to throw away the chance of making a good deal of money.[8]

He told his father that 'the value of de Beer's shares depends a good deal' on the success of the new colony, 'for if Chartered [Company] shares rise, de Beers must rise with them.'[9] This suggests that his father had advised him on what to do with Rhodes' £2,000, indicating an ongoing paternal influence. Though he and the British public were not to know it, Rhodes had structured De Beers in a way that insulated the company from possible losses on the Mashonaland gamble – for a gamble it was. From a commercial point of view the success of the Chartered Company relied on the discovery and exploitation of a gold reef to rival the Witwatersrand discoveries.

Fred's correspondence with his parents makes it clear that he did not intend to stay in Africa. As soon as he saw his way clear, he would retire to England, ideally setting up in the family's country house on the Thames.

In the meantime, the Chartered Company needed his expertise to shore up its position to the east. Whatever Rhodes had said about the scope of the Rudd Concession in negotiations over the Royal Charter, he knew that claims to eastern Mashonaland needed to be backed up. Selous accompanied a BSA force to the region known as Manica. The aim was to negotiate agreements with chiefs like the one Selous had made with Mapondera the previous year, disavowing any allegiance to Portugal and granting access to natural resources in their territories. The first of these was concluded in September 1890 with Chief Mtasa. Selous then accompanied the Administrator of Chartered Company territories, A.R. Colquhoun, on horseback over the mountains to a Portuguese outpost where they deposited a copy of their treaty, knowing full well it would provoke a furore. Rhodes intended nothing less than to bully the Portuguese into making over a corridor all the way to the Indian Ocean.[10]

With national pride now aroused to fever pitch, Portugal was not about to back down. A well-armed force of seventy men under the command of Colonel Paiva d'Andrada arrived at Mtasa's village early in November, intending to coerce a retraction from the terrified chief.

A few days later Captain P.W. Forbes arrived with a contingent of soldiers to press the BSA Company's claims. The stand-off was eventually resolved when Forbes surprised the Portuguese commander from the rear, arrested him and marched his humiliated soldiery back to Mozambique. Several months passed before the impasse was resolved through diplomatic channels in London and Lisbon. In the end the implacable opposition of the British Foreign Office stymied Rhodes's bid to extend his dominion to the sea. His audacity was rewarded to the extent that the Anglo-Portuguese convention of 1891 pushed the border of BSA territory to a line running along the summit of the range that lies east of the Save River. Selous had never been in doubt about the outcome. He assured his mother that should 'a single Englishman' be killed in any armed clash, the Portuguese 'will lose all their east African possession to a dead certainty'.[11]

Meanwhile, Selous was employed to map the region and negotiate further treaties with chiefs that would shore up the Chartered Company's claims against any challenge from the Portuguese. He does not record how much he paid any particular chief to sign one of these treaties, but a list of the supplies he carried survives.[12]

15 rifles
15 bandoliers with ammunition complete
150 rounds of ammunition.
30 white blankets. 6 for guides, 1 to Mangwendi
10 coloured blankets
5 soldiers coats
2" overcoats
1 cord coat
1" trousers
3 hats
4 shirts
3 coils fine wire
4 flints and steels
20 snuff boxes
2 harmonicas
10 packets needles
1" thread
100 lb coarse salt

On the other side of this list is the notation: 'Motoko and Mangwendi', so it seems that, apart from the rifles and ammunition, most of these goods were to be used in the negotiations with those two chiefs.

What Selous got in return for his gifts is set out in a printed treaty with Motoko, held in the archives of the Royal Geographical Society.[13] It gives an insight into the nature of the treaty-making that went on everywhere during the great imperial carve-up of Africa. Before Selous even laid eyes on the chief it was expected that Motoko at:

> a full meeting of the Council of Mabudja nation on the [blank] day of November 1890 [would] grant unto F.C. Selous, in his capacity as the representative of the British South Africa Company ... the sole, absolute and entire perpetual right and power to the following acts over the whole or any portion of the territory of the said nation, or any future extension thereof including all subject and dependent territories.[14]

The enumerated acts included the rights:

(A) To search, prospect, exploit, dig for and keep all metals and minerals.

(B) To construct, improve, equip, work, manage and control public works and conveniences of all kinds, including railways, wharves, canals, reservoirs, waterworks, embankments, viaducts, irrigations, reclamation, improvement, sewage, drainage, sanitary, water, gas, electric or any other mode of light, telephonic, telegraphic power supply, and all other works and conveniences of general or public utility.

(C) To carry on business of miners, quarry owners, metallurgists, mechanical engineers, iron founders, builders and contractors, shipowners, brickmakers, warehousemen, merchants, importers, exporters, and to buy and sell and deal in goods and property of all kinds.

(D) To carry on the business of banking in all branches.

(E) To buy, sell, refine, manipulate, mint and deal in bullion, specie, coin and precious metals.

(F) To manufacture and import arms and ammunition of all kinds.

(G) To do all such things as are incidental or conducive to the exercise, attainment or protection of all or any of the rights, powers, and concessions hereby granted.[15]

In other words, the company could do pretty much as it pleased. For example, farming was not specifically mentioned but it could be argued that growing food for the miners, bankers, builders, etc. was 'incidental or conducive' to the other activities.

There would not be any going back on this agreement either, for the Mabudja nation bound itself not to 'enter into any treaty or alliance with any other person, Company or State or to grant any concessions of land without the consent of the Company in writing.'

For his part Selous, on behalf of the BSA Company, promised to defend the territory against external attacks and to maintain 'the said Chief and his lawful successors in the constitutional maintenance and exercise over his subjects of his powers and authority'. As a 'token of the amicable and friendly relations subsisting between the King and the Company', the Company would pay the full cost of maintaining 'a British Resident with a suitable retinue and a suite of British subjects and an escort of British Police for the due maintenance of law and order'. And if this was not enough, at some undefined time in the future the Company would 'aid and assist in the establishment and propagation of the Christian religion and the education and civilization of the native subjects of the King by the establishment, maintenance and endowment of such churches, schools and trading stations'.

Incredible as it may seem, Selous fully expected that after some gifts and conversation conducted through an interpreter, Motoko would sign away his country by putting an X on the dotted line. He was annoyed to find when he arrived in November that the chief had shut himself away and the people were hostile. Thinking that he might do better by himself, he returned in December, accompanied by W.L. Armstrong, an interpreter, and a Zulu servant, William Hokogazi. Selous found Motoko and his Budja people to be very different from the Shona societies he had previously encountered. While they spoke a similar dialect, they were more closely related to the Batonga people of neighbouring Mozambique. Approaching the chief was no easy matter. Selous arrived in Buja country on 27 December. For the next four days he waited in the driving rain while the Mondoro, a ritual specialist known as the Lion God, decided whether he could be permitted to speak to the chief. On 2 January word came that he could advance to Motoko's capital.

Another four days passed while the leading men questioned Selous about the proposed treaty. There was no problem about letting white men look for gold, but why must their chief mark an X on the paper? About the time Selous's 'diplomacy and patience was well nigh exhausted', the chief's eldest son announced that he might approach Motoko. On the morning of the sixth, he and his party picked their way through a great throng of menacing warriors, armed with guns, spears, battle-axes and bows and arrows. He could well believe they had beaten back a determined Portuguese assault the previous year.

This was Armstrong's first encounter with African royalty and he was mightily impressed:

> Having crossed a valley about a mile in width, we arrived at the foot of a rocky hill, on which Matoko's kraal is built. Here we were requested to leave our horses and ascend a shelving patch of granite about 300 yards in length. We found the whole hilltop covered with sitting warriors, about 2000 strong, all armed to the teeth, but silent as the grave. A patch about two yards wide had been left for us, but as we passed onwards, preceded by the Prince and his Indunas, the warriors closed the path behind, until we reached the top, where, seated in a leafy arbour upon a white blanket, sat his sable majesty. King Matoko. A piece of blue limbo was twisted round his head, whilst his nose was smeared with a kind of snuff, and he presented the shrivelled, bent remains of a once powerful frame, looking at us with a stolid ice-like gaze. As we were the first white men they had ever seen, he looked very hard at us for some time, but spoke not a word. Indeed there was perfect silence until at a given signal two warriors on the King's right struck their calabashes, and the air was rent by the most ear-splitting unearthly yells and shrieks from warriors and people in every direction, as if to strike terror into the hearts of the two lonely white men. Twice this was repeated.[16]

Motoko sat under a makeshift arbour of boughs, with a few old men on either side, marimbas played softly in the background. A woman broke into a high soprano ululation. As the signal was given for him to approach, something like a shudder ran down Fred's spine. He had never met anyone so ancient. Motoko looked close to a hundred – old enough to have known Shaka, Mzilikazi and the other great conquerors of the 1820s. He now began to speak in soft but deliberate syllables. He had heard of the BSA Company's treaty with Mtasa, and saw the value of an agreement that would protect him from the Portuguese, the Gaza kingdom and other potential enemies. If white men wished to look for gold, they might come. Selous then said:

'If the words you have spoken come from your heart, I will write your name and my own on the paper which has been translated to you, and you must make an "x" behind your name.' He then placed his hand on mine whilst I wrote my name and made the 'x', as he was too old and shaky to actually hold the pen. Siteo and Kalimazondo then made crosses as witnesses for Motoko, whilst Mr. Armstrong and William Hokogazi did the same on behalf of the Company, and the treaty between Motoko and the British South Africa Company was concluded.[17]

It is impossible to say what Selous foresaw as the result of his treaty-making. His comments on the fertility and climate suggest he anticipated white settlement at some stage. He probably did not anticipate that five short years later the BSA Company's Native Commissioners would come to punish the Budja for failing to pay their hut taxes. They told the chief's emissary they:

were going to burn and shoot everything and destroy everything we saw until he sent to stop us, and ask for mercy, but before we would cease he would have to fill the valley with cattle for us to pick from for hut tax and that he was also to furnish us with 200 of his picked men to go and work in the mines.[18]

All this was no doubt covered by the clause in Selous's treaty permitting anything 'incidental or conducive to the exercise, attainment or protection of all or any of the rights, powers, and concessions hereby granted'.

Not a Fighting Man

For the next five months Fred was once again cutting roads through difficult country, connecting the new capital of Salisbury (Harare) with the town of Umtali (Mutare) near the still undefined border with Mozambique. In May news arrived that a Portuguese regiment was advancing on Umtali with the evident intention of driving out the British. The Administrator asked Selous to reinforce the defence with a contingent of men and two wagonloads of ammunition. Selous responded by saying he was 'not a fighting man'. He did not look 'forward with enthusiasm to the prospect of being shot', nor did he 'feel any strong desire to shoot anyone else'. Nonetheless he 'prepared to lend a hand in the coming struggle if necessary'.[19]

There is no record indicating that up to this point in life he had ever fired at a human target. To his evident relief, when he arrived at Umtali he found that the British garrison had routed the Portuguese without the loss of a single man. All that remained for him to do was to retrieve some wagons from a deserted outpost. Selous naturally took this as an opportunity to shoot at more congenial prey. When hippos proved elusive, he turned his attention to lions. He had not far to look, for on one moonless, starlit night a pride of five big cats seized and devoured one of his oxen. Fred and his companion Armstrong set themselves up with rifles in a flimsy shelter of boughs, determined to wait out the night. From time to time they heard the crunch, scrunch of lions feasting on the ox.

In the dead of night one of them got close enough to be dimly seen, giving Fred a shot at a point-blank range. No sooner had he slipped in another cartridge when a second came in sight. This time he succeeded in gravely wounding the beast, judging from the furious grunts. Meanwhile, a third could be heard behind the hut sniffing and poking at the boughs. Armstrong and Selous wheeled their rifles round just in time to fire. This time there was no doubting the result. In about five minutes they had got three lions. Before the night had passed they added a hyena to the bag. Selous prepared one skin for his collection and returned to Umtali with a lion hunting story he never tired of repeating.[20]

On his return to Salisbury in July 1891 he disappointed his mother by signing up for another year with the company. Since his father continued in good health, there was no compelling personal reason to return home. Besides, the company would be paying him £1,000 plus expenses, 'a sum that I could not afford to let slip'. He was also keen to do something with the farm the company had assigned him four miles out of Salisbury, and his gold claim, even though the full possibilities for development must await the railway.[21] The year, he insisted would pass quickly and then – quoting S.J. Arnold's ode, *The Death of Nelson* – for 'England, Home and Beauty'.[22] The reference to beauty was sure to revive his mother's hope for a marriage at last.

Apart from road-making, his last significant work for Rhodes was a fruitless search for a tsetse-free route through Mozambique between the Pungwe and Buzi Rivers. Unless one could be found there was no alternative to a rail line. With every passing week Salisbury was filling up with white settlers who regarded Selous as a living legend. A gymkhana held on Christmas 1891 attracted a large crowd, according to a report published in *The Field*: 'The shooting race was rather amusing. The competitors were expected to dismount four times, run twenty paces from their horse, fire, mount and ride on. The betting was in favour of Selous, the famous hunter, whose pony all thought would be sure to obey orders.'[23] There was no problem dismounting and shooting but, amid much hilarity, when he looked round he found his horse had cantered off with another pony.

By May of the following year, as there was no more work for him, he terminated his contract with the company. Feeling no sense of urgency, he resumed his proper business of hunting and collecting. From June to October he travelled in eastern Mashonaland before making his way down to the port of Beira. Along the way he shot his last lion and his last elephant, a 'tusker' whose ivory tipped the scale at 108 lb – a fitting conclusion to his long years in the wild.

14

England, Home and Beauty

At Cape Town Selous learnt that he would not have the pleasure of talking business with his father. Not now, not ever. While the son had been hunting and collecting overseas, his father, the former Chairman of the Committee of the Stock Exchange, died peacefully at his Regent's Park home in July 1892. Uncle Henry the painter had passed away late in 1890, so his nephew was now the eldest male of the Selous tribe.[1] There was a lot to mull over on the voyage home.

A Reuters correspondent was on hand when Selous strode down the gangway of the ss *Hawarden Castle* on 18 December 1892. In the course of a long interview he spoke glowingly of Rhodesia and its prospects. A number of rich gold reefs had already been discovered; mining would commence as soon as the railway under construction from Beira reached Umtali. English women and children were thriving in the healthy climate of Salisbury. For the first time he spoke about conserving big game in appropriate places. The 'fly' district 'was one enormous game preserve, swarming with buffalo, Burchell's zebras, and many species of antelope'. The Matabele, of course, remained a threat, but he very much doubted that Lobengula would risk a war with the settlers.

Selous may well have anticipated the dockside interview but could hardly have imagined the surprise his mother had prepared for him at Barrymore House in January. Her houseguest was a young lady of nineteen from Gloucester named Gladys Maddy.[2] Whether there was a deliberate plan to throw them together cannot be known. One suspects that two of Fred's sisters had a hand in the business because they were married to her cousins, sons of a prominent Gloucester family. In October 1890 Ann ('Tottie') had married Richard Jones, whose home, Hatherley Court, was close to Down Hatherley church where Gladys's father had been vicar since the 1850s.[3] Ann's husband had spent time in Johannesburg, and the couple paid Fred a visit in October 1891 before returning to live permanently in Gloucester. Less than a year later Fred's younger sister Sybil ('Dei') married the Revd Charles Jones, a younger son of the same family.[4] In his letter congratulating her on the marriage Fred asked: 'what is to become of me when I come home, with no sisters to comfort me? I suppose I shall remain a wanderer in far countries to the end of my days. At my age marriage would be very risky. It might turn out well, but ____. Well! no one knows what is in store for him.'[5] He certainly did not. In all probability one or both of the sisters came down to Barrymore House with Gladys. The impressionable young woman would have had every reason to be dazzled by her beau during the ensuing months of courtship. Never before had Selous been the subject of so much public attention and adulation.

At the time they met, Rowland Ward featured African hunting trophies and curiosities at his Piccadilly showrooms, drawing on the collections of 'F.C. Selous, the finest hunter since the time of Du Chaillu's exploits', and Captain Frederick Lugard, lately returned from a stint as the first British Military Administrator of Uganda.[6] Visitors could not fail to register that big game hunting and empire-building went hand in hand. Ward used the exhibition to promote himself as a prince of his profession. A feature article in the *Pall Mall Gazette* remarked that 'Sport would lose half its charm and all its glory were there no trophy to bring back as a demonstration of the prowess of the hunter; and skins and skulls would make but a sorry show had we not the skilled taxidermist to give them the verisimilitude of life.'[7] Ward let the interviewer in on some secrets of his craft while extolling the merits of hunting trophies as ornaments for every home. When pressed to say how specimens of big game could possibly suit a private house, Ward explained that he made them light enough to be moved around easily. Properly cared for, they should 'last for all time'. Nor should people restrict their attention to whole animals:

In the case of an elephant or a rhinoceros we preserve the heads and convert the skins into innumerable articles of domestic utility. The thick folds of the hides can be turned into tabletops, trays, caskets, and other articles. I have produced a large table out of a massive hide for the Prince of Wales, and a liqueur-stand out of an elephant's foot for the Duke of Edinburgh.[8]

Ward was pleased to announce that he was going into the publishing business. His first production would be a new book by F.C. Selous, *Travel and Adventure in South East Africa*.[9]

A week later the Council of the Balloon Society awarded its gold medal to 'Mr. Frederick Courteney Selous, in appreciation of the services he has rendered to zoological and geographical science, and in the advancement of British interests in Central Africa.' On the 13 February Fred addressed a packed meeting of the Royal Geographical Society on his 'Twenty Years in Zambezia'. The Duke of Fife, the Earl of Carnarvon, various geographical luminaries and 'a large number of ladies' attended. He followed this up with lectures on the same subject to the Manchester Geographical Society, the Philosophical Society of Glasgow and the Royal Scottish Geographical Society in Edinburgh.[10] To top it all, the Royal Geographical Society presented him with its Founders' Medal 'in recognition of the services he has rendered to geographical science by his prolonged travels in South Africa'.[11]

The March edition of the *Review of Reviews* devoted several pages to a 'Character Sketch' of Selous.[12] The author was W.T. Stead, the most famous journalist of his era. Since his first appointment as an editor at the age of twenty-two, Stead had been making as well as reporting news. By 1882, when he succeeded John Morley at the *Review of Reviews*, he was renowned for his exposé of squalor in London slums and his crusade against the alleged 'Bulgarian atrocities' perpetrated by the Ottoman Turks. Innovative in both the style and layout of stories, Stead had no qualms about mixing reportage and opinion. Poet and critic Matthew Arnold credited him with the invention of 'the New Journalism'. He made and broke reputations. An interview he did with General Charles ('Chinese') Gordon in 1884 pushed Gladstone's Liberal government into a near catastrophic intervention in the Sudan, while elevating Gordon to secular sainthood. Another ruined the career of politician Charles Dilke. Not everyone shed a tear when Stead went down with the *Titanic*.

He looked upon Selous as a second Gordon. 'He is almost as fair as

Gordon, and there is at times almost the same kind of light in his eyes. Like Gordon, he is extremely modest and unassuming, with a kindly soul in him and a passionate devotion to England.' The great point of difference was that Selous believed in the iron laws of Darwinian nature rather than the simple truths of the Christian Bible. Cruelty, suffering, struggle and death ruled both the human and animal worlds. For Stead, Selous represented everything noble, brave and self-sacrificing in the ancient profession of hunting. Although it had become a cliché to call every hunter a Nimrod, Stead perceived a more profound truth in the Old Testament story of the hunter-king:

> The wild beast was the enemy in those days – the universal enemy – of the human race, and the warfare against the four-footed lord-lings of the wilderness was the highest and most universal form of patriotism and of humanity. Primitive man had as his enemies not smooth-skinned bipeds, speaking different dialects, like Frenchmen or Germans and Russians, but fierce carnivores, who respected no truce, who observed no frontiers, who gave no quarter, and with whom he and his lived on terms of ceaseless war, to the knife and to the death. Nor was it only that the hunter was the hero-patriot, defending the commonweal against the savage incursions of ruthless foes, he was also the food winner. In him militarism and indus-trialism found their original point of union. He was the soldier to smite and to slay; but the same sword that smote and the spear that slew also provided food for the larder and clothes for the wardrobe. Small wonder, then, that in primitive times, 'the mighty hunter before the Lord' was regarded as the first of men, the father of the people, the champion of the race.[13]

Stead brought out aspects of Selous's life and character which readers of his published work would hardly have suspected:

> Mr. Selous is not like many a famous Nimrod, without education or breeding ... [he] is an English gentleman, educated at Rugby, whose country home is at Wargrave, on the Thames, and who finds his natural level among the cultured and well-to-do classes, who, demo-cratic changes notwithstanding, practically keep the government of the empire in their hands.[14]

What is more, he did not regard himself as a 'hunter by nature'. Had he been properly trained and employed, he would have devoted his life to collecting 'specimens instead of slaughtering elephants'. He omitted to say that for the last fifteen years he had been doing precisely that, while bagging no more than about one elephant per year.

Stead also elicited some surprisingly frank political opinions. Selous claimed to be a Liberal at home and an Imperialist abroad. Whereas he had once derided the Transvaal Boers as 'the most ignorant and stupid of all white races' and had condemned Gladstone for surrendering the Transvaal in 'a most humiliating peace', he now claimed it was 'a mystery to him why Mr. Gladstone did not restore the republic to its rightful owners in 1880' ahead of the Boer rebellion. Had their oppressors been any nation than Britain he would have gladly fought on their side. It is hard to say what motivated this backflip; perhaps it was his reading of G.M. Theal's *History of the Boers in South Africa* (1887), which condemned British policy leading up to the Great Trek of the 1830s.[15] His newly acquired enthusiasm for Transvaal independence would cause him a good deal of trouble over the coming decade. Why, when he understood so clearly their wish to be masters in their own house, did he not extend the same moral reasoning to the African people? That is the great blind spot in his thinking and writing about colonialism. Not once in all his writing and correspondence does he ever envisage a future South Africa where black voters determined the composition of government.

He clung to the position he had already staked out in relation to the Matabele. Unlike the Boers they had no rightful claim on the land they invaded in the 1830s. BSA Company rule would afford the Shona people the protection they needed to ward off the Matabele and the Portuguese.

Stead's interview was widely quoted and reprinted. In May the presentation of The Royal Geographical Society's gold medal brought Selous more publicity.[16] Somehow, amid all his speaking and dinner engagements, he found time to woo Miss Maddy and write his new book. By the beginning of June the completed manuscript was in the hands of the printers.

The finished book differs in many respects from his first, which chronicled his experiences on an almost daily basis for the eight months of each year that he was in the field. Although the subtitle to

166

the new book promises a 'narrative of the last eleven years spent by the author on the Zambezi and its tributaries', there are huge gaps. Whole years get summarized or dismissed in a few paragraphs. He says little or nothing of his life during the off-seasons. There is no telling where he stayed, the company he kept, or how he passed the long days from December to April. Needless to say, Selous does not even hint at the existence of 'his woman' and the children. Bits and pieces of articles he wrote for *The Field* and the Royal Geographical Society are slotted into chapters. Some of the animal stories concern the 1870s. His comments on the technical aspects of hunting are confined to a few pages on the merits of the 450-bore express rifle which 'can kill anything that walks the earth'. About half the book deals with his role in the colonization of Rhodesia and the future prospects of the country. Much of that reads like blatant BSA Company propaganda, especially in relation to the cruelty of the Matabele and the richness of the gold fields.

A few days after handing in his manuscript Selous addressed a meeting of the Royal Colonial Institute on 'Incidents of a Hunter's Life'. On a table were the heads and forepaws of six of his lions, set side by side and artfully arranged as if crouching by Rowland Ward. The audience would have had no idea they were about to hear anything other than a celebration of big game hunting as a way of life. Selous began by reiterating that he was a naturalist rather than a hunter. When he arrived in South Africa the great herds of elephants known to hunters like Cornwallis Harris and Gordon Cumming were already in retreat. Animals once plentiful now teetered on the verge of extinction. The quagga was already extinct in South Africa and the white rhinoceros appeared likely to go the same way. Professional hunters accounted for only a tiny fraction of the ongoing slaughter. 'In reality,' he continued, 'the possession of firearms by the natives, and the inducement which the traders offer to them to slaughter all wild animals whose horns or hides or tusks are saleable, have, with the spread of civilization, been the real agents in bearing off the game from South Africa.'[17]

At the conclusion of the lecture, the great explorer Henry Morton Stanley rose, as everyone supposed, to propose a vote of thanks. Instead, he launched into a vituperative attack on big game hunters as a species. He did not at all 'like the idea of people going into Africa to shoot lions and elephants and hippopotami and other game indiscriminately.'[18] Selous should not boast about shooting 800 head of game. There were gasps and protests heard round the room. What business had Stanley to speak of shooting indiscriminately? Was he not the man who praised Maxim's machine-gun as 'a splendid instrument for spreading Christianity and civilization among the savage races of Africa'? Had he not shot his way across Africa twice with an army of mercenaries at his back? Selous suppressed his inner rage as he had so often with African chiefs. He calmly replied that neither as a naturalist nor elephant hunter had he ever shot animals for sport. Of course, he had shot elephants for their ivory and other animals to feed his African followers.

The altercation with Stanley was widely reported, usually with the addendum that the sympathies of the audience were entirely with Selous. Gladys Maddy would have read one of those reports in her local paper, the *Gloucester Citizen*.[19] Even as he inwardly rejoiced in seeing his name coupled with Stanley, Selous wrote to editors correcting garbled accounts. Some even reported that he had killed 800 lions.[20] In any case the figure of '800 head of game' was Stanley's not his. It had never been his custom to boast of his bag.[21]

A measured reflection on the 'curious episode' appeared a few days later. 'That one traveller who has made his way, according to his own book, across Africa only by the expenditure of many cartridges, and with an army at his back, should publicly taunt another traveller for shooting lions and elephants, is a most incomprehensible thing.' On the other hand, Stanley had probably not meant to mount a hypocritical attack on Selous, who was well known for 'his humane treatment of the natives amongst whom he moved as a solitary traveller, unsupported by the rifles of a number of armed retainers'. He merely meant to express in his characteristic bull-headed way his well-known antipathy to the sport of hunting in general.[22]

At a deeper level the debate signalled a change of the tone in discussions of big game hunting. Hunters like Selous still shone in the public eye as exemplars of manliness, but the implications of the mass slaughter of African elephants and the extinction of species were sinking in. People flocked to the Wild West show of 'Buffalo Bill' as they had queued for a glimpse of Jumbo at the London Zoo and in P.T. Barnum's circus. But precisely because they had come to appreciate the values of the animals on display, they would no longer have applauded a buffalo or elephant-shooting contest. Rowland Ward, even though he made his living from mounting big game, was horrified to hear that the German animal dealer Carl Hagenbeck proposed to let a Dutchman shoot a rogue elephant in front of a large audience in a Hamburg square. It was not just wrong, but also dangerous, Ward protested. (The animal had to be put down, but it was eventually done by strangling it with a large chain away from public gaze.)[23] A late-Victorian version of today's campaign against 'blood ivory' was already under way well before Selous's lecture to the Royal Colonial Institute. Stanley was on record as saying that 'He who buys ivory nowadays buys an article which has been obtained by murder, theft, and rapine.'[24]

Evidently the business did nothing to diminish her hero in the eyes of Miss Gladys Maddy, whose parents announced their daughter's engagement on 21 June. The couple were to be wed in the autumn after Fred's return from a North American lecture tour. It was an excellent match as far as his mother Ann was concerned. The bride's father had taken his BA degree at Trinity College, Cambridge, and, in 1856, had been appointed Rector of Down Hatherley, a highly desirable and prestigious post, which was in the gift of the Lord Chancellor. In 1889 he was made an honorary canon of Gloucester Cathedral and later elected Chairman of the Gloucester Rural Council and the Board of Guardians.[25]

Historian Arthur Keppel-Jones plainly had Selous in mind when he wrote that it is hard 'to judge charitably a man who "got rid of" his African concubine and children before returning to England to marry respectably'.[26] To be fair, five years intervened between Fred's break-up in Shoshong and his first meeting with Gladys. He had, on several occasions, told relatives he was likely to remain single. Even after he became financially secure he spoke of having enough to live comfortably in England 'as a bachelor'. Whether he ever paused to think wistfully of his nomadic family life in the middle 1880s lies entirely in the realm of conjecture.

The engagement plunged Fred into a new round of social engagements with prospective in-laws, friends and relatives. There were proofs from the printer to be checked and lecture notes to be recast to suit US and Canadian audiences. About this time he also accepted an invitation to stay with Rider Haggard on his Norfolk estate.[27] On

3 July he was the guest of honour at a gathering of Rugby old boys.[28] More invitations began to flow in from owners of private hunting reserves, among them one from Murdoch MacLean, Laird of Lochbuie in Scotland, who subsequently became a good friend. In August he came away from MacLean's estate with a bag that included grouse, ptarmigan, a wild goat and a sea trout.[29]

Meanwhile, newspapers reported that all was not well in Rhodesia. In mid-July Henry Loch, the South African High Commissioner, wired the Colonial Office with a disturbing account of recent events at Fort Victoria in Mashonaland. A large Matabele *impi* had attacked Shona villages in the vicinity, killing many people and seizing large numbers of cattle. Subsequent telegrams from the BSA Company's Administrator, Dr Jameson, reassured the public that the situation had been brought under control.[30] He had been in touch with Lobengula, who was as anxious as anyone to avert a conflict. Over the next few weeks it emerged that negotiations over compensation to be paid for the raids had not gone well. The king had dismissed an ultimatum laid down by Jameson and war was definitely on the horizon.

That was enough for Selous, who announced that he was cancelling the North American tour and would sail for South Africa on 26 August aboard the ss *Drummond Castle*. He told a Reuters reporter that he was going out at his own expense, not as an employee of the BSA Company. If the threat proved less serious than it presently appeared he would return at once. Succinctly put: 'My position is simply this. I am one of those who assisted in opening up the country. I am a burgher of Mashonaland, and have personal interests there, and on receipt of that serious intelligence from that country I thought and still believe it be my duty to give a hand.'

15

Wounded, Lionized and Bagged

Within a month of his embarkation Selous had signed on as a scout with the Bechuanaland Police, who had already moved out of their own territory to Fort Tuli, south of Bulawayo.[1] The situation as he understood it was that, back in July, Lobengula had sent regiments to attack Shona villages near Fort Victoria. They had spread terror in all directions, burning huts, stealing cattle, and killing unoffending men, women and children. This unwarranted invasion of BSA Company territory provoked an understandable response from Dr Jameson and Sir Henry Loch, who began organizing military forces to confront the Matabele peril.

Today's historians see things differently.[2] The boundary between Matabeleland and the company's domain had been left undefined at the time the Pioneer Column marched in, for the very good reason that the Rudd Concession was premised on Lobengula's right to the entire country as far east as the Mozambique border. So there could be no doubt about the king's right to move through the territory. The immediate cause of the affray in July 1893 was that Shona people not under Lobengula's protection raided cattle from other Shona who acknowledged their tributary status. The king sent an *impi* to restore the stolen property to its rightful owners, stressing that under no circumstances were they to bother the white men. They made their presence known to the Chartered Company's agents at Fort Victoria before proceeding to pillage in their customary fashion. When Jameson asked for military reinforcements, Rhodes replied that the company was out of money, so he had better sort things out with Lobengula. Meanwhile, the little community of white settlers had worked themselves up into fits of indignation and were demanding war – paid for, of course, by the company.

Rhodes did not exaggerate the company's dire position. As a capitalist venture it depended absolutely on the exploitation of the promised great, deep reef of gold: the second Rand. For three years prospectors had swarmed over the rocky wastes and had found little beyond fragmentary shallow quartzite reefs and patches of alluvial sands. All this time the company had been burning money. Funds spent on roads, telegraphs, surveys, fortifications, administrative offices and rail lines would never be repaid unless they found the gold. However rich the soil, agriculture alone was never going to sustain a central African colony. The wavering faith of investors turned to panic when they heard the troubling news from Fort Victoria. In May 1893 Chartered Company shares sold at £2.8s. In July they dropped to £1.1s. By the third week in August they had slipped to 16 s.[3] Since proposing to Gladys, Selous had seen the value of his shares drop by two-thirds. Rhodes's convoluted financial engineering could not prevent De Beers shares, which Fred also owned, from moving down in tandem. The prospect of financial ruin as much as indignation over 'Matabele outrages' prompted his dash to the Plymouth docks on 26 August 1893. More than likely he had talked to other influential investors ahead of his departure.

A successful war against the Matabele would curb the panic and dispel some of the lingering doubts about the BSA Company's rights to the land. The question was how to pay for it. When Jameson demanded a second time that Rhodes find the money, he dipped into his own pocket and sent £50,000. Jameson used this to equip and recruit a force of mounted volunteers, mainly from South Africa. By the terms of the Victoria Agreement drawn up in August, each man was promised 3,000 *morgen* of farmland (about 2,568 hectares or 6,300 acres), in addition to fifteen reef and five alluvial gold-mining claims in conquered Matabeleland. Considering that the Colonial Office had told Loch it would not countenance anything other than a defensive war, this was outrageous. Keppel-Jones calls it 'nothing less than a contract for robbery under arms'.[4]

*

The Matabele Campaign

Thus the die had been cast well before Selous arrived on the scene. Ever-obliging King Khama sent nearly two thousand BaTswana – most of them armed with Martini-Henry rifles – to join the mounted volunteers and Bechuanaland Police forces massing at Tati, Fort Tuli and other spots along the frontiers of the Matabele heartland.[5] All they awaited was some sign of aggression from Lobengula.

This the king stubbornly refused to provide, relying on Sir Henry Loch's promise that 'if there are no *impis* out I shall not allow the white people to attack you'. Since June he had sent repeated messages disavowing any hostile intentions and denying he had any *impis* out in the field. By September Jameson's forces were in the field searching for Matabele; on two occasions there were vague reports that shots had been fired by people who may well have been Lobengula's men. In the hope of drawing them out, Jameson had agents provocateurs spread the word among the Matabele that white *impis* were on the move. When a black *impi* did move south to check out the rumours, the 'alarming news' was immediately telegraphed to Cape Town. Loch insisted that Lobengula should send some of his 'Chief Indunas to talk over matters with me, so that there may be peace'. While grumbling that he had already talked enough, he nonetheless sent a delegation to Tati bearing a letter addressed to Loch. They included the king's brother, Ingubogubo and two other high-ranking *indunas*. Neither they nor Lobengula were aware that newspapers in South Africa and Britain had been reporting on a war they said had begun a fortnight earlier.

Selous was on the spot at Colonel Hamilton Goold-Adams's head-quarters when the king's envoys arrived on the evening of 18 October, accompanied by one of his oldest friends, James Dawson. They bore a letter from Lobengula addressed to Sir Henry Loch. The king said he was 'tired of hearing the lies which come to me every day'. What proof was there that any British forces had come under attack? Could Loch point to any white corpses, injuries or stolen cattle? 'You send me no answer,' he complained, 'to all the letters I send you.' He had just heard of more Matabele cattle taken by the British. 'This is now four times my cattle have been taken.' How many cattle had the British lost to the Matabele who allegedly fired on them? If Loch would send envoys to

Bulawayo he would offer every assistance in finding those responsible for any attacks.[6]

These were all very good questions, to which the hapless king would never get answers. Before Loch's letter could be delivered, Colonel Hamilton Goold-Adams had the three envoys arrested. Soon afterwards two of them were 'shot while trying to escape'. Such incidents abound in the annals of empire. The astonishing thing is that Selous and Dawson did not intervene. When questioned later, Selous claimed the whole fiasco was an unfortunate accident. Because of its bearing on his integrity and reputation, his account merits quoting in its entirety:

> I was at Colonel Goold-Adams's camp when the affair happened, and I know exactly what occurred. Late in the afternoon of the day in question, when standing at the door of one of the houses belonging to the Tati Concession Company, I saw my old friend Mr Dawson ride up, accompanied by three mounted Matabele. Colonel Goold-Adams was not far away, and he also saw the arrival of the men. As I had sent a letter to Dawson only a few days before, urging him to try to get out of the country with Fairbairn and Usher, and as he looked very much fatigued, my impression first was that he had made his escape, and that the three men with him were Matabele who had seceded from the King. One of these men, namely, Ingubungubo [sic], the King's brother, I know well, and went up and shook hands with him, but my only thought at the moment was to minister to the personal wants of my friend Dawson, and I urged the latter to come into the Concession and get a cup of tea. Thus I am to a certain extent responsible for Dawson not having immediately reported the arrival of himself and the Matabele Embassy to Colonel Goold-Adams. Whilst I was absent with Dawson the Colonel, seeing three Matabele, all armed with rifles, looking curiously at the British camp, which was situated opposite the Concession station, and on the other side of the Tati River, sent Mr Taylor, of the Tati concession who speaks the Matabele language fluently, to call them to him and ask their business. One of the envoys, Muntus, when asked by Mr Taylor what he wanted, assumed a haughty bearing, and, spitting on the ground, said in a great rage, 'What are the white men doing in my King's country?' He then turned to his companions, and said,

'Hau gubi lapa' – meaning 'Things look nasty' – and added, 'Where are our horses? They have taken them away.' On this being inter-preted, Colonel Goold-Adams, who, it must be remembered had no conception that the men were envoys from the King, thinking that if they were not watched they would very likely make a bolt back to Matabeleland and give notice of the approach of the white men, informed them that they would have to go over to his camp on the other side of the river, at the same time assuring them that they would be well treated, but should they attempt to escape they would be shot. The men made no remonstrance and did not ask to see Dawson, but at once walked quietly across the river-bed to the camp, escorted by a corporal's guard of half a dozen men. When I came out of the house with Dawson after an absence of half an hour we heard that the Matabele had been taken over to the camp under guard. Dawson said he was sorry he had left them, for, as he had told me whilst we were in the house, the natives were envoys from Lobengula, and he himself had been sent in charge of them by the King. He said, 'We had better go across at once to the camp, and then you can report yourself to Colonel Goold-Adams.' By this time the sun was down, but it was a bright moonlight night. Dawson and I had just reached the bank of the Tati when we heard a shot from the direction of the camp, and on getting to the British quarters we were told that one of the *indunas*, after stabbing two men, had been shot in attempting to escape, while another had been stunned by a blow on the head from the butt end of a musket. The latter was still alive, and Dawson went to see him, but found him to be uncon-scious. Dr. Garriway was at once sent by Colonel Goold-Adams to attend to him, but by this time he had expired. What had happened was this: The three envoys were being escorted to the guard, but they were in no way bound and their limbs were unconfined, though of course their rifles had been taken from them beforehand, and three men of the Bechuanaland Border Police with loaded rifles were walking on either side of them. Suddenly Muntus seized the handle of the bayonet banging by the side of one of the troopers, drew it from its scabbard, and made a rush through the guard, stabbing right and left. Two troopers were stabbed, and Muntus had got quite clear of the guard and was running towards the place where the horses were picketed. He was about twenty-five yards distant when one of the guards fired and hit him, the bullet passing clean through his body and wounding a Bechuana trooper in the foot. The second Induna Inguba, a cousin of Gambos, made a rush to escape at the same time as Muntus, and as he did so one of the troopers who had been stabbed struck him a heavy blow on the back of the head with his musket. From this wound he subsequently died. The old Induna Ingunbogubo, the King's half-brother, was seized round the waist by Sergeant-major Hore. He at first struggled violently, but finding no harm was intended him sat down and remained perfectly quiet. On the following morning the Induna resumed his journey to Palapye with Dawson. It is ... very evident from the above story that although the death of the two men was a most deplorable accident, it was nevertheless an accidental occurrence, for which no one can possibly be held responsible. It is only the persistent malice of certain individuals, as ignorant as they are malicious, that leads them constantly to misrepresent the matter and to brand honourable men as most infamous criminals.[7]

Selous gave this account to a newspaper reporter in February of the following year, so we can only wonder at his precise recollection of all the details. Perhaps this is just one more instance of the prodigious feats of memory associated with his hunting stories – or the way his nimble imagination could fill in the blanks. In the absence of any contrary evidence from the Matabele side, it is impossible to construct an alternative explanation for the killing. It does seem remarkable that all the business with the *indunas* could have happened during the half-hour Selous spent indoors with Dawson. And we can say with certainty that if two white envoys to Lobengula had been 'accidentally' slain at Bulawayo, there would have been hell to pay. Within a week, news of the killings had reached England, confirming the humanitarian lobby's worst fears about Rhodes and the whole BSA Company enterprise.

Anyone eager to find out what was really going on in that part of the world could turn to *Travel and Adventure in South East Africa* by F.C. Selous, which Rowland Ward brought out the last week of September that year. Within the next four months the book went through three editions. 'There is no getting Captain Selous's latest book at Mudie's,' said one report, 'so incessant has been the demand.' Thanks to the war, it continued 'to be read as largely at the libraries as it was immediately after publication'.[8] His established public persona as modest, honest hunter Selous enhanced his credibility. Two hospital nurses writing of their *Adventures in Mashonaland* said he was universally known as 'the man who never tells a lie'. They had feared they might miss seeing the great hunter at Umtali, 'but their message to him was delivered, and the prompt reply came back that he would come as soon as he could get his shirt washed.'[9] Rider Haggard advised an interviewer to rest assured that the war would be fairly and successfully prosecuted by colonial forces whose 'general movements are governed by such men as my friend Mr Selous, whose experience at such a juncture will be worth a regiment'. (Haggard's brother, who was present, hereupon ejaculated, with considerable fervour, 'Worth an army!')[10] The endorsement was understandable coming from brothers who were heavily invested in the Chartered Company shares, but it only fuelled the legend that Frederick Courteney Selous was indeed Allan Quatermain. As it turned out he played a very small part in the Matabele campaign.

For several weeks the war went on with only one side in action. At the eleventh hour, when it was obvious to everyone that diplomacy would achieve nothing, Lobengula finally sent the Matabele army out to fight. His enemies had been advancing on Bulawayo in two columns: one commanded by Major P.W. Forbes approached from the north east and the other under Colonel Goold-Adams moved up from the south west. By 24 October Forbes's column had reached the Shangani River about 60 miles north-east of Bulawayo. At dawn the next day a Matabele force of about 3,500 attacked. Although armed with Martini-Henry rifles they had no chance against the Maxim guns which spread mayhem among their ranks. At the end of four hours more than a thousand Matabele lay dead on the field and their living comrades had retreated in disarray. Losses on the opposing side were four killed. A week later, Forbes did battle again at the Bembesi River with similar results: some eight hundred insanely brave warriors mown down by the Maxims; three killed and seven wounded on the company side. The road to Bulawayo was now left undefended. On 4 November the main column entered an empty town, burnt to the ground by order of the king, who had moved his people north.

Selous did not figure in either engagement as he was attached to Goold-Adams's force, which lagged far behind the other column. They were still more than 30 miles out of Bulawayo when, on 2 November, one of the wagons in their train came under attack. By the time Fred galloped up to assist, bullets were flying in all directions. Like the seasoned hunter he was, he dismounted and began firing from a less precarious position. Although he had clipped the bridle to his belt as a precaution, his horse – driven wild by the excitement – pulled it loose. Holding the belt in one hand and his rifle in the other, Fred scrambled to remount. That's when a bullet caught him on a rib. Had it not been for some of Khama's men and the Bechuanaland Border Police who appeared at that very instant, he was done for. With two Maxim guns in place the tide of battle turned and the day ended with six casualties on the British side and ten times that number of Matabele dead.[11]

It was the end of Fred's war and nearly the end of Lobengula's. Selous was invalided out, while the king died soon after moving north with the remnants of his regiments. Some say he died of the smallpox that had been raging in Bulawayo during the preceding six months. Others say he took poison, or died of a broken heart. The precise circumstances and place of his demise early in 1894 remain matters of dispute and conjecture. A few small skirmishes were fought before the country settled into peace, but there were no more pitched battles. The BSA Company claimed victory and set about confiscating land and cattle. However, most of the Matabele military leadership and regimental leadership remained intact, perhaps to fight another day.

Two days after his injury Selous wrote to Gladys and his mother to say he was all right apart from his very stiff and sore right side. The wound was not dangerous and he looked forward to marrying his fiancée 'unless the wear and anxiety of this campaign has made me look so old that she will not have me'.[12] Long before the letters reached England the news was in all the papers. Comrades spoke of his gallantry under fire. One report stated with considerable exaggeration that 'he performed prodigies of valour, and he is now recommended for the Victoria Cross'.[13] None of them noted that this was his first and only experience of battle. Never before had he fired a shot at a human being. Whether any of his bullets found its mark while he struggled with his horse is not known. One thing was beyond doubt. He was as cool-headed and fearless on the battlefield as in the hunt or on the run.

His subsequent reflections on the downfall of Lobengula suggest a somewhat confused state of mind. This was, after all, the king who had allowed the untried youth of twenty to try his luck with elephants, who congratulated him on becoming a man, and invited him to court the girls of Bulawayo in 1871. Lobengula had loaned him a 'salted' horse when he needed one and had entertained Fred with stories of his youthful hunting exploits.[14] Even after the war he spoke 'in high praise of Lobengula. A very capable man ... with a thorough understanding of the position, and much craft in controlling it so as to serve his private ends.'[15] Selous paid fulsome tribute to the discipline and courage of the Matabele regiments who were 'as brave as men could be'. He had spoken before the war of his belief that Lobengula would eventually tire of his troublesome white neighbours and found a new kingdom north of the Zambezi. In 1894 he reiterated the prediction almost as a wish:

> I think he would keep enough fighting men to cross the Zambesi and conquer a country to the north of that river, in the same way as his father established himself in Matabeleland after being driven out of the Transvaal. The high plateau known as the Batoka country is a very fine country, and is like Matabeleland in its physical aspects.'[16]

In his last surviving letter to his mother he expressed it slightly differently, hoping that Lobengula would move over the Zambezi rather than submit, as he would not 'like to see too many Matabele remaining in the country'.[17] Is this is a veiled expression of moral unease over the expropriation of land that he knew was coming, an expropriation that would be far easier to justify if the people decamped? Or did he anticipate, correctly, that the Matabele were not truly conquered and could create plenty of trouble when they saw their grazing lands being carved up and parcelled out to white farmers?

His public statements on the war and its aftermath combined moral outrage, Darwinian fatalism and a Pollyanna-ish optimism about the future of the country. The Matabele had brought the war on themselves by their raids near Fort Victoria back in July. The settlers were not going to stand idly by while their Shona servants were massacred. 'The white man had to leave Mashonaland or smash the Matabele.' It was 'absolutely necessary, if the work of colonization was to be carried on in Mashonaland, to assert the supremacy of the white race at once and for always.'[18] There would be no problem establishing the new

179

colonial order in Matabeleland:

> As soon as the rainy season is over and the natives have got in their crops a magistracy will be established at Bulawayo and the question of the location of the natives will be thoroughly gone into. No wrong to the natives is in contemplation. The country is large, and there is plenty of room to locate the natives in reservations, with which they will be perfectly satisfied, and at the same time leave room for European and colonial farmers.[19]

This accorded pretty well with the views of nineteenth-century colonizers across the globe. Outmoded ways of life had to go; land needed to be more efficiently utilized; white settlers would be more effective agents of modernization than uneducated indigenous peasants. From a twenty-first-century perspective, however, the case is dubious. If, as alleged, Lobengula was a savage despot who dragooned male warriors into regiments which he used to extract booty and tribute from his neighbours, why did it follow that the common people should give up their land and cattle to the white troopers who deposed him? It was yet to be shown that white farmers and graziers could use the land more effectively than Africans, and the distribution of income was bound to be skewed sharply in favour of settlers who had done nothing to earn it. Without cheap black labour, every enterprise in Rhodesia was doomed to fail because of the high transport and infrastructure costs involved in getting products to distant markets. And then there was the heavy cost of policing a subject population that was to have no say in government. Selous's prophecy that the 'natives will be perfectly satisfied in reservations' proved to be wildly optimistic.

Lionized

After convalescing in Matabeleland Fred spent his forty-second birthday in Bechuanaland before proceeding via the Transvaal to Cape Town.[20] When the ss *Spartan* docked at Plymouth on 4 February 1894, brother Edmund was on hand along with a representative of Rowland Ward, who had been keeping the British public up-to-date with the valorous deeds of 'the mighty Nimrod'. With his new book now in its third edition, the publisher had already planned a UK lecture tour. As Selous descended the gangway he acknowledged the cheers of the passengers with a wave of a soft felt hat with 'a brim as big as a parasol'. A reporter walked him over to a nearby hotel.[21]

Slipping instantly into his modest hunter persona, he said he had nothing to add to what had already been printed in the newspapers about the Matabele campaign. As he warmed to his topic, another altogether more vivacious personality emerged. 'Once get Mr Selous interested in his narrative,' wrote the reporter, and he is like 'a runaway locomotive that has no intention of leaving the track.' Pacing up and down the reading room of the Duke of Cornwall Hotel, he barely paused to draw breath:

> I will tell you in a few words why there was a war … The white man had to leave Mashonaland or smash the Matabele. The Chartered Company had to give up much of its property, and to undergo great loss in various ways, or smash the Matabele. The Matabele did everything to the white man in Mashonaland except kill him. They sometimes ran off with or killed his stock, but on all occasions, when an opportunity presented itself, they assegaied his Mashona boys. For fifty years the Matabele have been ruining the country all about them. They are responsible for not one, but hundreds of massacres of men, women, and children.[22]

Matabeleland was certainly a fine country for agriculture and probably for gold. The only immediate impediment to its development was the braying of so-called humanitarians like Labouchere. 'From the commencement of the war Mr. Labouchere has systematically misrepresented everything that has taken place. His conduct has been one constant *suppressio veri, suggestio falsi*', said 'the simple hunter'.

Henry Labouchere was a very rich Liberal politician who had edited the magazine *Truth* since 1876. A journalistic gadfly, he had, over the years, pursued numerous pet causes and moral crusades. His enormous wealth meant he could face libel suits with equanimity. More often than not he came off the victor. The particular charge to which Selous took personal exception was that he had been paid £2,000 by Rhodes to stop saying that Lobengula had no authority over Mashonaland. Selous insisted he had been paid £2,000 for his mineral concession, not his silence. Labouchere would hear from his lawyers and see him in court.[23] At least one paper foresaw an even contest:

> Mr. F.C. Selous is a famous slaughterer of big game, and he apparently thinks that the methods of the Shikari can be adapted to the pursuit of a libel action. He fired his writ at Mr. Labouchere with the same absence of notice or justification as he would discharge a rifle at an African lion. But, fortunately, the result has not proved quite so fatal, and Mr. Selous will have a good deal of difficult stalking to accomplish before he adds the skin of the editor of *Truth* to his other trophies.[24]

It would be months before the warring parties arrived at an out-of-court settlement, with Labouchere publicly retracting his accusation of bribery.[25] In the meantime Selous found the court of public opinion overwhelmingly on his side.

'Mr. F.C. Selous', said one widely reprinted report, is back in England where 'he will be the lion of society, if he allows himself to be lionised'. He did not seem to mind at all. He was seated among the luminaries at a Chamber of Commerce dinner for the Chancellor of the Exchequer, Sir William Harcourt, on 21 February. A week later he was the guest of honour at a Sports Club dinner where rising political star and future Viceroy of India, George Curzon, rose on behalf of the assembled guests to say that 'the very large majority' of the House of Commons 'sympathised with Mr. Selous as much as they admired him and those who had fought with him in South Africa'. On 5 March Selous joined Curzon, Sir George Goldie of the Royal Niger Company, and John Kirk, the long-time British Consul at Zanzibar, at a special meeting of the Royal Geographical Society to mark the five-hundredth anniversary of the birth of Prince Henry the Navigator. The next evening he was out to dinner at the home of English humourist Henry Lucy with Sir William and Lady Harcourt.[26] Six days later he spoke to the Royal Colonial Institute on 'The history of the Matabele, and the Cause and Effect of the Matabele War' with the Marquis of Lorne presiding. Among other beneficial consequences of the war was that 'the Dutch Boers had been checkmated, and English prestige lost at Majuba Hill [in the first Anglo-Boer War] had been regained.'[27]

The World weekly magazine featured Selous in March as the subject of their series, 'Celebrities at Home'.[28] Fred took the *World's* journalist on a tour of Barrymore House at Wargrave where, he explained, he would soon be settling down with his bride Gladys. Moving from room to room, he pointed out artworks by his Uncle Henry and the 'fine and bearded head' of his late father, who 'had the distinction being eight times elected Deputy-Chairman, and for six years in succession sat as Chairman of the London Stock Exchange. He was a man, too, well known to the votaries of chess as a fine player, and had been pitted against the champion Morphy with credit to himself.' Entering the drawing room the interviewer encounters a wall-mounted lion's head and a grand piano covered by leopards' skins. There he meets Ann Selous, 'a charming old lady, who, after a residence of twenty-five years in Wargrave, is able to chat pleasantly of the beautiful scenery of the vicinity, and of her neighbours'. She points out her husband's beloved clarinet, sketches by her daughter and other 'evidence of the artistic and literary talents' of the Selous family. Her son's taste for adventure and sport come, she explains, from her side of the family: 'the fox-hunting Sherbornes of Dorsetshire, who trace back on the mother's side to the eleventh century'. Beyond the ancient oak-beamed dining room and kitchen lies the former billiard room, now transformed into a museum. 'Here a surprise awaits you, for, the door being opened, the fierce eyes of 16 tawny lions' and lionesses' heads, placed in a double row, glare at you in the most life-like manner.' Above them, extending in serried rows around the room, are the heads and horns of 150 antelopes. Interspersed at a lower level are 'numerous rhinoceros horns, both the white and black varieties, hippopotamus skulls, elephants' tusks, ears, and tails.' On a side table lies his old muzzle-loading smooth-bore elephant gun. As Fred in his 'knickerbocker suit, leans against the mantelpiece' light streaming in from the windows illuminates his smiling face, showing up the scar on his cheek caused by the explosion of another gun. He goes on to speak enthusiastically of Rhodesia as a destination for capital and settlement.

Clearly Selous and his mother pictured him already installed with his bride as master of Barrymore. Something subsequently derailed the plan, probably a shortfall in funds caused by the plunging fortunes of Chartered Company shares, which left him unable to buy out the interests of his siblings. Whatever it was, the portrait of the 'Celebrity at Home' signalled that his intention was to live permanently in

England in the fashion to which the Selous family had always been accustomed. Life under the African stars would, like the old elephant gun, be laid aside.

Bagged

A Philadelphia newspaper reported in April that 'Frederick C. Selous, world famous as a hunter, has at last been bagged himself.'[29] In England the event was more politely billed as 'Fashionable Marriage Near Cheltenham'.[30] The wedding of the well-known materialist on 4 April featured a gaggle of Anglican clergy. Canon Maddy gave his daughter away in a ceremony conducted by her uncle Walter Jones, assisted by Fred's brother-in-law Charles. Africa was represented by Fred's old hunting sidekick, George 'Elephant' Phillips, and ostrich feathers in the bride's white felt hat. Among the gifts was a pair of candlesticks from Mr and Mrs Rider Haggard. The happy couple departed almost immediately for a lengthy honeymoon in Switzerland, Italy, Hungary and Constantinople, returning to England in July.[31]

No sooner had Selous disembarked than he was caught up in negotiations to exploit the potential of land taken from Lobengula. Maurice Heany had grabbed a property comprising 221,550 acres of land (346 square miles) and 488 gold reef claims near Bulawayo. Considering that white members of the invading forces had, according to the Victoria Agreement of the previous year, been promised 6,000 acres and fifteen gold claims each, this figure suggests that Heany had aggregated around thirty-five separate grants by buying them at a discount from individual members of the Volunteers and Bechuanaland Police. He then sold all of the land for £60,000 to a corporation called the Matabele Gold Reefs and Estates Company Limited, in which he held 30,000 shares. Another 80,000 shares were offered for sale to the public at £1 per share, with 50,000 shares being held in reserve.[32] This meant that if all the shares were taken up Heany would have done exceedingly well. His suggestion that Selous join him in the management of the company must have met with Gladys's approval, because he announced at the end of July that they would be going out to Rhodesia the following spring. His service with the company would probably last two years, after which they would come back to England.[33]

Meantime, the plan to buy Barrymore House had been abandoned.

Ann Selous sold the house at Wargrave and bought another, Longford House in Gloucester, in order to be near her daughter Annie. Fred showed he was serious about returning to England by buying a country property called 'Alpine Lodge' near Worplesdon in Surrey.[34] He immediately began building an adjoining museum for the trophies and collections that had previously been displayed at Barrymore House.

In the months ahead of their departure for Africa, Fred and Gladys lived the life of the leisured class. On three separate occasions they hunted and fished on the Lochbuie estate of his friend, the Laird MacLean. In September Fred hunted goats in Turkey for the first time. For part of the time he and Gladys travelled as tourists in fine style, with tents and five servants.[35] Selous remained in demand as a speaker. A week after a caricature of him representing 'Sport and Adventure' appeared in *Vanity Fair*, he spoke without notes at the Imperial Institute. He amused the large audience by saying that:

> no title had given him greater annoyance than that of 'great hunter' and 'mighty Nimrod', that had been freely bestowed upon him by the Press. He had often been ready to sink into the ground when he had missed a rabbit in front of a Scotch ghillie, who had no doubt been told that he was 'the great hunter, Mr. S'. (laughter). An elephant was a much larger and a more sedate animal than a rabbit, and he had often lost the results of a good stalk by a bad shot.[36]

The Duke of Fife, Vice-chairman of the BSA Company, moved the vote of thanks at the close of the meeting, saying that 'in the future Mr. Selous would be known among those who had advanced the cause of civilization and had helped to extend the British Empire'.

Selous also kept in touch with his friend J.S. Keltie, Secretary of the RGS, assisting him in revisions to his book, *The Partition of Africa*. He insisted that references to him as 'great hunter' and 'mighty hunter' be cut, 'as they grate on me and are quite superfluous'.[37] On 16 March he spoke again on 'Travel and Adventure' at Exeter Hall, in the presence of minor royalty: the Duke and Duchess of Teck. The following week – just before sailing for the Cape – he was honoured at a gala dinner by old Rugby School students and teachers, including his headmaster, now the Bishop of London. His former tutor presented a silver salver inscribed, 'to Frederick Courteney Selous, Esq., by his Rugby friends, in admiring recognition of the qualities he has shown and services he has rendered as an African traveller and explorer, March 21st 1895.' Selous replied by saying that until this moment his proudest achievement had been the award of the Royal Geographical Society's gold medal, 'but that his career should have been followed by his old school companions he considered a greater honour'. He hoped that should any of them ever travel to Rhodesia they would 'not hear of anything that he had done but what would become an Englishman and a gentleman'.[38]

He probably did not picture his friends conversing with the Matabele.

16

A Rhodesian Idyll and the Rising

Fred and Gladys sailed for South Africa aboard the Union Castle steamer *Norman* on 30 March 1895. For the better part of two months they were the guests of Cecil Rhodes at his Cape Town residence, *Groote Schuur*, recently remodelled by architect Herbert Baker. Rhodes was then at the zenith of his power and influence. He had crushed Lobengula, consolidated control of the diamond industry, and entered upon his second term as Prime Minister of the Cape Colony. He would not have had much time to spend with Selous, but certainly would have talked about Rhodesian business dealings.

In addition to his farm near Salisbury and his stake in Heany's Matabele Gold Reefs and Estates Company, Selous had been appointed as a director of another land corporation, The Matabeleland Central Estates Company. In this case it was Sir John Willoughby who was capitalizing on 350,000 acres of land seized from Lobengula's people, which was to be rolled into the new corporation with a capital of £150,000, with 60,000 shares to be offered to the public at £1 each. As with Heany's company, the idea was to profit from the anticipated rise in value of the shares, while developing farms, grazing lands and gold mines. According to the prospectus, 'the whole area has been most carefully selected, and is considered one of the finest in the British South Africa Company's territory. An appraisal of the fine prospects for the country was supplied by the impartial and unbiased hand of F. C. Selous.'[1]

At the end of their stay at *Groote Schuur*, Rhodes took Gladys aside. 'Mrs Selous', he said 'your life will be very dull without a good horse, so when you arrive at Bulawayo go to the Standard Bank and you will find a sum of money and buy the very best horse you can.'[2] It is evident that they parted on the very best of terms. Still taking their time, Fred and Gladys did some shooting in the Orange Free State before travelling by ship to Beira. They took a meandering route over two months by wagon to Salisbury, which gave Fred an opportunity to introduce his wife to the places that had been his most common haunts for the last twenty-five years. On the way Fred shot what he thought was a jackal, but turned out to be a leopard.[3] Collecting was still a preoccupation despite his business entanglements. Fred had hired a Scotsman called Mr Notman as a full-time assistant in preparing specimens for the Natural History Museum.

Finally, in August, they reached their new home on the Essexvale Estate, named for the Earl of Essex who was Chairman of the company. While awaiting delivery of a prefabricated iron home from England, they lived in a thatched, two-room wattle-and-daub cottage. Gladys did not seem to mind roughing it in a structure that she found 'beautifully cool in the very hot weather'. Rhodes proved as good as his word. When Gladys arrived at the Bulawayo bank she found a money order made out for £500, enough to buy a first-rate horse and a small black pony. 'Housekeeping' she wrote, 'is no playwork in Africa, especially when you are far from town. If it were not for birds and a little game I don't know what I should do.' The most interesting social event was the visit of two Matabele queens, wives of the kingdom's founder Mzilikazi. To young Gladys, they seemed 'very ugly old women, and at least seventy years old. I thought I had better give them a present, so I opened a tin of fruit and gave them to eat. They were delighted.'[4]

By December the 'collapsible house' had been erected on 'a very picturesque position' Fred had selected on the top of a cliff about eighty feet above the Ingnaima (Ncema) river. They named it Hatherley Cottage after Gladys's parental home. Within a short time English flower gardens had been set out and 5,000 eucalyptus trees planted.[5] The company supplied 1,000 head of cattle, which were loaned out to Africans on the estate, who would bring milk in every day, which Gladys churned into butter to be sold in Bulawayo. There they spent 'a very happy 3 months on the most friendly terms with all natives living near us'. From time to time they would ride twenty miles into Bulawayo to spend the night with friends.[6]

The Jameson Raid

Since 'signing on with the devil' Fred had enjoyed an unprecedented run of good fortune. With each audacious move Rhodes's drive to build an African empire had prospered. When he spoke of Cape to Cairo people listened – and believed. At the end of December 1895 he pushed a step too far and left his minions scrambling for safety on the ledges of a precipitous mountainside. Within a few months practically everything that could go wrong, did.

The fatal misstep was a scheme to overthrow the Transvaal government in a coup. Rand gold had vastly enriched President Paul Kruger's republic. As in years gone by, his ruling maxim was government of, by and for the Boers. British and European immigrants could invest and buy land, but they enjoyed no more voting rights than Africans, which were no rights at all. Believing that the interests of the British Empire in general and those of the deep-level gold mines in particular would benefit from regime change, Rhodes set about stirring up rebellious sentiments among the immigrant population. The idea was that, at a given signal, they would seize control of the capital Pretoria and declare Kruger's government deposed. A picked force of well-armed British South Africa Company Police under Rhodesian Administrator L.S. Jameson would ride to their assistance.

During the month of December Jameson augmented his ragtag contingent of BSA Company and Bechuanaland Police with a number of colonial volunteers. They were very well armed but not nearly so numerous as he had hoped. For weeks they cooled their heels at Pitsani, just across the Transvaal border, waiting for a signal that the Johannesburg uprising had begun. When it did not come, Jameson and Rhodes decided to kick-start the revolution by a lightning strike on Johannesburg.

On 29 December, as Gladys was preparing for Fred's forty-fourth birthday, Jameson's men rode forth to inglorious calamity. The Boers had got wind of their movements and had no trouble rounding them up. By 3 January it was all over. Jameson and his men were locked up. Rhodes's political position was perilous. The British Government, which had known about the plan, repudiated the whole enterprise and threatened to revoke the BSA Company's Charter. Representatives of the Boer population of the Cape Colony, which had up to this point given their votes to Rhodes, now recoiled in a fit of nationalist horror at the perfidious attack on their fellows in the Transvaal. His political career in South Africa was finished, along with any hopes he might have cherished for a knighthood or the House of Lords. Germany's Kaiser Wilhelm II sent President Kruger a telegram congratulating him on having secured a decisive victory without the help of 'friendly Powers', which meant the Jameson Raid was now an extremely serious international incident.

Many people expected to hear that Selous had been in the thick of the fight, but he was totally out of the loop. When he heard the news he was genuinely shocked at the scale of miscalculation and foresaw the impact it was sure to have on Boer public opinion. He was not sure what effect the raid would have on his immediate situation. His friend Keltie at the RGS had written to ask about investment prospects. His reply of 20 February 1896 showed he was still sanguine:

> Our Company is in a very sound position, as we hold a lot of valuable properties, especially one reef on which I hope that a battery will soon be working. Of course, recent events in the Transvaal, and the transference of all the leading men of this country from Bulawayo to Pretoria Gaol have had a retarding influence on the prospects of the country, but if Rhodes comes up here as he is said to be about to do, he will soon set everything going again.
>
> As tor tips, I know nothing, but if our crack reef is floated separately you won't do wrong to take a few shares at par.'[7]

There was a danger, however, that the flotation of the company would be delayed 'through Heany's complicity in this TransVaal business and consequent arrest'.

That's right. His friend and employer Maurice Heany, Managing Director of Matabele Gold Reefs and Estates, had galloped off with Jameson without so much as a word to Fred. His US passport got him out of Kruger's prison and – although Fred did not know it – he was already in England. After a whirlwind romance he married a girl he had only just met, the day before he sailed for America on the ss *St. Louis*. On 7 March, the pair were besieged at New York's Fulton Street pier by pressmen eager to hear Heany's take on the Jameson Raid. On that subject he would not speak, except to say he 'was sorry for Jameson and the other boys, for they seem to be in a ticklish mess'.[8] The *New York Times* reporter went on to say that Heany was of Irish descent and after growing up in Baltimore had gone twenty years ago to seek his fortune in South Africa. He had come back to America to 'place himself under the protection of the American Government'. For the time being the couple would make their home in Baltimore.

Some English papers speculated that Selous might be appointed Administrator of Rhodesia in place of the gaoled Jameson.[9] The choice fell however on Albert Grey (soon to be Earl Grey), one of the few Chartered Company directors who possessed a reputation for humanitarian views on southern African affairs. He arrived too late, however, to exercise a decisive influence on the affairs of the country which were rapidly approaching crisis point.

Rinderpest and Rebellion

However much Selous may have speculated on the fate of Captain Heany, he had a new and more pressing worry. Rinderpest had come to Rhodesia and he had been appointed Inspector of Cattle for southern Matabeleland. This devastating disease, whose German name means 'cattle plague', infects and generally kills cattle, buffalo, large antelopes, warthogs, giraffes, wildebeests and other ungulates. The African epidemic of the 1890s swept down from Ethiopia and before it burnt itself out killed an estimated 80 to 90 per cent of all the cattle in southern Africa. For Selous the hunter, the death of so much game was heart-breaking. For the Bantu-speaking peoples it was a once-in-a-century catastrophe. It was not just the loss of milk and meat. Cattle were central to economic and social relations: exchanges of cattle cemented marriages; personal wealth was measured in cattle; chiefs wielded power through the distribution of cattle and grazing lands. In popular discourse a man without cattle was no better than a bushman or a slave.

Selous had expected the disease to be halted, at least for a time, by 'the fly zone' of the Zambezi valley. But thanks probably to the wild game as a vector it was already killing cattle in northern Matabeleland by February 1896. He went conscientiously about his duties as an inspector, but in reality he knew no one could stop its grim march down to the Cape.

Even before the rinderpest arrived in his neighbourhood, loss of cattle was the number one grievance for Matabele. The BSA Company had not handled the cattle issue at all well. After the war of 1893 they had confiscated vast herds on the completely mistaken assumption that most belonged to Lobengula. Nothing could be more calculated to foster a burning sense of grievance. Men fumed to see cattle they had tended as herdboys distributed to white farmers on land that rightfully belonged to them.

The company erred in other ways. To make up shortfalls in revenue and to encourage Africans to become waged labourers, hut taxes were imposed throughout Rhodesia. South African experience since the 1840s showed this to be the most efficient way to collect a tax from black peasants. It was difficult to evade because huts were easily counted. White settlers did not live in huts, so they escaped this impost as they escaped most others. The company justified the tax in Matabeleland by pointing to Lobengula's guilt. It justified the tax in Mashonaland by saying they should be grateful for protection against Matabele raids. Hut taxes were levied through chiefs and if they did not pay on time, cattle were seized – lots of them. The company also imposed a labour tax, which required young men to supply their labour at a low rate of pay for a certain number of days. Added to these taxes and levies was the hurt and humiliation suffered by the principal chiefs and *indunas* who now felt themselves to be nobodies under the new regime.

After talking to the veteran missionary Charles Helm, Selous understood the full extent of Matabele grievances, but still did not imagine that a widespread challenge to company rule was contemplated.[10] By mid-March he was fully occupied in cattle inspection. Gladys looked on him as her strong but silent protector. She understood that his work 'meant a great deal of riding about the country, but he was always very careful not to leave me alone at night. While on these trips he heard many rumours about native unrest but never mentioned it to me.'[11] On Monday 23 March Fred heard from H.M. Jackson that a number of black police had been assaulted by a gang of angry Matabele. He did not imagine this to be a prelude to a general rising, but felt apprehensive about having left Gladys home alone that night. Next day he was relieved to find nothing amiss at the house. Gladys had, however, received an odd deputation that morning:

Several men came and asked if they could buy or borrow some axes and sharpen them on our grind stone. They wanted them to strengthen their cattle kraals. We kept large stores of many things for the natives, beads, calico, etc. Little thinking I sold them and noticed they would sit around watching me and talk and tell me I was their white Queen etc, but always wanted know when was the boss coming back, was he coming that night. He turned up earlier than expected as he had heard things were getting more unsettled and even 2 or 3 white people had been murdered. I told him what I had done selling axes etc, but he never told me anything as he was most anxious not to make me nervous but he told the 2 men to have their rifles ready and be on the look out. ... Well we had a quiet night & I never even noticed that my husband had a loaded rifle by his bed.[12]

Fred's recollection is slightly different, but agrees with Gladys on a husband's duty to maintain a discreet silence on disagreeable subjects. A man in his employ took him aside to say his wife had heard that a native commissioner on the other side of the hills had his throat slit by his own black police. While that was disquieting news, he did not anticipate an attack on his own place, as they had shown nothing but kindness to Africans on the Essexvale Estate:

I, of course, said nothing to my wife as to what I had heard, but I told Mr. Blöcker and the young Scotchman to keep their rifles handy in case of accidents. I had, too, some very good watch-dogs that I knew would give me warning if any Kafirs came near the house, and I kept awake all night with my rifle and a belt full of cartridges alongside of me.[13]

Next morning he rose to find that armed men had seized cattle from pens on the estate. Gladys was nonplussed when the watchman ran up to their house shouting:

'Bring the horses, bring the horses, make haste!' I could not understand it. Then my husband told me all he had heard and said 'Eat what you can, pack a few clothes, collect all the money and we must ride hard into Bulawayo.' So we locked up the house and with our 2 men started off for town. Luckily we had 4 horses at the time. Our two most faithful servants took my little dog and bag of clothes and walked and ran into Bulawayo.... I was just about dead beat when I did arrive at my kind friend's house where I stayed ... many had already been murdered. My husband went off to collect some men and horses to return and save our house, which was eventually looted and burnt and I was left with only a change of clothes![14]

Historians have struggled over the past century to explain how the leaders of the revolt coordinated their movements in secret without arousing suspicion. There has also been a lively debate about how they conceptualized their movement. Special attention has been paid to the role of religion and the supernatural. Did ritual specialists known as *Mlimo* or members of something called the *Mwari* cult play a key part in infusing the rebels with a sense of togetherness and a larger purpose? Or did Rhodesian settlers and officials resort to mumbo-jumbo about *Mlimo* and *Mwari* to divert attention from the cattle seizures, labour imposts and hut taxes which had driven the African people to rise up against their oppressors? These remain very interesting questions, on which scholars will differ. They do not, however, have much bearing on Selous's experience of the war. He confessed frankly that he had not expected a rising and was at a loss to explain how it could have grown from a spark into a conflagration without his noticing anything amiss. He also admitted that the Matabele had perfectly rational reasons for resenting the alien rule that had been foisted upon them without their consent. They could not be expected to understand that colonial rule would bring more long-term advantages to African families than a reversion to the old regime. What he did know was that he and the other settlers needed to organize the defence of their families and property – without an instant's delay and without much reflection on the righteousness of their cause.

As settlers poured into Bulawayo and organized temporary quarters for women and children, many gave way to panic and despair. Gladys wrote to her parents to say that even though people crowded into the Bulawayo Club as in the Black Hole of Calcutta, she was not the least frightened. A drunken man made his uncertain way down the main street shouting, 'The Matabele are coming, the Matabele are coming'. Children began to cry and many of their mothers fainted dead away.[15]

It is said that Kipling had Dr Jameson in mind when he praised the man who could keep his head when all about were losing theirs. The aphorism would be even more aptly applied to Selous on 25 March 1896. He did not panic but instantly set about recruiting a corps of volunteers with horses and guns. He could not turn to the British South Africa Company Police because they had all been diverted by the failed Transvaal coup. Selous thought and later wrote that the Matabele rising was precipitated by the absence of those forces. Had there been no Jameson Raid, there would have been no uprising.

Soon after his arrival in Bulawayo on 25 March, he stood on the veranda of the Chartered Hotel, and called for volunteers to ride with him to Essexvale and help secure the property.[16] His on-the-spot survey of the forces available was not encouraging. Something like a thousand men were present in Bulawayo but only about half of them had guns. Horses were likewise in short supply. At least 400 men would have to stay to guard women and children gathered within the hastily erected *laager*. There was only one Maxim gun in working order. Perhaps 300 mounted men could be spared for military operations in the countryside.

The military situation was nothing like the war of 1893. This time the Matabele had the advantage of numbers, firearms and surprise. Their forces were dispersed and they refused to join the whites in pitched battles where they might be destroyed by the Maxims. Instead they adopted hit-and-run guerrilla tactics with the avowed object of killing as many white people as possible. Selous's opinion was that, had they made a direct strike on Bulawayo at the end of March, it would have been all over for the settlers. Reinforcements could not possibly have arrived from the Cape in time to save them. An added worry was the rinderpest. Lacking a railway, transport of heavy equipment and supplies depended on oxen, which had begun to die in their thousands. Fortunately for the settlers, Bulawayo did not come under attack. Instead, the Matabele struck at isolated farms and tiny villages, killing several hundred colonists.

It was 2 a.m. by the time Selous and his volunteers reached Essexvale. At first glance everything seemed to be as he had left it, however at daylight he discovered that all the company cattle had been driven off. After some hard riding they recovered those cattle and another large herd being driven through an adjacent valley. These he *kraaled* at Essexvale, fearing that they would certainly perish of the rinderpest if driven to Bulawayo. On the morning of Sunday 29 March, Selous and his men started back along the road to town. As they passed the granite-strewn Matopos Hills, he made an impulsive decision. In the coming weeks the Matabele would undoubtedly establish fortified strongholds in that region. It seemed a good idea to reconnoitre. He drew his mounted patrol up in parade order and told them that he was going into the Matopos. They were welcome to join him or not as they wished. To a man they chose to ride with him. Within an hour or so they were in the narrow cleft of a deep gorge and heard the crack of rifles above them. A little further on they came across corn-fields and a sizeable herd of cattle. Unwilling to leave them to their foes, and lacking the ammunition to shoot them all, Selous decided to try driving them back to the main road. They had not got far before they ran into an ambush. For an hour or so they traded shots with the Matabele, among whom were several deserters from the Company police. When it became evident that the attackers would not leave the shelter of the boulders, Selous decided to abandon the cattle and pick their way up the gorge to safety. The Matabele lost several men, while there were four horses killed and two men wounded on the other side.

In a letter home, a young trooper attested to Selous's leadership and courage:

[I] started off with Selous, whom I knew before, with about thirty-five others. We had a very exciting time. ... Selous is splendid man to be under. He is always to the fore. We had a pretty hot time of it in the Matoppo Hills. There were fellows there who had been all through the Basuto and Malaboch campaign, and they said they had never been in a hotter place. Had the native police against us, who have been taught to shoot, and armed with Winchester rifles, and they put their bullets closer than was pleasant. There were some raw niggers with them, too, but you know they are far more formidable with their assegais than with old-fashioned muskets that shoot round the corner, loaded with pot legs, scraps of iron, and buckshot, to say nothing of pebbles. ... We lost four horses and two men wounded. I was one of the chaps who held the retreat, and had the bullets whistling round us, I can tell you.[17]

Gladys, who had seen fear written on the faces of men in Bulawayo, told her parents she would 'be most awfully ashamed if I was in any way a relation of some of the men up here. But ... I have a husband that everyone looks up to and respects.'[18]

Pending the arrival of reinforcements, the defenders of southern Matabeleland organized themselves into three units: the Bulawayo Field Force in which Selous was enrolled as a captain; an Afrikaner (Boer) Corps; and a corps comprised of over a hundred 'Colonial Boys', mostly Zulu and Xhosa from the Cape Colony. Selous's main job was to establish forts along the road to Tati, so as to ensure it remained open to supplies coming up from the Cape. By chance he spent the night of 18 April in Bulawayo and so was on the spot when the news came next morning that Matabele *impis* had been seen only three miles south of the town. Fred rode out to see what was going on, arriving in time to assist in a skirmish on the banks of the Umguza River. He was put in charge of a small company of Afrikaner sharp-shooters who cut a swathe through the attackers. He does not say whether any of those killed fell to his rifle, but by the end of the action he found he had fired nineteen cartridges, before the order was given to move back to Bulawayo.

Selous was allowed leave from his fort building and two days later was again in the thick of a fight on Umguza. The officers on his side were intent on drawing the Matabele out into the open where their artillery could direct deadly fire. The Matabele were equally determined to fight from positions in the bush. At length a cavalry manoeuvre forced a number onto the banks of the river and battle was joined. Selous had been ordered to ride forward with the 'Colonial Boys' and expected that the Maxim gun would do its customary slaughter. He was dumbfounded to find that the gun crew stood idly chatting while waiting for the command to shoot. Meanwhile the order came for his men to fall back. Thinking to get a couple more shots at the enemy, he dismounted and took up a firing position far ahead of his own forces. When the retreating Matabele saw him in this vulnerable situation, they turned and began to fire. Turning to grab his horse by the bridle, he found that the frightened animal had run off. Had not Lieutenant Windley, one of the officers leading the Colonial Boys, galloped to his assistance, he surely would have caught a bullet. With Windley covering him he dashed back towards the lines, running as he had not run since his elephant hunting days in the 1870s. One of the Xhosa soldiers, John Grootboom, gallantly offered him his own horse. Even then he barely had the strength to mount but, being among friends, had no trouble getting back to Bulawayo.

His next assignment was to move out on 11 May with a combined force marching north-west, where they were to join up with a relief column advancing toward them from Salisbury under Sir Charles Metcalfe and Cecil Rhodes. The two contingents met on 20 May and the officers shared a mess that evening. Selous thought Rhodes looked pretty well considering the circumstances. Only his 'fast grizzling hair and a certain look in the strong face' betrayed the mental strain of the last six months. This was one of two occasions during the subsequent weeks when he and Selous were thrown together, but there would scarcely have been time for any private chat on personal matters. Selous was given command of a portion of the Bulawayo Field Force and over the next month was engaged in destroying crops and burning the huts of Matabele – all of whom were treated as enemies equally guilty of the murder of innocent settlers. He gives no detailed account of the work, but acknowledges in his book about the war that the colonial forces went about their work with a pitiless ferocity borne of their rage against the brutal murderers of their fellows. By late June military command had passed to officers of the regular British Army, including Major Baden-Powell, whom Selous encountered for the first time.

On 4 July Earl Grey disbanded the Bulawayo Field Force with a speech paying tribute to their valour and resourcefulness. Fred, a civilian once more, rejoined Gladys in Bulawayo. Because he was one of the few genuine celebrities involved in the early stages of the war, British newspapers made him the focus of their hero-worship. One wrote in early April that 'the utmost zeal has been shown in the work of suppressing the revolt, and Mr. Selous alone has been worth a whole company of ordinary soldiers, thanks to the great influence which he wields'. The *Globe* asked if there was any way he might be suitably honoured for his splendid services by the British Government: 'In any other country in the world the devotion of a private citizen, who, in a time of the greatest danger, freely offered his life for the service of the State, would immediately be brought to the notice of the Fountain of Honour and suitably rewarded'. In September the *Yorkshire Post* said the 'substantial services rendered by Mr. Selous will, it is understood, be recognized at the end of the year by the bestowal of a knighthood'.[19]

The public adulation, gratifying as it must have been to friends and family, exaggerated his part in the war. He had, after all, only seen a few hours of action on three separate days, not nearly enough to warrant being dubbed Sir Frederick. Another factor in play was that the war in Rhodesia had not ended with the disbandment of the Bulawayo Field Force. Two weeks earlier a fresh insurrection had broken out in Mashonaland, blasting any hope of an early return to tranquillity. It also showed that protection from Matabele raids was not enough to counterbalance the burden of the company's new taxes and labour laws. A long and difficult campaign would be required to 'pacify' the country. With each passing month more evidence emerged of questionable tactics and brutal measures employed against the African population. As with more recent 'small wars', public enthusiasm waned in Britain. The BSA Company had promised to extend Britain's African empire with no expense to taxpayers at home. Now it was the British Army that had to rescue the company. Coming so soon after the Jameson Raid, the uprising further shredded Rhodes's now threadbare reputation.

The Inexorable Law

Knowing how much the first Matabele campaign boosted sales of his *Travel and Adventure* in 1893, Selous worked furiously during June and July to bring out a book on the war of 1896. In addition to recounting his own experiences, he collected oral history from fellow officers, which makes it an important historical source on the conduct of counter-insurgency warfare in that era. From a biographical point of view *Sunshine and Storm in Rhodesia* is notable for its strident defence of the colonial forces against accusations that they had brought this war on themselves and pursued it with excessive ferocity. His starting point was that the Matabele strategy of indiscriminately killing white settlers justified an equal and opposite reaction. He confessed to feeling waves of revulsion that drove him to a high pitch of bloodlust.

Speaking of one particular cavalry charge in which Matabele were shot in the back as they fled in disorder, he observed that :

no quarter was either given or asked for, nor was any more mercy shown than had been lately granted by the Kafirs to the white woman and children who had fallen into their power. [He could not] dispute the horror of the picture; but I must confess that had I been with Captain Grey that day, I should have done my utmost to kill as many Kafirs as possible, and yet I think I can claim to be as humane a man as any of my critics who may feel inclined to consider such deeds cowardly and brutal and altogether unworthy of a civilised being.[20]

He went on to say that experience showed that in every man 'somewhere deep down below the polished surface of conventionality there exists ... an ineradicable leaven of innate ferocity, which although it may never show itself except under the most exceptional circumstances, must and ever will be there.' It was this 'cruel instinct which, given sufficient provocation, prompts the meekest nature to kill his enemy – the instinct which forms the connecting link between the nature of man and that of the beast.'[21] Nothing was more certain than:

> the horrors of a native insurrection – the murders and mutilations of white men, women and children by savages – to awake this slumbering fiend – the indestructible and imperishable inheritance which, through countless generations, has been handed down to the most highly civilised races of the present day from the savage animals or beings from whom or which modern science teaches us that they have been evolved.[22]

Selous used the same Darwinian reasoning to argue that there was no point regretting the displacement of indigenous peoples by European colonialism across the globe. Just as the 'noble red man' had been exterminated by the tide of white pioneers advancing westward in America, Matabeleland was 'doomed by what seems a law of nature to be ruled by the white man, and the black man must go, or conform to the white man's laws, or die in resisting them'. No amount of humanitarian concern could avert that destiny. The British settler was 'but the irresponsible atom employed in carrying out a preordained law' – the 'inexorable law which Darwin has aptly termed the "Survival of the Fittest".'[23]

Not knowing how far the war had yet to run, Selous closed his book with the dateline, 'Bulawayo, 26th August 1896'. When he finally had an opportunity to revisit Hatherley Cottage, he found it a blackened ruin. Until the rinderpest had run its course there was no way Essexvale could return to normal operations. Without cattle there was nowhere to live and nothing for Fred to manage. With the Rhodesian economy paralysed and his work for the Matabele Gold Reefs and Estates Company at an end, there was no alternative but to return to England. At the end of August 1896 he moved down to Kimberley, where Gladys stayed with friends, while he traveled down to southern Mozambique in search of the nyala, a rare antelope that he had for many years longed to add to his collection. He took the recently completed railway from Pretoria to Lorenço Marques (Maputo), and from there made his way by boat up the Maputo River. Along the way he had the opportunity to converse in French with a cultivated Portuguese official, and to compare notes on colonial administration. Speaking of the war in Rhodesia, the Portuguese officer said it showed the defects of the British system of recruiting African police from the local population. The Portuguese practice was to employ Africans from distant regions who would not be likely to form close bonds with the subject people.

Fred found that the southern Amatonga (Tsonga) spoke excellent Zulu and so could understand the Matabele dialect of that language. He had no trouble finding his nyala and took several specimens away. Here he encountered a version of the men among whom he had spent his early years elephant hunting:

At Gugawi's I met an Englishman, who informed me that he had come down from Barberton, and was travelling about amongst the Amatonga, buying skins of wild cats, jackals, etc., which he hoped to sell again at a profit to the Kafirs working in the mines in the Transvaal. He seemed much surprised when I told him that I had only come to Amatongaland in order to shoot an *inyala* [sic], and frequently remarked in the course of our conversation, 'Well, I'm ————; so you've come all this —————— way to shoot a —————— buck.' He also informed me that he was not very well, as he had been 'on the burst' for the last three days; but this confidence was superfluous, as no one could have approached within ten yards of him without realising his condition.[24]

No doubt the figures of Westbeech, Cigar and other legends of the bush came to life again in his imagination. It was a life he had left forever.

Two months later, Rhodes's house *Groote Schuur* burnt down. Selous's testing years of temptation were over.

17

My Dear President Roosevelt

The usual gang of journalists had gathered at the docks on 20 November 1896 when Fred walked down the gangway with Gladys on his arm. This time the reporters wanted answers to hard questions raised by Henry Labouchere and a great many others about the inhumane conduct of the Rhodesian campaign. *Sunshine and Storm in Rhodesia* had just appeared, to a more mixed set of reviews than his previous books. Selous had been itching to level both barrels at the 'misguided philanthropists' who failed to understand the realities of savage warfare. Before they could corner him a representative of Rowland Ward pulled him aside to caution him against saying anything controversial. Labouchere had once again made Selous the target of criticism, but his cutting remarks were by now old news, which it was best not to stir up.[1] So Fred held his tongue.

Other things he had written in the book had a more decisive impact on his standing as a public figure. He had reiterated his assertion that, by drawing troops away, the Jameson Raid had precipitated the rising in Matabeleland. That was not to say that Jameson had shrunk in his estimation. Like any man 'Dr Jim' made mistakes; this was one of them. The worst consequence of the raid in the long term was that the Dutch population of South Africa, hitherto divided in its loyalties, was now united in their loathing for Rhodes and the conspirators. The 'deplorable invasion of Transvaal by a British force in defiance of all international law, to accomplish I still fail to understand what', had aroused anti-British 'national sentiment'. It raised the spectre of a coming 'war between the two races' (Dutchmen and English) which 'would retard the general progress of the country for a generation'. Those who expected the burgeoning population of British and Europeans attracted by the mineral boom to swamp the descendants of Dutch settlers were mistaken. Most of the newcomers were single men. The Boers married early and bred prolifically.[2] They would, in fifty or eighty years, still constitute the great majority of the white population. Motivated by national sentiment they would almost certainly unite as a republic under a flag of their own – unless Britain pursued a conciliatory policy that would halt the drift toward war.

As a long-term prophecy this stands up fairly well. In the short run it could only have the effect of alienating Rhodes and the clique of speculators with whom Selous had been so closely entangled for the last seven years. Although Rhodes was now finished as a political force, he was still a very rich man. Fred's stance on the Jameson Raid ensured that the magnate would take no more interest in the fortunes of Fred and Gladys. Maurice Heany returned to Rhodesia and got his business back on its feet. In July 1900 he told Rhodes that he had outlaid £5,000 restocking Essexvale with cattle and that 'matters at the Mines are going exceedingly well'. The Matabele Gold Reefs and Estates Company was liquidated about the same time and the assets rolled into a new corporation that was the largest landowner in Rhodesia. Heany did not, however, consider calling Selous back to Hatherley Cottage.[3]

For a time it appeared that the British Government was eager for his advice. Colonial Secretary Joseph Chamberlain, who the year before mispronounced his name in the House of Commons as *See*-loo, called him in for a consultation on southern African affairs on 22 January 1897.[4] While he continued to praise him in Parliament, Chamberlain ignored Fred's advice on how to deal with the Boers. In April he appointed as the new High Commissioner for Southern Africa, Sir Alfred Milner, who set Britain on a collision course with the Transvaal.

The return to England brought a bevy of speaking engagements. At a Sports Club dinner in January Selous praised hunters as pioneers of Empire and civilization. 'Big-game hunters were always in the forefront of the march of civilization' and had 'done as much in that respect as missionaries.'

The quality which led men to penetrate into new regions for sport had been most useful to England as a colonising nation. The Boers of the Northern and eastern portions of the Transvaal were all big-game hunters, and it was owing to this circumstance that they were the most formidable guerrilla troops that could be found in the whole world.[5]

Selous spoke as warmly as ever about the prospects of Rhodesia, but without the stridency of the previous year. At the Anglo-African Writers' dinner he spoke 'of peace in the Transvaal and goodwill towards the Boer and the native, the mighty hunter being as pacific as a little child'. Although less sanguine about mining in eastern Mashonaland, he still held out hope for big discoveries in the west. Putting his money where his mouth was, he 'had been buying the shares of his own companies at a premium'.[6]

Money did not seem a pressing concern at the moment and hunting was very much back on the agenda. He and Gladys spent January holidays shooting with their friend MacLean of Lochbuie.[7] In February they were off to Turkey again. Gladys remained in Smyrna (Izmir) while Fred tried his luck with stags, goats and vultures' eggs in nearby snowy mountains.[8] He kept careful notes and wrote them up, but they inevitably pale in comparison with his African adventures. Knowing little of the people, the language or their history, his ethnographic observations on the Turks rarely rise above the level of an ordinary tourist.

When he returned to Smyrna from one of his little excursions into the mountains at the beginning of March he found a letter waiting from a Mr Theodore Roosevelt of New York City.

The Last of the Real Wilderness Life

There was no reason why Selous should take any particular notice of the Roosevelt name. He was just one of many star-struck fans with whom he corresponded on the finer points of big game hunting. Fred's reply dated 3 March 1897 was written the day before William McKinley's inauguration as President of the United States. Roosevelt's influence in local New York Republican politics won him a minor appointment in the new administration as Assistant Secretary of the Navy. What piqued Selous's interest was his correspondent's extensive experience of the Rocky Mountains. He and Gladys had been talking for some time about a trip to the American West, and were eager for information about the best hunting spots in Wyoming.

As a lad Roosevelt had shared Selous's enthusiasm for nature and collecting. At the age of seven he practised rudimentary taxidermy for what he called the Roosevelt Museum of Natural History. Roosevelt had not, however, been endowed with Fred's 'strong constitution'. He was a sickly boy, plagued by asthma. He cursed his own timidity and longed to be like 'men who were fearless and could hold their own in the world'. He could not distinguish himself in ball games but, by dint of application, he learnt to box and shoot and ride. His love of the outdoors led him to buy a ranch in North Dakota, where he might have spent his life but for the fatal allure of politics. He shared his generation's love affair with the grandeur of America's western wilderness and travelled into it at every opportunity. Like Selous, he aspired to make a real contribution to natural history through the close study of animal specimens.

Characteristically, Fred's letter of 3 March begins with a reference to money troubles. 'Some months ago' he and Gladys counted on touring for several months in the West, but just now things were 'so bad in South Africa' that it would be impossible. Instead of setting aside £1,200–1,500 for the trip, they would have to manage on £400 all up.[9] They would be delighted to accept Roosevelt's invitation to pay a visit in New York, but Fred confessed to some apprehension about his fitness. In his elephant hunting days he could stand any amount of fatigue, but his recent experience in Turkey showed that mountain work was 'a little trying'.

The planned meeting in New York did not eventuate because in April Selous accepted an invitation to address a conference of the British Association in Toronto. He and Gladys crossed the Atlantic on the liner *Parisian* in early August. His chosen topic for the British Association was 'The Economic Value of Rhodesia'.[10] To twenty-first-century eyes it reads as an optimistic appraisal of the colony's future. But contemporaries – speculators and investors in particular – regarded it as a wet towel cast on the bonfire of their aspirations. The rinderpest, he said, had wiped out the cattle, but in time the herds would recover. Other dreadful diseases like lung sickness could be controlled by timely vaccination. While recent locust plagues had been dreadful, they would probably die down. The country above 5,400 feet of altitude was as healthy for white people as any on earth, so if settlers avoided the lower districts they would not fall victim to the deadly fevers. Horse sickness afflicted Rhodesia as badly as South Africa, but with careful management it was possible to raise 'salted' stock. Rice and wheat could be grown but would never be cheap enough to compete with Indian and Australian production. There was no problem getting black workers for farms but almost nothing would entice them into underground mining.

Selous wrote some two decades later that this paper caused the capitalists of South Africa and Rhodesia to 'cast me into the outer darkness' because 'I told the simple truth about the economic value of the country, without any attempt at exaggeration, which of course did not please those who only wanted to boom the country and sell their holdings.'[11] Only a year earlier he had been leading the cheer squad. His altered tone suggests faltering faith in his own Rhodesian investments. He may also have heard from Heany that Rhodes, Jameson and their clique had no further use for him.

From Toronto he and Gladys went by rail to Sheridan, Wyoming. For the next two and a half months they lived in cabins and tents while exploring the countryside of the Bighorn River country and nearby mountains.[12] Gladys took as much delight as Fred in the scenery. Though she does not appear to have shot any game, she showed great skill at fishing.

The mighty peaks of the Grand Tetons, the forests, the lakes: everything delighted the eye. Selous 'could imagine no more perfect country in which to hunt than the Rocky Mountains must once have been, when game was still plentiful'. Having read numerous accounts of the western plains he was astonished by the rapid decline in wildlife. Where bison had roamed in tens of thousands there were only bleaching skulls to remind the traveller of their thundering herds. The great wapiti (elk) which had once been a common sight had now to be sought out high on forested mountainsides. Fred considered himself fortunate to bring back a couple of fine heads. Because it was his country, Roosevelt reacted emotionally to Fred's account of Wyoming which made him:

realize so vividly how almost the last real hunting grounds in

America have gone.... A very few more years will do away with all the really wild hunting, at least so far as bear and elk are concerned, in the Rocky Mountains and the West generally ... I feel rather melancholy to think that my own four small boys will practically see no hunting on this side [of the Atlantic]... I was just in time to see the last of the real wilderness life and real wilderness hunting. How I wish I could have been with you this year![13]

There was no epiphany in Fred's life when he committed himself to the cause of wildlife conservation. From his first elephant hunt he had been aware that herds were dwindling. By the 1880s he feared for the survival of the white rhino. Part of the motivation for collecting for museums was preserving specimens of rare and extinct species. His vision for the settlement of Mashonaland in 1890 included hunting reserves in 'the fly'. Not long before departing Rhodesia in 1896 Selous was elected first President of the Bulawayo Society for the Preservation of Game. He had encouraged the formation of a London-based Committee for the Preservation of African Game, which persuaded Cecil Rhodes to set aside 200,000 acres as the first designated wildlife reserve in Rhodesia.[14]

In the 1890s he became acquainted with African hunters who shared his views on conservation. It was not surprising that E.N. Buxton, H.A. Bryden and J.G. Millais became congenial companions. Like Selous they wrote books about hunting, with the eye of a naturalist. Fred introduced Roosevelt to their work, which reinforced his commitment to the budding international conservation movement. In February 1898 Roosevelt wrote to thank Selous for sending one of Millais's books with exquisite drawings (which is no more than one would expect from the son of a Pre-Raphaelite painter). 'I do wish,' he said, we had a Millais on this side of the water to do for American game something of the same kind.' A few days later he wrote to congratulate Fred on the news that Gladys was expecting. 'After all, there is nothing that in any way comes up to home and wife and children.'[15] Roosevelt had, of course, no way of knowing that Fred had previously known the delights of domesticity with an African family. His first English child, Frederick Hatherley, was born in April 1898 and his second, Harold Sherborn, in 1899.

More than a year went by before Roosevelt and Selous resumed their correspondence. While Selous settled into family life as a country gentleman, Roosevelt was catapulted onto the world stage as a national hero. Two days after he posted his letter congratulating Gladys on her pregnancy, the US battleship *Maine* exploded and sank in Havana Harbour, precipitating the Spanish-American War of 1898. Roosevelt resigned as Assistant Secretary of the Navy and joined a volunteer unit of the US Cavalry popularly known as the Rough Riders. In many ways it resembled Selous's volunteer Bulawayo Field Force, right down to the slouch hats and jackets. Its miscellaneous riders included cowboys, ranchers, miners, amateur athletes and Hispanics eager to support the overthrow of the Spanish regime in Cuba. The big difference between this outfit and the Bulawayo volunteers was Roosevelt's insistence that they be well drilled and equipped. They took the name Rough Riders from the Wild West of 'Buffalo Bill', who billed the show as 'Buffalo Bill's Wild West and Congress of Rough Riders of the World'.

Newly commissioned as a colonel, Roosevelt led his irregulars in a daring charge up San Juan Hill and into the hearts of his countrymen. The timid boy had become the fearless hunter/soldier of his dreams. New York newspapers and political operatives clamoured for him to return to public life. In November the man who had failed in a bid to be Mayor of New York City was triumphantly elected governor of his state.

Meanwhile, Selous enjoyed a less fevered life as a minor celebrity back on the lecture circuit. In January 1898 he attracted enthusiastic audiences in Hull, Manchester, Middlesbrough and Birmingham. The next month he visited Scotland, with talks in Glasgow, Edinburgh and Perth. From published reports it appears that he said little about the war in Rhodesia. There was no talk about vengeance or nature's inexorable laws. Instead, he fell back on tales of charging elephants and menacing lions. He paid tribute to the loyalty and service of his African hunting companions:

Describing the warmth with which his black followers welcomed him after an attack in which they thought he had been killed, he said he was not of those who regarded the natives of South Africa as incapable of gratitude and destitute of good feelings. (Hear, hear.) His experiences led him to an entirely different opinion. If a white man gave a Kaffir reason to be grateful he probably would be. Mr. Selous had met many good Kaffirs, had many friends among them, and could say that they were always grateful for any kindness he did them. (Cheers.)[16]

Selous also discovered a previously unknown ability to engage with schoolboy audiences. Having heard that Fred was visiting his mother in Gloucester following the Scottish tour, the headmaster of nearby Cheltenham College inveigled him into a performance at the school hall. As he had all his lecture apparatus with him – pictures, skins, lantern slides – Selous soon had the boys enthralled. Perhaps they would like to know, he asked, what it was like to dine with a savage king? He had sat down with Lobengula on many occasions. The king used his knife and fork in a most enterprising manner:

He cut off a large piece of meat, stuck it on the fork, held it to his mouth, seized as much as he could with his teeth, and then cut it off with the carving knife as near his lips as possible (laughter). He ate several pounds of meat at each meal, but no vegetables. (cheers) As a rule he washed his dinner down with copious draughts of native beer (laughter).[17]

Apart from lectures, Selous devoted himself to his private museum and meetings of various societies. His wife renamed their Worplesdon house 'Heatherside' and set about filling it with her own collection of curios, recently enhanced with the addition of some highly polished elks' teeth.[18] In November Selous made another brief expedition to Wyoming with even more disappointing results than the year before. A newspaper caption said it all: '12,000 MILES FOR LESS THAN 20 SHOTS.'[19] Part of the problem was that November snowfalls had been light, so the elk and deer could seclude themselves in the higher altitudes. The more basic situation was that there had been a precipitous decline of wildlife of all kinds. Once birds of prey would have devoured a discarded carcass within hours. In the stillness of the new West, meat left out overnight would be found untouched in the morning. Conscious of the conservation imperative, Selous stressed that his only interest was the collection of fine specimens of animals that are 'likely to become extinct within the next generation or two':

I would like to state ... that my visit must not be considered a hunting trip. I made no attempt to secure a big bag. In fact, I never shot anything unless I was satisfied that the creature would make a good specimen, when killed, for mounting. I fired less than twenty shots from the beginning to the end of my three weeks' sojourn in the Rockies, and in no instance did I shoot a female animal of any species.[20]

Strange bedfellows

Paradoxically, despite their many shared enthusiasms, Selous and Roosevelt moved in opposite political directions in the last two years of the nineteenth century. 'TR' (as the newspapers called him) rode a wave of war fever into the governor's mansion while Selous was drawn into a peace campaign aimed at halting Britain's slide towards war with the Transvaal Republic.

At one level Fred's stand followed logically from the position he had staked out in 1896. He was on record as condemning the Jameson Raid and forecasting that a war with the Transvaal would sound the death knell of British rule in South Africa. He had told his friend Keltie at the RGS that it would 'require as many troops to conquer the Dutch in South Africa fighting in their own country and with the right on their side, as were employed for the invasion of the Crimea'. From a financial point of view 'no matter which way it ends, it must be disastrous to the future prosperity of the country'.[21] Britain might win the war, but would certainly lose the peace. The conflict would unite everyone of Dutch descent in antipathy to all things English and hasten the birth of an independent Afrikaner Republic of South Africa. As a person Selous had grown more consciously proud of his ancestral line over the years. He believed that his forefathers had been Huguenots who had fled to Jersey to escape persecution by Louis XIV, just like the Huguenots who had moved via Holland to the Cape after 1685. So there was a strengthening sentiment of fellow-feeling. However, a new and totally unexpected ingredient in his political attitude in 1899 was the loathing he expressed for the 'capitalist clique' that was pushing on the war.

As the crisis drew nearer he wrote warning letters to *The Times* and joined the South Africa Conciliation Committee, which aimed to avert war through a negotiated settlement.[22] As Vice President, Selous was thrown into strange and unaccustomed company. The President, Leonard Courteney, was a lifelong Radical. The Secretary, Emily Hobhouse, was a noted pacifist. Several left-leaning clergymen joined, as did the so-called 'Radical Countess' of Carlisle. Octogenarian Herbert Spencer – despite being the man who coined the phrase 'survival of the fittest' – was a lifelong opponent of militarism and imperialism. John A. Hobson would write a hugely influential tract against imperialism, with special condemnation directed against the Rhodesia labour laws which Selous had praised. Even further to the left was Walter Crane, who had been introduced to socialism by William Morris and whose illustrations adorned the magazine *Justice*, the propaganda organ of the British Social-Democratic Federation. One of Selous's letters to the *Morning Post* drew an admiring notice from H.M. Hyndman, Britain's most prominent apostle of Karl Marx.[23]

More than a few people would have been scratching their heads at the spectacle of a big game hunter in such company, especially one so recently tied up with Rhodes and the crushing of the Matabele. After the formal outbreak of war in October 1899, Selous lent his support to efforts to interest Roosevelt in the cause of conciliation. Montague White, who had been the Transvaal's Consul-General in London before the war, used Selous's name to wangle an appointment with the governor in February 1900. There was some thought that Roosevelt's Dutch family background would incline him to sympathize with the anti-war cause.[24] White found him willing to listen but not especially well-informed on the conflict. TR failed to see why the Dutch and English should not meld as completely into one people in South Africa as they had in the United States. Most of the pro-Boers he knew were motivated by anti-British prejudice, a sentiment with which he found difficult to sympathize. In any event, the current state of American politics made it impossible for him to take a public stand on the war one way or the other.

He was, however, interested enough to ask Selous for his frank assessment of the situation. This led to a most revealing exchange of correspondence in March 1900. Fred was despairing and despondent. 'It is a very bitter grief to me not to be able to side with my own country in this war, & I feel it so much that were I a younger man and unmarried, I would leave this country & settle in America.' It was hard to believe that the 'the Imperialists & Capitalists ... have captured the Press both of South Africa & of Great Britain & persuaded the great majority of the British people that the present war is just & was necessary.'[25] But for the discovery of gold, matters would not have come to this sorry pass. Had it not been for the Jameson Raid the Transvaal would not have set out to acquire heavy artillery. He blamed Rhodes for stirring up public opinion at home:

> Mr. George Wyndham (the present under secretary for war who had spent four months with Mr. Rhodes in Matabeleland and had become thoroughly imbued with all his political ideas for the future of South Africa, one of which was the elimination of the Dutch Republics & their absorption into a confederacy of all the states of South Africa under the British Flag) came to England & started the South African Association.... This Association has preached a Jehad [sic] against the S. African Dutch ever since, has sent paid lecturers all over England & Scotland, & also sent a man named Allen to Canada, who interviewed all the principal people there, & educated them on the Transvaal question from the mining Capitalists' point of view.[26]

With these words he utterly repudiated the man and the cause to which he devoted all his energy between 1889 and 1896. After reiterating his prediction of the Afrikaners' demographic dominance in post-war South Africa, he closed by recommending J.A. Hobson's new book on the South African war, which exposed the machinations of the capitalists of Johannesburg.

Roosevelt responded with a masterful and astonishingly even-handed essay in comparative historical analysis.[27] Passing over the analogy some might have drawn with the capitalists and journalists in his own country who recently clamoured for the war with Spain, he went back to the 'struggles which put the Americans in possession of Texas, New Mexico and California' in the 1840s. Then it was the Americans who were the 'uitlander' settlers and the Spaniards who were the rightful owners. 'This Outlander population rose, and was helped by raids from the United States, which in point of morality did not differ in the least from the Jameson raid, although there was back of it no capitalist intrigue, but simply a love of adventure and a feeling of arrogant and domineering race superiority.' The USA then annexed Texas, 'made its quarrels our own, and [went on to] conquer both New Mexico and California.' From 'the standpoint of technical right and wrong, it is impossible to justify the American action in these cases, and in the case of Texas there was the dark blot of slavery which rested upon the victors; for they turned Texas from a free province into a slave republic.' Although morally and legally reprehensible, the American conquest advanced the larger interests of civilization. Even the 'Indo-Spaniards' of the new territories found a better life. 'In my regiment which was raised in the South-west I had forty or fifty men of part Indian blood and perhaps half as many of part Spanish blood, and among my captains was one of the former and one of the latter – both being as good Americans in every sense of the word as were to be found in my ranks.'[28]

Selous could never have ascended to this lofty plane of vision. There were implications in Roosevelt's line of reasoning that, had he grasped them, might have made him rethink his position on the future of South Africa. He simply lacked the imagination to visualize a society in which men of many races might serve side by side in an army composed of equal citizens.

Though it took some time, he gradually recovered from his disappointment at the Conciliation Committee's failure to achieve a negotiated peace. When it became clear that Britain would pay any price for victory, he stopped making public statements on the war. In August 1900 he wrote to the secretary of the Conciliation Committee, stating that he would not sign their protest against annexation of the conquered republics. There was no putting back the clock. Even so, he continued to believe 'that sooner or later the people who actually live in South Africa – as distinguished from those, whose only interest in the country is the exploitation of its mineral wealth – will govern the country themselves'.[29] Would that his vision had extended to all 'who actually live in South Africa'.

Two noteworthy pieces of correspondence survive which show that his stand on the war resonated on both sides of the battle lines. One came from Transvaal President Paul Kruger in April 1900 via an old acquaintance, Piet Greyling. When the old man heard that he was writing to Selous to express appreciation for his work with the Conciliation Committee, he asked Greyling to 'tell Selous I always respected him as a just, brave and capable "Rooi Nek".' His one hope had been that his 'white hairs should find eternal rest without seeing the two dominant Races of our continent shedding each other's blood in such an inglorious cause'.[30] The other is a confidential letter from George Wemyss in British Military Intelligence dated 24 March of the same year. It appeared likely, he wrote, that after the surrender of the Transvaal, there would still be Boers who would 'refuse to be bound by any terms of peace'. He hoped Selous would use his reputation among his former hunting companions to compile a list of names of Boers in the northern Transvaal who might be counted on to give their compatriots a realistic idea of the awful consequences they would suffer by fighting on. There is no record of his response to either letter, so the biographer is left regretting he cannot add 'agent for MI5' to Selous's curriculum vitae.

'That Damned Cowboy is President'

As expected, the National Convention of 1900 renominated William McKinley as the Republican candidate for president. To strengthen the ticket with a halo of military glory they put the hero of San Juan Hill on the ballot for vice-president. TR told Selous he had 'a pretty lively campaign in running for the vice-presidency. The office itself is to me distasteful, but I was glad to have the chance of doing efficient work against what I regarded as a most dangerous and unAmerican party movement.'[31] McKinley and Roosevelt swept to a comprehensive victory and were sworn in on 4 March 1901.

Six months later, an anarchist assassin, Leon Czolgosz, caught up with McKinley at the Pan-American Exposition in Buffalo New York and put two bullets in his abdomen. Eight days later he died. McKinley's campaign manager, Senator Mark Hanna, who had opposed Roosevelt's nomination because he regarded him as a loose cannon, remarked in disgust, 'Now that damned cowboy is President of the United States'.

It had been a meteoric ascent and turned the relationship with Selous on its head. It was now Fred who was the star-struck correspondent of a great man. The decline of the wilderness became the predominant subject of their letters. The slight book *Sport and Travel, East and West* (1900) in which Selous bundled up accounts of his hunts in Turkey and the Rockies, made TR reflect with melancholy on 'the great mountain forests now growing bare of life, in the very places where as late as 1891 I saw the elk in herds of thousands; where in 1889 I killed eight different kinds of game in a single trip.'[32] It strengthened his resolve to extend the scope of national parks and forests. During his presidency he created the US Forest Service and established 51 Federal Bird Reservations, 4 National Game Preserves, 150 National Forests, 5 National Parks, and 18 National Monuments – comprising more than 230 million acres of public land.

Selous shared his disappointment at the disappearance of large fauna: 'It is indeed melancholy to reflect upon the rapid disappearance or great diminution of many noble forms of animal life both in North America and Africa.' While TR had been on the campaign trail Fred had made his first trip to Newfoundland, where he had witnessed 'the most reckless and unsportsmanlike destruction of Caribou, on migration.'[33] How he would have liked 'to have spent a year in America 20 or 30 years ago, before the bison had disappeared and when bears and wapiti antelope and mule deer with big heads were common.' Similar observations pepper their accounts of the short trips each was able to make from time to time. With two young children it was no longer possible for Gladys to travel with Fred. He hunted now to collect new specimens for his own collection and to keep up his reputation – and book sales – with the public. Though the books were well-reviewed, none can compare with the early works on big game hunting in savage and unknown territory. Travelling to the hunt by rail and coach to the Rockies, British Columbia, the Yukon, Turkey or even Siberia, was not the same as seven months through the wilderness by ox wagon. His articles on these subjects for *The Field* hold little interest for present-day readers.

Selous confessed to Roosevelt that he was getting 'rapidly to the end of my tether as far as big game hunting is concerned'. He always hated leaving his 'wife and boys, and the distress I suffer on this account, takes away very much from the pleasure of my trips, and my desire to get home again makes me hurry in a way that militates against my success.'[34]

Apart from the short expeditions and lecturing Selous was turning into a homebody. He nearly resigned as a councillor of the Royal Geographical Society because he missed so many meetings in

London.[35] He assumed the presidency of his local cricket club, where Gladys was a loyal and appreciative spectator. A feature article in *Windsor Magazine* remarked that 'To see him sitting peacefully in his English country home, or watching the cricket on the village green, it would be difficult to imagine all that he has undergone and the perils which he met with so perfect nerve.'[36] Having once experienced the opprobrium that falls on those who oppose a popular war, he did not venture again into the realm of political commentary.

The great cause that continued to energize him was wildlife conservation. He was in frequent contact with E.N. Buxton and regularly met Henry Bryden in London at the Constitutional Club to discuss strategies for advancing the campaign.[37] The three helped to found the Society for the Preservation of the Wild Fauna of the Empire in 1903 and the Shikar Club, which held regular dinners at the Savoy to discuss preservation of reserves for big game hunters.[38]

A Trip Back to the Pleistocene

After nearly a decade of correspondence Selous and TR finally met in 1905 at the White House. Roosevelt recalled later that Fred stayed several days, and that they went riding and rock climbing together along the Potomac river. Despite having hobnobbed for many years with British aristocrats, tycoons, politicians and men of science, Fred was dazzled. 'I can't tell you,' he wrote, 'what a great satisfaction it was to me to meet you and Mrs. Roosevelt and to be so kindly received by you both.' It was by far 'the greatest honour I have ever received'. What most struck him about the encounter was the intense interest the president took in his work and the encouragement he provided. TR said he absolutely must write another book on the natural history of big game. 'You are the only man alive, so far as I know, who could do it.' Take, for example, H.G.C. Swayne's book, *Through the Highlands of Siberia*, recently published by Rowland Ward, which Selous had recommended:

It is an excellent book in its way, but really it is only a kind of a guide book. ... you have the most extraordinary power of seeing things with minute accuracy of detail, and then the equally necessary power to describe vividly and accurately what you have seen. I read

Swayne's book and I have not the slightest idea how the sheep or the ibex or the deer look; but after reading your articles I can see the lions, not snarling but growling, with their lips covering their teeth, looking from side to side as one of them seeks to find what had hurt it, or throwing up its tail stiff in the air as it comes galloping forward in the charge.[39]

If Selous would write the book, Roosevelt would do the introduction. He hoped that it would be possible to bring India and tigers into the book.[40] Fred had never encountered such a man, one who appeared to see into the very depth of his being and to grasp comprehensively his relationship to wildlife and the wilderness. When he spoke of the 'deep respect and regard' he had for TR, it was 'not because you are the President of the United States, but because you are Theodore Roosevelt, and because all your life, whether as ranchman, hunter of big game, governor of New York State, Leader of the Rough Riders in Cuba and President of your great democracy, you have always deserved the respect and esteem of your fellow men.'[41] Selous was not a deep thinker but he sensed, like so many others, that this was the most interesting intellect to occupy the White House since Abraham Lincoln.

He worked steadily on the book all through the next year and, by April of 1907, had despatched a manuscript to Roosevelt. Like his previous books it included articles he had published in *The Field*, knitted together with observations on different species of animals gathered over thirty-five years. Fred apologized to the president for the shortage of funds that precluded shooting in India, but hoped that his extensive material on lions would make up for the absence of tigers. He could not comprehend how Roosevelt could find time to read anything, let alone his manuscript, but assured the president there was no need for an immediate verdict because he would be away birds' nesting in Turkey for the next seven weeks.

Amazingly, TR read the manuscript with meticulous care and had his foreword ready by the end of May. This included a detailed consideration of the question of protective colouring from an evolutionary point of view. He and Selous did not adhere to the common opinion that colouration developed primarily for the purpose of camouflage. They could not see how the zebra's stripes served this purpose, nor the white-feathered coat of the snowy owl. He treated the subject at length and with all the scholarly insight he could muster. It is quite impossible now to picture a sitting president of the United States writing an analytical foreword to anyone's book. Minders of all sorts would scan the text for errors and gaffes. Selous himself would be subjected to extensive background checks and security clearances.

Fred had to cut short his trip to Turkey because he found the country around Smyrna 'overrun with brigands'. He thanked Roosevelt profusely for his care with the manuscript and explained that his new publishers, Macmillan, would delay bringing the book out so as not to have it compete with their re-issue of *Hunter's Wanderings*. By May of the next year TR was getting impatient. When would the book be coming out? Soon, he hoped. Africa was very much on his mind:

A year hence I shall stop being President, and while I cannot be certain of what I shall do, it may be that I can afford to devote a year to a trip in Africa, trying to get into a really good game country. How would it do for me to try to go in somewhere from Zanzibar and come out down the Nile, or vice versa? What time ought I to go? That is, what time ought I to make my entry into the country? Is there anyone I could write to about an outfit. Is there anyone who could give me an idea of how much the trip would cost; and, finally, could you tell me whether there are people to whom I could write to ask about engaging porters, or whatever it is I would travel with?[42]

He had not 'the slightest desire to be a game butcher, but I should like greatly to be in a land where I really saw multitudes of big game.' To put it succinctly, 'I want to take a trip back to the Pleistocene!'[43]

It may be that Selous's text for *African Nature Notes and Reminiscences* had planted the thought. He describes how, when on the hunt, he would sometimes 'seem to be carried back to some far distant period of the world's history ... My rude companions were palaeolithic men, and we were hunting strange beasts in the hot dry atmosphere of a long past geological era.'[44] The concept chimed in with the idea common in the Edwardian era that even the most highly civilized human contained within himself elemental drives and primitive instincts inherited from earlier aeons. Arthur Conan

Doyle's *Lost World* (1912) imagines a group of European explorers wandering into an Amazonian valley where dinosaurs live on, and where they must summon up their inner caveman in order to survive. Roosevelt found the idea of testing himself against primordial nature compelling. Taking a trip back to the Pleistocene also meant gazing upon an abundance of wildlife in Africa that the advancing frontiers of industrialization, settlement and agriculture had effaced elsewhere in the world. In his eyes the value of Selous's books had been the close observation of 'the great, splendid, terrible beasts whose lives add an immense majesty to the far-off wilds, and who inevitably pass away before the onrush of the greedy, energetic, forceful men, usually both unscrupulous and short-sighted, who make up the vanguard of civilization.'[45]

Thanks to the allure of the African savannah that Selous had done so much to foster, it was not so difficult to organize a trip to the Pleistocene. A good starting point was a stroll down Piccadilly. Not far from Rowland Ward's taxidermy 'Jungle' was the London office of Newland, Tarlton and Co., a safari firm begun by a couple of enterprising Australians in Nairobi. They could arrange all details of tickets, introductions, guides and porters. In Brakley Street, east of St Paul's Cathedral the firm of Lawn and Adler offered every conceivable item required for wilderness adventure. If TR would send an old shoe they would make up a set of boots suitable for all East African terrain, wet or dry. The democratization of travel that made Thomas Cook a byword for mass tourism and had commercialized the African safari. Selous promised that Roosevelt would see 'more different kinds of game than if you had lived in Pleistocene times, for you will be able to travel over thousands of miles of country whereas early man was probably confined all his life to a very small area of country.'[46]

Even so, Selous and Roosevelt spent months poring over every detail of the kit. Russian caviar would not be required; Boston baked beans would. American rifles by Winchester or Remington would do as well as any British firearm. On the trail Roosevelt never used beer or spirits; however, he would take champagne 'in case of fever'. China would not be needed; enamelled cups and aluminium plates would do just fine. The lists were passed back and forth across the Atlantic with numerous alterations and deletions – all this while Roosevelt went about his duties as President of the United States. Selous declined an invitation to act as a guide. This was country he had traversed only once before on a short and rather disappointing safari in 1903 at a time when high grass impeded pursuit of game. He was, however, able to recommend R J. Cunninghame, a man he had last met at Lobengula's *kraal* in 1889 and who had, for the last three years, been making his living managing porters and supplies for East African safaris.[47]

Some matters had to be left for TR's personal attention. For example, if it were found desirable to follow the game into German East Africa, visas and paperwork would be required. Roosevelt was pretty sure he could 'get a letter from the Kaiser telling his people there to give me a fair show'.[48] He was keen to see that any rare animals he collected were preserved for the American National Museum in Washington, D.C., so he arranged for two field taxidermists to join the expedition. His son Kermit would also come along. All that was missing by the end of 1908 was Frederick Courteney Selous, whose company the president craved. Fred explained that regrettably the current state of his finances would not allow him to join the grand safari. De Beers shares had plunged, dividends were cut and it was all he could do to hang onto the family home. Almost miraculously a rich American emerged to save the day. W.H. McMillan, who was well connected in Republican political circles, had chosen to take up ranching in Kenya. He looked forward to welcoming TR and would be pleased to pay all Selous's expenses.

'Three cheers', Roosevelt wrote on 26 December. 'I am simply over-joyed that you are going out. It is just the last touch to make everything perfect. But you must leave me one lion somewhere!'

18

'Who Could Wish a Better Death?'

Roosevelt was determined so far as possible to evade public attention on his safari, especially in Europe where the Press would make 'a raree-show' of him as an ex-president.[1] He arranged a passage to Naples where Selous could join him for the voyage on to Mombasa. That way they could share each other's company without the distractions of a media scrum. Fred was equally determined to escape the spotlight. He did not hunt with Roosevelt 'as his party is very large, and I don't want to be with a crowd'. Owing to commitments at home he could only spend three months in Kenya during the tail end of the rainy season when the grass was long and the chances for game at their worst. The most he dared to hope for was a male lion from the high country 'where they often grow fine manes'.[2]

As it happened, he missed getting a lion, but did bag some rhino, several species of antelope for his collection and 'a fine specimen of a five horned giraffe bull, after which I had a splendid gallop quite in the old South African style'.[3] When he caught up with TR again in Nairobi in July, he was greeted with Roosevelt's favourite exclamatory adjective: 'I tell you, Selous, it's bully!' To Fred he 'was like a boy out of school. His double chin had receded, and his waist measure had lost more inches than I could guess.' Not only had he got some very fine specimens – including white rhino – he had impressed the Kenyan hunting fraternity with his cool nerve in the field. 'He was a quick thinker, a quick mover and a dandy shot.'[4]

Back in England Selous worried over money. The previous year his De Beers shares had taken a dive owing to the discovery of rich new diamond fields. Without the usually reliable dividend income, Fred feared that he might lose his house and museum. In May 1908 he had written to the Royal Geographical Society, asking that his annual subscription be cancelled and his name removed from the members' roll:

> I have lost a lot of money lately but am still trying for my wife's sake to hold on to this place which we have made ourselves and which she loves. With two boys to educate, I am therefore cutting down all my expenses in every possible way, and that is why I resolved to give up my fellowship of the R.G.S., the Z[oologocial].S[ociety]. and the African Society.[5]

Rather than lose one of their illustrious gold medal winners, the RGS elected him to life membership. The secretary told him he was 'in excellent company as a free Life Member: there are only ten more altogether, all of them very distinguished men.'[6]

A compendium of his expeditions to Canada, *Recent Hunting Trips to British North America* (1907), was praised by some reviewers as the best-ever book on hunting in that country, but made very little money.[7] It occurred to him that a book of fiction for boys might tap into the burgeoning youth market. Macmillan was very interested and offered to make him a most 'suitable offer' for the completed manuscript. It should be no less than 90,000 words and might go over 100,000: '*Tom Brown's Schooldays*, for instance, is about 120,000.'[8] Selous may have had in mind a fictionalized version of his own boyhood adventures, because he was tinkering with a partially completed manuscript as late as 1914.[9] However, the projected book never saw the light of day, probably because a restructuring of diamond marketing returned De Beers to profitability in 1909.[10] Aside from his shares, Selous continued to serve on the boards of companies such as Dominion Saw Mills and Lumber Ltd.[11] He at last felt as financially secure as a man of his temperament could ever be.

His own boys were growing up, intended of course for Rugby. He took a keen interest in their physical development and hoped they would share his appreciation for the outdoors. Major-General Robert Baden-Powell, whom he had known briefly in Rhodesia, had become a national hero for organizing the defence of Mafeking during its

217-day siege in the Anglo-Boer War. Despite their slight acquaintance, Baden-Powell recognized in Selous the qualities he hoped to foster through the Boy Scout movement he founded in 1907. The first Boy Scout handbook pointed to Selous's escape from Mashukulumbwe country as a prime example of the 'Scout saying, "Never say die till you're dead"':

> Three weeks had passed since the attack, and the great part of that time Selous had been alone— hunted, starving, bitterly cold at night, and in sweltering heat by day. None but a scout with extraordinary endurance could have lived through it, but then Selous was a man who as a lad had made himself strong by care and exercise. And he kept up his pluck all the time.
>
> It shows you that if you want to get through such adventures safely when you are a man and not be a slopper, you must train yourself to be strong, healthy, and active as a lad.[12]

Even better in Baden-Powell's eyes was that Selous neither smoked nor drank. Flattered by the tribute, Fred agreed to be honorary scoutmaster of the local Worplesdon troop and led the boys through forest paths in practical demonstrations of tracking. He also delivered lecturers in aid of Baden-Powell's Scout Camp Fund.[13]

Probably because of his lingering resentment over the public reaction to his stand on the recent war, Selous never returned to southern Africa. However, he continued to work to protect African big game. When he was working for the BSA Company he envisaged white settlers living on high country farms that coexisted happily with reserves for African fauna down in 'the fly'. He was appalled and angered when he learnt that the Rhodesian government was actively engaged in the extermination of big game. The experience of rinderpest had shown the connection between trypanosomiasis and tsetse fly. Fred himself had written articles on the subject. However, the Rhodesian Administrator's authorization of a general cull of elephants in order to protect settlers' cows and horses struck him as worse than a blunder: 'To exterminate game of all kinds in a country in order to get rid of tsetse fly would not only be an abominable crime, but an absolutely unnecessary crime.'[14]

Step by step he was driven towards advocating more extreme

measures of conservation. For years he had been telling the public that indigenous hunters with firearms had done far more to exterminate wildlife than sportsmen. That led him to advocate reserves where only licensed hunters would be allowed. Now that he had seen with his own eyes the effects of white settlement and ranching in Africa and North America, he agreed with Roosevelt that there should be large national parks where shooters of all kinds were banned.[15] The man who had once exulted in every advance of African railways now feared for the future of his beloved Zambezi Valley: 'God knows what it may be now in these days of steamboats and railways, when the great game has disappeared before the march of civilization and the neighbourhood of the great river may have become a dreary, lifeless wilderness.'[16]

Why, it may be asked, did he continue to hunt and collect? From his earliest days in South Africa he had felt the reproach in the eyes of dying giraffes and antelopes. These days he refused to call his expeditions hunting trips, and emphasized that he did not shoot females of any species. His interests were purely scientific, he insisted. From a twenty-first-century perspective it does not seem very scientific to judge the value of male animal heads by the length and adumbration of their horns, which is what Selous continued to do on his North American hunts for elk, moose and caribou. The truth was, he doted on his collection and continued to enjoy the chase in distant mountains and forests for its own sake, even if for only a month or two every year. In his own mind as well as in the eyes of the public, hunting was his identity.

The contradiction between the naturalist and the hunter was borne home to him in a very personal, hurtful way by his younger brother. Edmund had grown up in the shadow of his dashing, self-reliant sibling. Better educated than Fred, he had been at Pembroke College, Cambridge, and admitted to the Bar. But he shared the family passion for wildlife. He too learnt to hunt and collect birds' eggs. In 1886 he had enquired shyly at the Natural History Museum about courses on natural history.[17] Soon he had abandoned the law in order to devote himself full-time to ornithology. His 1901 book *Bird Watching* not only coined a phrase to describe a new obsessive pastime for men and women; it repudiated the whole enterprise of specimen collecting. Calling himself a 'life-loving zoologist', Edmund railed against the cold-blooded scientists more in love with death than life – 'more comfortable dissecting a body in their study than studying a life out of doors':

> In their writings, these serenities are accustomed to speak calmly of the approaching extinction of this or that more or less lovely or interesting creature – say, for instance, the lyre-bird of Australia – if, 'happily', such and such a museum has been supplied, or if Professor somebody has ascertained this or that in regard to it; or professors and the public generally are exhorted to obtain such supplies or such information 'before the end comes'.[18]

Before the end indeed! 'Every effort should be exhausted, every nerve strained, to avert such end.' Each day 'some specific life that is, or was, of more value than all their individual ones put together, is getting scarcer, or ceasing to be.' Edmund had, he confessed, 'once belonged to this great, poor army of killers, though, happily, a bad shot, a most fatigable collector, and a poor, half-hearted bungler, generally'. Now, after closely observing birds, 'the killing of them seems to me as something monstrous and horrible; and for every one that I have shot, or even only shot at and missed I hate myself with an increasing hatred'.[19]

There could be no doubt what he thought about Fred and his bags and his private museum. As far as can be ascertained, he never set foot in the house at Worplesdon. Fred does not speak of Edmund in surviving letters or writings after the 1890s.

Roosevelt, on the other hand, made a special point of seeing the museum on his return from Africa. He, Mrs Roosevelt and son Kermit came down to Worplesdon on 1 June 1910 towards the end of a visit to London overshadowed by the death of King Edward VII in May. The previous week Selous had been one of a select number of luminaries invited to join Roosevelt for dinner at the London House of Lord Lonsdale: hunter, explorer, soldier, roué and bon viveur. E.N. Buxton was there of course, as was Walter Rothschild, whose private collection at his country house, Tring, is now an outpost of the Natural History Museum at South Kensington. Sir Frederick Lugard, future Governor-General of Nigeria and Lord Curzon , ex-Viceroy of India, represented both the Empire and the confraternity of big game hunters. Selous predicted that, on his return to America, Roosevelt would 'receive such a welcome as has never before been accorded to a human being.

I have been twice to America, and right across to the Pacific since I returned from East Africa, and I believe you will have to be President again.'[20]

Inspired by TR's success with giant eland and other prey in the Sudan, Fred made another African expedition at the end of 1910 with financial backing from the Natural History Museum and Walter Rothschild, who wanted particular specimens.[21] He was frustrated from beginning to end by British officialdom, which threw bureaucratic obstacles in his way, and by the elands which eluded his gun. Roosevelt totally sympathized. He had similar experiences with officials in Alaska who showed 'a wooden incapacity to understand the difference between the ordinary type of sportsman, who is merely a vigorous and unintelligent game butcher, and the hunter-naturalist of the higher type who is collecting for a great National museum.' It was even less understandable in the case of Selous. 'Without any flattery, your position among hunters is entirely unique. I regard you as one of your country's real assets, and I cannot understand any responsible Englishman, and above all any responsible Englishman in a wild country, failing to appreciate this.'[22]

His 'unique position' among hunters meant that manufacturers of guns and camping kits continually sought him out for endorsements and advice. In his early writings he had not said much about rifle types. Put a solid bore 450 bullet through the brain of an elephant, he wrote in 1893, 'and you will drop him as dead as if you had blown his head off with the 81-ton gun'. In his later years he wrote much more technical comments in response to requests from specialist hunting magazines. The Royal Geographical Society asked him to write the chapter on 'Guns, Rifles, Ammunition' for their new edition of *Hints on Outfit*. To meet these and other requests he continually updated a file of clippings on guns, accessories and specifications. He also wrote on the comparative merits of various bullets under the Hague and Geneva Conventions on warfare. His friend and first biographer, 'Johnny' Millais, believed that Selous's accuracy as a marksman in the field suffered as the result of too much experimentation with rifles supplied by manufacturers eager for his commendation.[23]

After his return from Kenya in May 1911 Fred experienced the first real bodily infirmity he had known. Doctors told him that removal of an enlarged prostate would have to be followed by a month convalescing in a nursing home. Typically, he insisted on being up and active within a fortnight. He told his friend Bryden that he had 'now got rid of the only organ in my body' he did not really need.[24] Roosevelt was not so sure. 'That was an ugly operation but I am glad you had it, and that, as you say you "healed up like a dog or a savage" after it.'[25]

His new friend and patron William Northrup McMillan now issued a second invitation to come to Kenya at his expense at the end of the year. McMillan must have been good company – Roosevelt said simply, 'he is a trump' – but, at nearly 7 ft feet tall and over 300 lb, he made the most unlikely hunting sidekick for Selous since Elephant Phillips. Viewed from any angle in old photographs the man mountain does not make an appetizing sight. The big attraction of his ranch was financial; a cheap base from which to collect specimens for the Worplesdon collection. That aside, why was Fred willing to spend nearly six months away from Gladys and his boys? Why did not Gladys travel with him at least part of the time? After all, the boys were now at boarding school. There are no obvious answers in surviving correspondence and nothing to hint at any cracks in their partnership. There is a suggestion that, in retrospect, the flight from Bulawayo in 1896 had soured Gladys on Africa. Selous, in contrast, felt increasingly constrained by the crush of people who 'spoil all the pleasure of going to a cricket- or football-match or a theatre'. More and more he 'was longing to be in Africa'. If only 'Mrs Selous would be happy there, I would rather live in East Africa than in this country'.[26]

Selous and Roosevelt discussed the coming trip in terms of fitness, which was a shared obsession. TR constantly fretted over his flab, while Fred determined to remain up for any physical challenge. When he expressed doubts about readiness for the coming safari, Roosevelt reassured him that it was 'idle to suppose that you can now do what you did when you were in the twenties'. There was no man of sixty on the planet 'who is physically as fit as you'. The fixation on strength and agility extended to discussion of their boys. Selous thought Kermit Roosevelt 'a wonderful fellow' whose 'disposition is as fine as his powers of endurance. He was born a generation too late, as with his walking and running powers he would have made such a splendid elephant hunter in the good old free days'.[27] As for his own children, the omens were excellent:

Our eldest boy has been Captain of his school's Rugby football team this season. Of course, it is only a preparatory school for the big Rugby School; but there are 120 boys there and he is by no means the oldest. He has passed his exam for the big school and will go there after the Christmas holidays. There he will have to remain for 4 or 5 years before going on to Cambridge. He will certainly get into the first football fifteen at Rugby when still very young, and I quite think he will be captain of the team before he leaves the school.[28]

No pressure!

On the way out to Kenya Selous stopped in Paris to collect a gold medal from the French Academy of Sport, one in a stream of honours piled on him in his later years. The previous year the Foreign Office picked him to represent Britain at the Second Congress of Field Sports held in Vienna. He carried a personal message from King George V recommending uniform measures for the protection of game birds, especially quail and woodcock. The St Hubert Society of France elected him to honorary membership, as did the National Geographic Society of the United States.[29]

He remained in demand as a speaker and increasingly beat the conservationist drum, especially in relation to extinctions. He was plainly struggling with the contradiction his brother Edmund saw between love of living wildlife and the hunter's business of killing. In a speech to the Authors' Club soon after his return from Kenya he explained hunting as an atavism born of early man's struggle for existence. Some 'races of low culture' such as Eskimos and pygmies still hunted to keep their families in food. For civilized people there was no real necessity. Men such as he hunted because 'the passion for it had been handed down' from 'remote ancestors' and 'that passion must now be restrained, both in savages and civilised men, otherwise owing to the great power of modern firearms and the facilities for travel, if there was no restriction all those beautiful and wonderful forms of wild life would soon be absolutely exterminated'.[30] He had run off to hunt elephants at the age of nineteen 'simply because he was the lineal descendant of prehistoric man'.

At other times and in different company Selous continued to laud the pursuit of dangerous big game as a test of manhood. Roosevelt drew the same parallels between courage in the wilderness, on the battlefield, and in daily life. In 1912 he ran as an independent presidential candidate on behalf of his newly founded 'Bull Moose Party'. On 14 October, as he stepped from his Milwaukee hotel into a waiting car, a crazed assassin stepped forward with a Colt revolver and fired at his chest. Fortunately, the thick coat he was wearing and the fifty-page sheaf of speaking notes in his right inner pocket slowed the bullet that lodged against a rib, missing Roosevelt's heart. 'You must drive on', he told the driver, so I may deliver my speech. He stilled the waiting crowd with a wave of his hand. 'I don't know whether you fully understand that I have just been shot.' Unbuttoning his vest to show the bloodied shirt, he roared, 'It takes more than that to kill a bull moose.' And then he went on with his scheduled ninety-minute address.

When Selous wrote to commend his 'magnificent behaviour, splendid pluck and great constitutional strength', Roosevelt protested that the injury was not as serious as the time your 'old four-bore gun was loaded twice over by mistake; and as other injuries you received in the hunting field'. Modern civilization, indeed all civilization:

> is rather soft; and I suppose the average political orator, or indeed the average sedentary broker or banker or business man or professional man, especially if elderly, is much overcome by being shot or meeting with some other similar accident, and feels very sorry for himself and thinks he has met with an unparalleled misfortune; but the average soldier or sailor in a campaign or battle, even the average hunter of dangerous game, would treat both my accident and my behaviour after the accident as entirely matter of course.[31]

Roosevelt went on to lose the election, even while scoring the highest percentage of votes ever cast for a third party candidate in American history.

A few months later they resumed their discussion of civilization and character in a different historical context. Ever since the priest of a Jersey church had written to him about ancestors mentioned in the parish records, Selous had taken a heightened interest in the history of his family and nation.[32] Early in 1913 he toured Jersey and northern France, marvelling at the achievements of the medieval Normans. The people who built the great Gothic churches and cathedrals 'must have possessed great brain power and great will power'. Surely the Norman

Conquest was 'the best thing that ever happened for Great Britain'. Combining the genetic inheritance of the Scandinavians and the Franks, 'they were certainly a much more highly civilized people, more cultured, more imaginative and more enterprising than the heavy, dull-witted, beer-drinking Saxons'. Roosevelt agreed, remarking that Fred's letters were 'always interesting, whether they relate to lions and elephants, or to Old English ballads, or, as this one does, to the Normans'. Those 'cathedrals represent the greatest architecture this world ever saw, with the sole exception of Greece at its best'.[33]

From the evidence of their correspondence neither man foresaw the imminent outbreak of the 'Great War for civilization'. By the end of 1913 Fred was 'pining to get to Africa again', but could not think of travel until he had settled the affairs of his mother, who had died in October at the age of eighty-seven. On 2 December he went up to Rugby to lecture the boys on African wildlife. It was a proud moment for both father and eldest son. Young Freddy had, as predicted, made the football XV in first year at the upper school. He also excelled at boxing and distance running. 'The Doctors pronounce him to be absolutely sound too', Selous told Roosevelt, 'so I hope to be able to get him into the East African Civil Service when he is 22'.[34]

Early the next year Selous was deeply involved in the conservation cause. He and Bryden spoke at the meeting of the Fauna Preservation Society. In March he joined the African explorer Harry Johnston in lobbying for a law to kerb the killing of rare birds by prohibiting the importation of feathers for any purpose other than scientific research.[35]

On 27 June 1914 a huge exhibition of hunting trophies opened at the Water Colour Society's gallery in Pall Mall, the last such event before Russia's ultimatum to Serbia set the armies of Europe irrevocably into motion. Never before had the links between hunting, royalty, the military and the British aristocracy been so visibly set out for all to see. Queen Alexandra sent one of her buffalo heads, as did the Duke of Connaught, along with other animals that fell to his rifle in East Africa. Prince Arthur of Connaught sent the head of an impala shot in Kenya. Prince Alexander of Teck lent a kudu he bagged in the Transvaal. Other trophies represented the Duke of Westminster, the Duke of Sutherland, Lord Wodehouse, Mr J.G. Millais, Lieutenant-General Sir A. Paget, Sir H. Rawlinson and Sir Owen Phillips. Selous's numerous contributions stood alongside the white-bearded gnu shot by the First Lord of the Admiralty, Mr Winston Churchill.[36] The idea that success in the hunt presaged success in battle, now firmly established in the public mind, was about to be put to the ultimate test.

Frederick Courteney [*sic*] Selous, DSO

Although the outbreak of war caught him by surprise, Selous immediately declared his intention to join the forces and go to the Front. The patriotic sentiment was commonplace but his determination to enlist requires some explanation. He came very late to soldiering. At no time in his early life had he considered an army career. At the age of forty he professed he was 'not a fighting man'. He had been a lusty advocate of the Matabele Wars of 1893 and 1896, but experienced only a few days of active combat as part of an irregular force of volunteers. Distaste for the cause kept him out of the second Anglo-Boer War. Yet here he was, aged sixty-two, eager to serve and convinced he could make a real contribution to victory.

Perhaps by this time he had so far internalized the concept of the hunter/soldier as to really believe in his superior qualities as a fighting man. Maybe his personal cult of fitness demanded continual validation. He seemed genuinely puzzled that the military high command failed to commission him directly for service in a battalion bound for France. The best he could manage was to enrol in the Legion of Frontiersmen, which was not an official part of the army at all but a paramilitary organization founded in the wake of the Boer War to guard against the threat of invasion from the continent. Rather than being actually composed of frontiersmen, the Legion celebrated the idea of the citizen soldier as exemplified in irregular units like Teddy Roosevelt's Rough Riders and the Bulawayo Field Force. Selous had not previously been aware of their existence but caught the spirit. In mid-September he told Roosevelt he expected to ship out for France any day. He had been present at a parade ground inspection the previous week:

and I never saw a tougher, harder or more serviceable looking lot of men, than the greater part of these 700 who were paraded. Col Driscoll tells me that he can mobilize 3000 men in a few days all of whom have led rough lives in various parts of the world and all of whom can ride and shoot, and it passes my comprehension why the War Office, who are crying out for recruits all of whom have still to be taught to shoot, will not at once accept the services of such serviceable, well seasoned men, as are the majority of the Legion of Frontiersmen. My age made it impossible for me to get to the front except with some irregular corps, but I hope that before long now, Col Driscoll will get the order to mobilize 1000 or 2000 of his men, and I have his solemn promise that if he goes to the front I shall go with him.[37]

Roosevelt was not surprised by the news. 'Kermit and I as soon as the war broke out said that we knew that you would go to the front, and that nothing would keep you back.'[38]

Both Selous and Roosevelt took for granted that cowboys and South African hunters who could ride and shoot would be crucial to winning the war. Had he reflected more profoundly on the lessons of the Matabele campaigns Fred would have grasped the transformation wrought by mechanized warfare. Lobengula's warriors – 'brave as men could be'– had fallen like mown grass before the hail of death streaming from the Maxim guns. At 600 rounds a minute the Maxim shot more bullets in three minutes than Selous had fired in his entire life as a hunter. Within a few months the big guns in Europe had fired more shells than all the artillery in mankind's previous wars. There would be no heroic charges of mounted riflemen from the trenches on the Western Front.

Weeks passed and it became evident that Selous was not going to the Front or anywhere else with the Legion of Frontiersmen. When Driscoll's offer to raise a thousand men to confront the Germans in East Africa was vetoed by the War Office, Selous took a certificate of fitness from his insurance company to a sympathetic member of Parliament who offered to intercede with Lord Kitchener on his behalf. He would be willing to serve in any capacity 'in which a good knowledge of French and some German might be useful'.[39] Kitchener said his age 'was prohibitive against your employment here or at the seat of war in Europe'. That appeared to be that. The best Selous could do was service as a special constable in his town, part of a scattered Dads' Army of what he called 'useless old buffers'.

By December, however, there had been a change of heart at the War Office. Perhaps some good could be done by despatching men from the Legion of Frontiersmen to East Africa where, if nothing else, they might divert German resources from the European theatre of war? Driscoll and Selous were charged with the task of recruiting a thousand men by February. Advertisements placed in the newspapers called for:

> picked men willing to serve together wherever ordered as infantry. They must be good rifle shots and of sober, steady habits. Strict medical test necessary. Preference will be given to frontiersmen and others who have lived abroad, age 25 to 45. Apply to Lieut.-Colonel D.P. Driscoll, D.S.O. (late Driscoll's Scouts), 6, Adam Street, Strand, London; or to
>
> F.C. SELOUS, Heatherside, Worplesdon, Surrey.[40]

Selous would have known by this time that his wife would soon give birth to another child, but that did not deter him from military service. (*The Times* reported the premature birth of a son on 12 July 1915; however, the child died a few days later.)

The only exceptions to the age limit in the Frontiersmen were Selous (sixty-three) and Driscoll (fifty-five). By March they had their men, who were inducted into the forces as a special unit, the 25th Service Battalion, Royal Fusiliers (City of London Regiment). Roosevelt was exultant, wishing only that his four boys could also join the fight. Had he been president, he could confidently say 'the United States would have been in a totally different position'. Young Freddy Selous appeared certain to distinguish himself whenever he entered the service. At the Rugby sports day in March he came first in shot-put, throwing the cricket ball, and the quarter mile race.[41] Instead of Cambridge the young man would directly enter officer training at Sandhurst.

Commissioned as a lieutenant, Selous shipped out for Mombasa, where he landed on 4 May 1915. His own company 'was indeed a mixed lot', including men from the French Foreign Legion, the Metropolitan Police, zoo and lighthouse keepers, music hall acrobats, and a former general in the Honduras Army.[42] Within a few weeks they were on their way by rail to Lake Victoria, from where they launched an amphibious attack on a German wireless telegraph station at Bukoba.

Even today Bukoba is a sleepy little backwater of bustling modern Tanzania. Guides can point out the houses formerly occupied by German officers, but know nothing of the wireless station or the British assault. The concrete pylons that once supported the tower still stand, but no plaque identifies their significance. My own guide in 2014 thanked me for drawing his attention to the place. The German post occupied an excellent defensive position among reedy swamps, protected on the seaward side by a small island. Steep cliffs deterred coastal attacks north and south of the town.

When the British troop ship approached the harbour a little after midnight on 22 June the sentinel island lit up like a fairground, alerting troops in the town to an imminent attack. Having lost the element of surprise, the ship steamed north around a point lying about three miles north of the German defences. Before the alarm could be sounded Selous and the rest of the assault force had scrambled up the cliffs and through banana plantations to a defensible position at the summit. From there they proceeded to advance in skirmishing formation towards the town. While the banana trees and granite rock-strewn landscape afforded plenty of cover, the British shared that advantage with the German defenders. Closer to town it was tough work wading through the river and adjacent swamps. By night-fall, the sodden, hungry British forces had fallen back to their former position. The next day the struggle resumed. German machine-guns chattered wickedly from scattered bunkers. At various spots Selous and his platoon had to slither among the rocks while bullets whizzed overhead. He saw several men killed at his side but, by the end of the day, the town had fallen. He had, he reflected, spent many happier hours: 'Yet what a small and miserable thing this was in the way of a battle compared with the titanic combats which have been taking place in Europe.' He could 'well imagine how the nerves of any man, however strong, may be shaken to pieces, by the awful clamour of the giant shells and the concentrated fire of many machine-guns, and countless numbers of rifles, and the terrible havoc wrought by these fearful weapons of destruction.'[43]

Some who were present that night said the victors had looted the German officers' quarters, drunk the wine cellar dry and run riot through the town. Selous remarked only that a good deal of wine and beer was found, but he 'saw no drunkenness among the men'. The German wireless tower impressed him as a marvel of modern engineering, 'something like an Eiffel Tower', some 200 ft high 'with immensely strong concrete foundations'. Latter-day military historians have speculated that its destruction may actually have inhibited the war effort. With the telegraph silenced the British lost the chance to intercept messages. The men clambered aboard their ship next day and were back in Nairobi by 27 June. It was far and away the most exciting week of Fred's war. Roosevelt wrote to congratulate him on 'a first-class little fight at Bukoba'. Surely, if the Germans kept sinking ships with US citizens on board (the *Lusitania* had been sunk by a U-boat in May), Americans would come to their senses and override the 'professional pacifists' who had been keeping his country out of the war.[44]

For the better part of the following year Fred's platoon was occupied in guarding the Uganda railway that ran up from Mombasa. It was grinding, miserable work of which Fred very soon tired. Once he was through with this job, he swore, 'no more military duty for me. I hate all the drill and routine-work, and I shall be far too old to take any part in any other war after this one'.[45] The present conflict was not yet a year old and already he was 'hoping to God' that peace would be made soon 'or all our young men will be killed'. The worst of his present situation was that the British forces were outgunned, out-generalled and out-fought by the Germans in East Africa. It was all they could do to keep the trains running, while dysentery, fever and other diseases cut a swathe through their numbers. The Germans had the immense advantage of brave and resourceful native-born *askari* troops who knew the country well and stayed healthy.

The previous year he had been looking forward to his son Freddy signing up by and by. 'My eldest son,' he reminded Roosevelt, 'is quite big and strong enough to go to the front but he is only 16, and I don't want him to go just yet.' By the beginning of December 1915 the awful scale of the carnage was telling. Thinking of Freddy, who would be eighteen the next April, he expected he would 'be sent out soon after then, as he is big and strong for his age'. But 'if he gets killed it will break his mother's heart and mine too, if I should live to come home'. His friend Johnny Millais's son was also on the verge of military service so, Fred wrote, 'it will be the same for you and your wife if you lose Geoff; but I pray God he will be spared to outlive this terrible war'. Since Bukoba he had not been involved in any fighting but had seen enough of poor planning, bad soldiering and death from preventable disease to say that 'if the whole truth about everything out here is ever known it will be a revelation to most people'. It was 'certainly an evil day for British East Africa when the Indian Government took over the defence of this country'. Every day the African *askaris* on the German side were proving their superiority in the field. These were black soldiers recruited locally, many of whom had acquired legendary fighting skills in slave raiding prior to the establishment of the German colony.[46] Speaking for himself, Fred 'would much sooner wish to fight against Germans from the Fatherland than these well-trained and elusive blacks'.[47]

May came and the battlefield situation remained much the same. Selous was practically the only man in his battalion who had not lost a day's service through illness. However, he had lately begun to suffer embarrassing trouble with haemorrhoids and 'another [unnamed] problem' that necessitated his return to England for an operation in June. He had feared he might never see his family again, especially as Freddy had joined Royal West Surrey Regiment as a lieutenant in April. His haemorrhoid operation was a complete success and he was soon on his way back to East Africa. During his time at home he had a chance to show off one positive fruit of his war service: a collection of 3,000 Kenyan butterflies.[48] Not long after he landed at Mombasa, newspapers reported that he had been awarded the DSO (Distinguished Service Order) for his part in the fight at Bukoba and a skirmish with the enemy on the rail line in May 1916.[49] By 16 November he had heard the news from friends but still had not received official notification. He asked a friend to collect all the clippings from newspapers, especially from South Africa and Rhodesia. Perhaps the award would restore him to the esteem he had enjoyed in that part of the world before the Boer War. As for the progress of the war in East Africa, things had been looking up since General Jan Smuts took command of the forces. All the main coastal towns and railways in German East Africa had been taken. However, rather than surrender, the enemy had retired into wild and little-known country between the Rufiji River and Portuguese Mozambique, from which it would be very difficult to prise them. Worse, the rainy season was coming on, which 'will see the end of all the white troops out here', finished off by the fevers. The Germans suffered too, but that hardly mattered as most of their fighting was done by the black *askaris*. Selous expected that an advance into the interior would happen soon.[50]

And it did come. He wrote to Gladys on 15 December to say that his platoon was moving to Kissaki, preparatory to an attack on the Germans at the Rufiji River. Every day was a rain-sodden forward march and the troops were dropping like flies. His detachment had shrunk in the last few weeks from 384 to 170. On Christmas Day he wrote from Kissaki to say that the attack would be made in the next few days: 'The German forces are sure to be entrenching, and as they still have a number of machine-guns, it may be no child's play attacking their positions, and we may meet with heavy losses.'

While marching his troops toward the Germans at a place called Beho Beho, Selous's luck ran out. One of those damned, elusive *askari* sharpshooters put a bullet in his side. Before he could recover his footing, he received another bullet – a clean shot that entered at the mouth and travelled through the brain. He would not have suffered. The next day he was buried there, where his remains still lie, beneath a marker in the Selous Game Reserve.

When Roosevelt got the news, he remarked simply, 'He closed his life exactly as such a life ought to be closed, by dying in battle for his country while rendering her valiant and effective service. Who could wish a better life, or a better death, or desire to leave a more honorable heritage to his family and his nation?'[51]

19

The Legacies and Afterlife of Selous

The weight of grief fell heavily on Gladys. Thanking J.S. Keltie for his letter of condolence on behalf of the Royal Geographical Society, she acknowledged for her husband 'it has been a fine ending to a wonderful life – full to the brim right up to the end'. But that hardly compensated for 'the sorrow and loss and for my boys so sad just at a time when they need a Father's help and advice'. She expected that 'The fine Tributes of the world & all his many friends will in time help and comfort me a great deal & I am very proud of them.'[1]

Memorials

The circumstances of his death won Selous an extra measure of fame in a nation weary of trench warfare and hungry for heroes. Johnny Millais, who had already won plaudits for the biography of his father, was a natural choice to write a commemorative volume. He began collecting material for the book almost as soon as he heard the news. His task took on added poignancy the following year when, as Selous had feared, their sons, Captains Geoff Millais and Freddy Selous were both killed in action. Young Freddy's brief, glamorous life in the Royal Flying Corps ended abruptly when the wings on his flimsy craft collapsed during a dogfight over France.

A star-studded committee raised money for a memorial, including Roosevelt, Smuts, Lord Rothschild, Rider Haggard, Harry Johnston, the American millionaire Solomon Guggenheim, E.N. Buxton and his cousin Lord Sydney Buxton, the High Commissioner for South

Africa.[2] Some consideration was given to erecting a monument in the Matopos Hills of Rhodesia near Cecil Rhodes' grave, but in the end the committee decided on a bronze sculpture by W.R. Colton to be placed in the Natural History Museum, and a Rugby scholarship, with preference to be given to sons of fallen officers. The government of the Union of South Africa donated a block of syenite to frame the sculpture and the Union Castle Line carried it free of charge to England. Boy Scouts formed a guard of honour and members of the Legion of Frontiersmen lined the stairs when the bust was unveiled on 10 June 1920.[3] Viscount Grey, Foreign Secretary during the war and a noted advocate of bird sanctuaries, gave the main address. Selous would have been pleased that his memorial occupies a niche at the right hand of the statue of Charles Darwin. Inevitably, he is shown with his trademark slouch hat and 450 Gibbs rifle, riding shotgun, so to speak, for the scientist whose writings so profoundly shaped his views on life and the universe.

The committee faced an added expense correcting the sculptor's error in showing Selous's birthdate as 1853 rather than 1851 – doubly significant because the death of a fighting soldier at age sixty-five was deemed more remarkable than sixty-three.[4] The Natural History Museum was further enriched by Gladys's gift in 1920 of the entire contents of Fred's private museum. In addition to the large number of mounted specimens, there were over 7,000 birds' eggs. According to the curator:

> The great feature of the collection is that Capt. Selous personally took every egg from the nest himself. He would never accept for his collection any egg or clutch of eggs offered to him by a friend nor would he purchase one from a dealer.... For this reason, no less than for the amazing neatness and methodical care with which it was arranged, to say nothing of its comprehensive range, the collection is a particularly valuable one.[5]

His most appropriate memorial was the gazetting in 1922 of the Selous Game Reserve in the British mandated territory of Tanganyika, which became independent Tanzania. It is today a UNESCO World Heritage Site and one of the largest faunal reserves on earth. Fred, whose grave lives within the reserve, would have appreciated that controlled hunting is permitted.

Legacies

Gladys could afford to give the collection away because, for all his fretting about money, Fred had left her in very comfortable circumstances with an estate worth more than £33,000.[6] She was not left, however, with a son to keep her company. The surviving child, Henry Sherborn Selous, followed the career his father had mapped out for his elder brother, joining the East African colonial service in Nyasaland (Malawi) where he died in 1954.

Whether Fred left anything to his African children, supposing that they still existed, has long been a subject of unverifiable speculation. A *Wikipedia* entry claims, without a supporting reference, that he had children by three different African wives. Another unreferenced online article, under the heading 'Selouse', says:

> He married a Ndebele woman from Southern Rhodesia now Zimbabwe by whom he had a daughter Magdalen Selous born in 1874, a Tswana woman from Bechuanaland now Botswana, who was a sister of the Bamangwato King Khama III, by whom he had a son John Selous born in 1900 and a Manyika woman from Eastern Zimbabwe by whom he had a son, Frederick Fisher (influential settlers could register the births of their half-caste children under different last names in order to protect their reputations). Frederick Fisher was born after his marriage to Marie and maintained correspondence with F.C. Selous for years.[7]

The names and dates lend an aura of authenticity but there are reasons to doubt the story. African children allegedly born after his marriage to Gladys (whose first name was Marie) must have been sired between November of 1895 and August 1896, because this is the only period he was resident in southern Africa after his English marriage. The year 1900 is quite impossible. Secondly, there is no reference at all to children by 'his woman' of the middle 1880s, who undoubtedly did exist and whose names and fate are unknown. Both Stephen Taylor and Kathryn Tidrick heard stories in Zimbabwe in the 1980s of descendants of Selous living in Harare, some of whom lived in a house supposedly left to them by Fred.[8] A Mrs Lydia Selous told Taylor that her husband James John Selous, born 1900 had, as a child, gone riding with his father on bush expeditions.

Historians like verifiable, documented facts. When verification is impossible they prefer the explanation that best fits the available evidence. In this case confusion over children named Selous most likely arises from the fact that another man took that name. Some or all of the children named above are probably descendants of Jan the Korana, born around 1850, who for most of his life was known as John Selous. On Fred's very first African trading expedition in 1871 he encountered what he called a 'Korana clan ruled over by Klas Lucas'. A young man named Jan from that clan took the opportunity to escape his 'Griqua master' and joined Selous as a servant. Writing in 1907 Fred said they had remained together for the better part of twenty-five years. Moreover, 'he is still alive to-day and long ago christened himself John Selous'. This implies that they kept in touch.[9] By all accounts John Selous became a skilled hunter. The story of the Griqua hunters like him and Cigar has yet to be told. Assiduous research may yet uncover the full and undoubtedly fascinating story of this John Selous and his progeny.

Great White Hunters in Life and Legend

Selous never called himself a great hunter. Other people did. The concept of Selous as 'Africa's greatest hunter' is a legacy of the Victorian and Edwardian period that deserves more scrutiny than it has received. Selous cannot have earned the title through numbers of animals killed, for the simple reason that there is no census available for comparative purposes. He often spoke and wrote of other white hunters who had shot more African game, but gave no figures. He knew for a fact that far more elephants had been killed by Africans in his own time than by European hunters. There are, however, no bag lists for any African hunter. So if 'greatest hunter' means anything, it means greatest *European* hunter.

Selous kept very careful track of the big game he killed. Near the end of his career he reckoned he had shot altogether nearly a thousand head of big game. Among them were 175 buffaloes, 106 elephants, 26 black rhinoceros, 23 white rhinoceros, 31 lions and 4 leopards.[10] Of the 106 elephants, 78 were shot in his first three seasons of hunting – before his twenty-fifth birthday. Even someone who calculated greatness by quantity would not number Selous among the top elephant hunters. It should be emphasized that more than two-thirds of all the big game animals he killed over his whole lifetime were shot during his first eight years of hunting when no one outside of South Africa had heard of him.

He shared the obsession of other European hunters with male animals and horns. None of his elephant tusks and only a few of the antelope heads he collected rank among the biggest or longest of those mounted by taxidermists like Rowland Ward. So Selous does not stand out as the greatest collector of horns, if measured by size, length, number of points, etc. By his own testimony he was not a crack shot either in the field or at targets. Part of the charm of his books lies in accounts of animals he missed when shooting at close range.

People like Baden-Powell believed Selous's greatness expressed itself in his character: his manly bearing, refusal to boast, good manners, fitness and utter fearlessness in the face of danger. Because he was a fine man, he must therefore have been a great hunter. Baden-Powell frequently cited him as the example of what a Boy Scout ought to be, morally straight, physically strong, brave and trustworthy. Because he was these things, he must be the greatest hunter. As Baden-Powell told the story, Lobengula:

was very much surprised to find that in a short time Selous proved himself not only a very brave and clever hunter, but that he was far better than any of the best warriors and hunters that the tribe could produce. He could run mile after mile following up elephants; he was a wonderful tracker and a nailing good shot with the rifle. He could always manage with very little food; by being always in fit condition and never having drunk anything stronger than water. ... He could get what he wanted to eat by shooting and cooking ... He never smoked cigarettes or any kind of tobacco, so he kept his wind, and could quickly outrun the quick footed Matabele and they could run 40 miles in a day. He was the truest type of Scout that you could find anywhere. No man ever hunted so many elephants or so many lions as he did.[11]

This story of Selous excelling the best of the Matabele warriors points to another important aspect of the 'greatest hunter' label. It is understood that what we are talking about is 'the great *white* hunter'. Other people do not count. Yet a striking feature of Selous's African books is that he never hunts alone. He is always part of a team that includes black guides, interpreters, wagon drivers, porters and shooters. Many of them prove to be equally able, brave, strong, loyal and self-sacrificing. The 'great white hunter' myth extracts him from his historical context and exalts him as the self-sufficient, masterful man. By the same token, excessive emphasis on racial identity distracts attention from nineteenth-century big game hunting as a collective, international, multi-racial juggernaut of destruction.

Where Selous clearly showed his superiority was in writing. Roosevelt was not alone in his belief that no man ever wrote so well about hunting. It was the evocative writing and factual detail in Selous's first book that caught Rider Haggard's attention, rather than the persona of the hunter. It enabled Haggard to populate *King Solomon's Mines* with a multitude of geographical, botanical, zoological and technical details about big game hunting, a sport about which he knew very little from personal experience.

Selous continued to be a source of inspiration for creative writers after his death. Ernest Hemingway kept a copy of *A Hunter's Wanderings* and used details gleaned from his reading of Millais's biography in his short story, 'The Snows of Kilimanjaro'.[12] The great white hunter assumes his modern form in another story, 'The Short Happy Life of Francis Macomber'. The character Robert Wilson is a man of few words, knowledgeable about animals, who knows where to aim for deadly effect and is utterly without fear. Kenyan big game hunting is for him – and Hemingway – about freedom and mastery. Macomber, a slim, athletic and very rich American, takes his beautiful wife on a Kenyan safari. He worries when Wilson insists they leave their car to hunt a lion on foot and panics when the lion appears. By running away he earns the contempt of everyone, even the African gun-bearers. That night his wife, who has been unfaithful many times before, creeps into Wilson's tent and onto the folding double cot he keeps for such occasions. 'He had hunted for a certain clientele, the international, fast, sporting set, where the women did not feel they were getting their money's worth unless they shared that cot with the white hunter'. By becoming a hunter Wilson freed himself from the money that enchains his clients. Confronting deadly animals confers on him the mastery that gives him access to animal excitement of all kinds, most especially sex. When, next day, Macomber conquers his fear in the face of charging buffalo, his wife, realizing that her dominance in their relationship is finished, shoots her husband.

Hemingway's stories set the scene for many future books and films about great white hunters. Over time, however, as in Selous's own transition from hunting to preserving, the emphasis shifted from shooting animals to saving and caring for them. One of the last of the successful East African safari films, *Baby Elephant Walk* (1962), casts John Wayne as the laconic fearless white hunter, but in this quest his aim is to capture animals for a zoo. By the time the South African comedy *The Gods Must be Crazy* became a hit movie in 1980, the white male protagonist has evolved into a professional game park ranger totally devoted to saving big game from African poachers. Tongue-tied and clumsy in the presence of women, he is nonetheless up to the test when a force of black terrorists takes hostages from a local school. Whiteness, bravery and strength win the girl after all. Beneath the comedic storyline Hemingway's themes of mastery – over animals, black men and white women play out pretty much the way they did in 'The Short Happy Life of Francis Macomber'.

One of the most popular latter-day writers of African adventure, Wilbur Smith, makes no secret of his admiration for Selous. The hero of his novel *When the Lion Feeds* (1964) is Sean Courtney [not Courteney], whose dates (born 1860, died 1925) place him squarely in Fred's generation. Subsequent novels in the Courtney series, introduce readers to his son, a World War I flying ace, German snipers and numerous episodes recalling Selous's career. Smith's fictional Courtneys display heaps of bravery and resourcefulness, which is rewarded by bevies of willing women in the Hemingway tradition.

Selous Scouts

Selous's name lives on in Zimbabwe. There is, for example, still a Selous Hotel and a Selous Street in Harare, while Rhodes Street and Jameson Street have been changed to Herbert Chitepo Avenue and Samora Michel Avenue. Altogether 148 'offensive and objectionable' colonial names have been banished to the cartographical underworld in Robert Mugabe's Zimbabwe. It is all the more remarkable that Selous survives on a street sign because, in the late stages of the Rhodesian War for liberation, his name was attached to a notorious special forces unit, the Selous Scouts, whose clandestine counter-insurgency operations became a byword for state-sponsored terror.

It may be that some Zimbabweans remember Selous's defence of the Shona as the rightful owners of the land and the builders of Great Zimbabwe. Perhaps the memory of his less-than-glorious part in the conquest of Rhodesia has faded, while his promotion of 'the fly' regions as game parks has been realized beyond his dreams.

Man versus Wild

In the wider world, Selous's name has fallen practically into oblivion, along with admiration for the hunter, the colonizer, and the specimen collector. The scholars' rediscovery of the connection between hunting and conservation has yet to percolate through to the general public. The cult of manliness exemplified in Selous's life no longer takes the form it did in the days of Roosevelt or Hemingway, but it is by no means dead. Perhaps it can't be killed and maybe it shouldn't. Adventurers still seek freedom and mastery in physical contests with wild beasts and wild places. The spirit that sends young men free-climbing up sheer rock faces a thousand feet high, that inspires them (fatally) to live with brown bears or cross Antarctica on foot is the same that caused Selous to pack his bags for Africa in 1871. Individual bravery in battle is honoured as much as ever it was in his day. The great revolution of our time is that so many young women have gone out on similar errands, sailing single-handed round the world, climbing Everest, living with gorillas in the mist.

The presenter of the popular television series, *Man versus Wild*, exemplifies how far the ideal of masculinity has altered in our time. In certain ways Bear Grylls resembles Selous. Son of the politician Sir Michael Grylls, Grylls attended Eton College before doing military service as a reservist with the SAS. He speaks French and Spanish. He has survived a parachute accident at 4,900 metres, climbed Mount Everest, and crossed the Atlantic in an inflatable boat. In 2009 he became the youngest-ever Chief Scout of the Scout Association founded by Baden-Powell. On the other hand, he does not hunt or kill animals. He is an observer in the tradition of Edmund Selous the bird-watcher rather than Fred the collector. His twenty-first century masculinity expresses itself in contests with wild nature rather than mastery of beasts, men or women.

Notes

Preface

1. Selous boots from www.westleyrichards.com; the R8 Selous Rifle, made by Blaser Jagdwaffen, www. blaser.de for sale at sales@eurooptic.com; Owen's portrait can be seen at www.responseabilityalliance. com/html/artist.html; and the engraved crystal at www.africahunting.com/threads/ frederick-courteney-selous.1866/.

2. J.A. Mangan and C. McKenzie, 'Martial Conditioning, Military Exemplars and Moral Certainties: Imperial Hunting as Preparation for War', *The International Journal of the History of Sport*, Vol. 25 (2008), p.1154.

3. R. Brown, *Blood Ivory: The Massacre of the African Elephant*. The History Press: Stroud (2008), Ch. 4; J. Finke, *The Rough Guide to Tanzania*. London: Penguin Rough Guides (2007), p. 291.

4. *The Guardian*, online edition, accessed 18 April 2004.

5. Key works include P. Mason, *Birth of a Dilemma: The Conquest and Settlement of Rhodesia*. Oxford: Oxford University Press (1958); T. Ranger, *Revolt in Southern Rhodesia 1896–7*. London: Heinemann, (1967); and A. Keppel-Jones, *Rhodes and Rhodesia: The White Conquest of Zimbabwe 1884–1902*. Kingston, ON: McGill-Queen's University Press (1983).

6. J.M. MacKenzie, *The Empire of Nature: Hunting, Conservation and British Imperialism*. Manchester: Manchester University Press (1988).

7. K. Thomas, *Man and the Natural World: Changing Attitudes in England, 1500–1800*. London: Allen Lane (1983); T. Griffiths, *Hunters and Collectors: The Antiquarian Imagination in Australia*. Cambridge: Cambridge University Press (1996).

8. *Journal of Southern African Studies*, Vol. 24, No. 4 (1998).

9. J.G. Millais, *Life of Frederick Courtenay [sic], D.S.O., Capt. 25th Royal Fusiliers Selous*. London: Longmans Green (1919).

10. J.A. Casada, *Africa's Greatest Hunter: The Lost Writings of Frederick C. Selous*, 2ⁿᵈ edn. Huntington Beach, CA: Safari Press (1998); J.A. Casada, *Frederick C. Selous, A Hunting Legend: Recollections by and about the Great Hunter*. Huntington Beach, CA: Safari Press (2000).

11. K. Tidrick, *Empire and the English Character: The Illusion of Authority*. London: I.B. Tauris (2008), pp.48–86.

Chapter 1 Bird's Nest, Butterflies and Mischievous Boys

1. J. Tallis, *Tallis's History and Description of the Crystal Palace, and the Exhibition of the World's Industry in 1851*. London: London Printing and Publishing (1852), p.55.

2. Roualeyn Gordon Cumming, *Five Years of a Hunter's Life in the Far Interior of South Africa*, 2 vols. London: John Murray (1850), Ch. 2, p.18.

3. J.M. MacKenzie, *The Empire of Nature: Hunting, Conservation and British Imperialism*. Manchester: Manchester University Press (1988), p. 29.

4. *Marketing History of the Piano*, www.cantos.org/Piano/History/marketing.html (accessed 5 November 2014).

5. 'The Boyhood of Mr. F.C. Selous', *Chums*, May 1894; reprinted in *Cheltenham Chronicle*, 5 May 1894.

6. Ibid.

7. H. Osborne and M. Winstanley, 'Rural and Urban Poaching in Victorian England', *Rural History*, Vol. 17 (2006), p. 204.

8. *Lloyd's Weekly Newspaper*, 24 March 1895.

9. *Dundee Evening Telegraph*, 25 May 1897.

10. Thomas Hughes, *Tom Brown's Schooldays*. London: Cassell and Co. (1907), p. 227.

11. *Pall Mall Gazette*, 22 March 1895.

12. George B. Muir to Selous, Macmillan & Co. Ltd, 7 November 1908, Selous Papers, Zimbabwe Archives (SE), SE 1/1/2/2.

13. Summarized from lengthy quotations in J.G. Millais, *Life of Frederick Courtenay* [sic], *D.S.O., Capt. 25th Royal Fusiliers Selous*. London: Longmans Green (1919), Chs 2, 3.

14. Ibid, p. 23.

15. J.A. Casada, *Frederick C. Selous, A Hunting Legend: Recollections by and about the Great Hunter*. Huntington Beach, CA: Safari Press (2000), p. 80.

16. Millais (1919), p. 40; I.F.W. Beckett, *Riflemen Form: A Study of the Rifle Volunteer Movement 1859–1908*. Barnsley: Pen & Sword Military (2007), pp. 116–17. For confirmation of Selous's membership of the rifle corps, see the recollection of his friend H.A. Bryden, in Casada (2000), p. 135.

17. Selous to 'Ma chére mere', 20 December 1868, SE1/1/1.

18. Selous to his mother, 18 November 1868, SE1/1/1.

19. Selous to Locky Selous, dated 21 April 1869, 'near Temple Bar' SE1/1/1; Selous to his mother, June 1870, SE1/1/1.

20. Selous to his mother, June 1870, SE1/1/1.

21. Ibid.

22. Selous to his mother, 22 July 1870, SE1/1/1.

23. Selous to his mother, 20 October 1870, SE1/1/1.

24. Selous to his mother 5 July 1870, SE1/1/1.

25. Selous to his father 22 July 1870, SE1/1/1.

26. Selous to Locky Selous, 21 April 1869, SE1/1/1.

27. Selous to his mother, 22 July 1870, SE1/1/1.

28. Quoted in Millais (1919), p. 25.

29. Selous's journal, SE 1/4/1.

30. Millais (1919), pp. 27, 29.

31. Stephen Taylor, *The Mighty Nimrod: A Life of Frederick Courteney Selous, African Hunter and Adventurer, 1851–1917*. London: Collins (1989), p. 32. Taylor also refers to medical studies at University College Hospital, but does not say when they might have happened.

32. SE1/4/1.

33. *Natal Witness*, 1 September 1871.

Chapter 2 Not-so-great White Traders

1. C. Payton, *Diamond Diggings of South Africa*. London: Horace Cox (1872), pp. 62–4.

2. Quoted in W.B. Lord, *Diamonds and Gold*. London: publisher unknown (1871), pp. 9–10.

3. N. Etherington, *The Great Treks: The Transformation of Southern Africa, 1815–1854*. London: Longman (2001), p. 95.

4. J.P.R. Wallis (ed.), *The Matabele Journals of Robert Moffat, 1829–1860*, Vol. 1. London: Chatto & Windus (1945), p. 29.

5. William Cornwallis Harris, *The Wild Sports of Southern Africa; being the Narrative of an Expedition from the Cape of Good Hope through the Territories of the Chief Moselekatse to the Tropic of Capricorn*. London: John Murray (1839), p. 106.

6. Etherington (2001), p. 249.

7. Harris (1839), pp. 202, 207.

8. J.M. MacKenzie, *The Empire of Nature: Hunting, Conservation and British Imperialism*. Manchester: Manchester University Press (1988), pp. 94–101.

9. J. Mackenzie, *Ten Years North of the Orange River. A Story of Everyday Life and Work among the South African Tribes from 1859 to 1869*. Edinburgh: Edmonston & Douglas (1871).

10. Probably Mahura; see C. Hamilton, B.K. Mbenga and R. Ross (eds), *Cambridge History of South Africa*. Cambridge: Cambridge University Press (2010), Vol. I, p. 354.

11. Selous's journal, 1 February 1872, SE1/4/1.

12. F.C. Selous, *A Hunter's Wanderings in Africa*. London: Macmillan & Co. (1907), p.8.

Chapter 3 Lost on the Missionaries' Road

1. N. Parsons, *King Khama, Emperor Joe, and the Great White Queen*. Chicago: University of Chicago Press (1998), pp. 39–40. On the generally slow progress of missionaries in Southern Africa, see N. Etherington, *Preachers, Peasants and Politics in Southeast Africa*. London: Royal Historical Society (1978).

2. F. C. Selous, *A Hunter's Wanderings in Africa, being a Narrative of Nine Years Spent Amongst the Game in the Far Interior of South Africa*. London: R. Bentley and Son (1881), pp. 14–15.

3   F. Morton and R. Hitchcock, 'Tswana Hunting: Continuities and Changes in the Transvaal and Kalahari after 1600', *South African Historical Journal*, (2014) No. 66, pp. 418–39.

4   E.C. Tabler (ed.), *To the Victoria Falls via Matabeleland: The Diary of Major Henry Stabb, 1875*. Cape Town: Struik (1967), pp. 29–30.

Chapter 4 In the Kingdom of the Great Black Elephant

1. Selous's open-minded approach to the evidence contrasts with that of British Major Henry Stabb, who on viewing the old workings in 1875 asserted 'they are certainly not the work of any race of people such as those now existing in this part of Africa who have no such knowledge of mining as these works give evidence of'; E.C. Tabler (ed.), *To the Victoria Falls via Matabeleland: The Diary of Major Henry Stabb, 1875*. Cape Town: Struik (1967), p. 58.

2. F. C. Selous, *A Hunter's Wanderings in Africa, being a Narrative of Nine Years Spent Amongst the Game in the Far Interior of South Africa*. London: R. Bentley and Son (1881).

3. Selous, a keen observer, thought he stood 'about 5 feet 10 or 11'. The higher figures are cited in Ian Phimister, 'Lobengula Khumalo (*c*.1835–1893/4?)', *Oxford Dictionary of National Biography*. Oxford: Oxford University Press (2004), (www.oxforddnb.com/view/article/52662, accessed 11 March 2015).

4. In modern Ndebele and Zulu, *qomisa*.

Chapter 5 Elephants Galore

1. As recounted by Selous's friend of later years, H.A. Bryden in his book *From Veldt Camp Fires: Stories of Southern Africa*. London: Hurst and Blackett (1900), p. 54.

2. E.C. Tabler (ed.), *To the Victoria Falls via Matabeleland: The Diary of Major Henry Stabb, 1875*. Cape Town: Struik (1967), pp. 90–91.

3. N. Etherington, *The Great Treks: The Transformation of Southern Africa, 1815–1854*. London: Longman (2001), pp. 214–15.

4. F.C. Selous, *A Hunter's Wanderings in Africa, being a Narrative of Nine Years Spent Amongst the Game in the Far Interior of South Africa*. London: R. Bentley and Son (1881), p. 66.

5. A position endorsed by present-day anthropologist E. Wilmsen in *Land Filled with Flies: A Political Economy of the Kalahari*. Chicago: University of Chicago Press (1989).

6. Selous (1881), p. 172.

7. Ibid, pp. 128–9.

8. Ibid, p. 173.

9. Ibid, pp. 173–4.

10. Ibid, p. 222.

11. Ibid.

Chapter 6 Hunter Heroes

1. W. Cody, *The Life of Hon. William F. Cody, known as Buffalo Bill, The Famous Hunter, Scout and Guide: An Autobiography.* Hartford, CT: Frank E. Bliss (1879), pp. 62, 154–5, 157, 161–2, 171–4.

2. F. Norton (ed.), *Frank Leslie's Historical Register of the United States Centennial Exposition, 1876.* New York, NY: Frank Leslie's Publishing (1877), pp. 86–7, 137.

3. R. Ward, *A Naturalist's Life Study in the Art of Taxidermy.* London: Rowland Ward, printed for private circulation (1913), p. 54.

4. These examples, and those in the following paragraph, are drawn from F. C. Selous, *A Hunter's Wanderings.* London: Macmillan & Co. (1907). The quotation on the eyes of wounded lions comes from F. C. Selous, *Travel and Adventure in South-East Africa.* London: Rowland Ward (1893). p. 166.

5. F.C. Selous, *A Hunter's Wanderings in Africa, being a Narrative of Nine Years Spent Amongst the Game in the Far Interior of South Africa.* London: R. Bentley and Son (1881), p. 90.

6. 'Notes of Travel and Adventure in the Interior of South Africa', *The Field*, 23 August 1890, pp. 293–4.

7   'Sport and Exploration on the River Chobe, South Central Africa', *The Field*, 12 February 1876, p. 174.

8   Selous to his mother, 23 February and 8 March 1876, SE1/1/1.

9   Selous to his mother, 29 March 1876, SE1/1/1.

10 Selous to his mother, 21 April 1876, SE1/1/1.

Chapter 7 'Elephants are Now Almost a Thing of the Past'

1. Selous to his mother, 24 May 1876, SE 1/1/1.

2. Selous his father, 19 July 1876, SE 1/1/1.

3. W.G. Grandy, 'Report of the Proceedings of the Livingstone Congo Mission', *Proceedings of the Royal Geographical Society*, (1875) No. 19, pp. 78–105. The expedition was abandoned while still on the lower Congo, when word came of Livingstone's death.

4. Quoted from an unpublished document in R. Sampson, *White Induna: George Westbeech and the Barotse.* USA: Xlibris (2008), Chapter 2; first published in 1972 as *The Man with a Toothbrush in his Hat.* I have been unable to locate the original of this document in the Zimbabwe National Archives, where author Sampson claims to have found it.

5. Selous to his mother, 15 October 1877, SE 1/1/1.

6. Selous to his father, 17 October 1877, SE 1/1/1.

7. Selous to his mother, 15 October 1877, SE 1/1/1.

8. J. Fage and R. Oliver (eds), *Cambridge History of Africa,* Vol. 6. Cambridge: Cambridge University Press (1985), p. 415.

9. First published in *The Worldwide Magazine* (1898), No. 2, pp. 321–8; reprinted in J.A. Casada (ed.), *Africa's Greatest Hunter: The Lost Writings Of Frederick C. Selous,* 2nd edn. Huntington Beach, CA: Safari Press (1998), pp. 7–16.

10. Selous to his mother, 25 January 1880, SE 1/1/1.

11. Selous to Bartle Frere, 4 February 1880, JMS 2/111, RGS.

12. Selous to his mother, 25 January 1880, SE 1/1/1.

13. Selous to his mother, 6 April 1884, SE1/1/1.

14. Selous to Bartle Frere, 4 February 1880, JMS 2/111, RGS.

15. Selous to his mother, 7 March 1880.

Chapter 8 Author, Collector, Explorer

1. Selous to his mother, 20 July 1878, SE 1/1/1.

2. Selous to his mother, 2 November 1880, SE 1/1/1.

3. Selous to his mother, 20 July 1878, SE 1/1/1.

4. Selous to Günther, 24 February 1884. Letters Zoological Department 1/25. Letters In, January–June 1884, Archives of the Natural History Museum (NHM), South Kensington, London.

5. Condition of existing displays mentioned in Selous to Günther, 29 October 1882, Letters In, Zoological Department 1/25, NHM.

6. Dane Kennedy, *The Last Blank Spaces: Exploring Africa and Australia*. Cambridge, MA: Harvard University Press (2013), p. 80.

7. *London Daily News*, 21 October 1881.

8. *Morning Post*, 29 December 1881.

9. *Pall Mall Gazette*, 2 February 1882.

10. *London Standard*, 22 June 1882.

11. F.C. Selous, *A Hunter's Wanderings in Africa, being a Narrative of Nine Years Spent Amongst the Game in the Far Interior of South Africa*. London: R. Bentley and Son (1881).

12. Selous to Günther, 3 February 1882, Letters In, Zoological Department 1/21, NHM; Selous to Henry Walter Bates, 10 November 1882, JMS2/225, RGS.

13. Selous to Günther, 3 Feb 1882, Letters In, Zoological Department 1/21, NHM.

14. Selous to Günther, 2 Aug. 1882, Letters In, Zoological Department 1/23, NHM.

15. A. Günther to Selous, undated, but certainly January 1883, Copies of Out-Letters 1883–1885, DF201/12, NHM.

16. Ibid.

17. Ibid.

18. Selous to Günther, 2 August 1882, 29 October 1882, 9 August 1885, Letters In, Zoological Department 1/23 and 1/28, NHM.

19. R. Ward, *A Naturalist's Life Study in the Art of Taxidermy*. London: Rowland Ward, printed for private circulation (1913), p. 33.

20. Selous to Günther, 15 January 1886, Letters In, Zoological Department 1/29, NHM.

Chapter 9 Neither Monk nor Saint

1. Dawson Papers, National Archives of Zimbabwe, quoted in S. Taylor, *The Mighty Nimrod: A Life of Frederick Courteney Selous, African Hunter and Adventurer, 1851–1917*. London: Collins (1989), p. 129. The first scholar to call attention to Selous's woman was A. Keppel-Jones in his book, *Rhodes and Rhodesia: The White Conquest of Zimbabwe 1884–1902*. Kingston, ON: McGill-Queen's University Press (1983), pp. 55, 97n. 2.

2. F.C. Selous, *African Nature Notes and Reminiscences*. London: Macmillan and Co. (1908), p. 333; elsewhere he is identified as a 'Koranna elephant hunter' who served apprenticeship with Selous. See W.M. Kerr, *The Far Interior: A Narrative of Travel and Adventure from the Cape of Good Hope across the Zambesi to the Lake Regions of Central Africa*, Vol. 1. Boston: Houghton Mifflin (1886), pp. 43, 68–9, 71, 76. Selous arranged for John Selous to serve as wagon master and interpreter for Kerr on his expedition to Lake Nyasa. It seems very likely that the Selous family that Stephen Taylor reports living in Harare in 1984 is descended from this man.

3. F.C. Selous, *A Hunter's Wanderings in Africa, being a Narrative of Nine Years Spent Amongst the Game in the Far Interior of South Africa*. London: R. Bentley and Son (1881).

4. Letter to Günther, 29 October 1882, Letters In Zoological Department, 1/23, NHM.

5. F. C. Selous, 'Explorations in the North Mashuna Country, Tropical South Africa', *The Field*, 17 April 1886, p. 501.

6. Selous to Günther, 29 October 1882, Letters In, Zoological Department, 1/23, NHM.

7. Günther to Selous, January 1883, Copies of Letters Out, Zoological Department, DF201/12, NHM.

8. In *The Field*, 28 July 1883, p. 153, Rowland Ward reported hearing that Lobengula was detaining Selous for his own safety during a period when Matabele raiding parties were active; this conflicts with Selous's record.

9. 'Mr. Selous's Original Map of Mashonaland', Zimbabwe. Spec. 20, RGS.

10. Selous to Günther, 24 February 1884, Letters In, Zoological Department, 1/25, NHM.

11. F.C. Selous, *Travel and Adventure in South-East Africa*. London: Rowland Ward (1893).

12. In Taylor (1989), p. 107, the author cites, as proof of a close relationship, that in 1882 Lobengula asked Selous to translate a letter from Piet Joubert, the Transvaal Republic's border agent, proposing an alliance – the evidence being a copy of the translated letter surviving in Selous's papers. It is more likely that the letter was written in order to inform Lobengula of Britain's retrocession of the Transvaal, which had just occurred. Lobengula showed the letter to other people, and boasted of his own sarcastic reply; see Keppel-Jones (1983), pp. 34 and 52, note 103. There is no indication that Selous translated the letter; many people in Bulawayo could have done so.

13. Kerr (1886), pp. 18ff.

14. Still thirsting for African adventure, Kerr mounted an expedition in relief of the beleaguered Egyptian official Emin Pasha, hoping to meet up with Henry Morton Stanley who was on the same errand. Malaria forced him back and killed him in 1888.

15. Selous to his mother, 6 April 1884, SE1/1/1. It is not clear when Edmund travelled up to the Zambezi, though it would most likely have been before the onset of the rainy season in the previous year.

16. Günther to Selous, 11 July 1884, Copies of Letters Out, Zoological Department, DF201/12, NHM.

17. F.C. Selous, *Travel and Adventure in South-East Africa*. London: Rowland Ward (1893), p. 190.

18. Selous to Günther, 15 January 1886, Letters In, Zoological Department 1/29, NHM.

19. Selous to his mother, 6 April 1884, SE1/1/1.

Chapter 10 Maholie Lies

1. R. Ward, *The Field*, 22 January 1887, p. 113.

2. Copy in English of Selous to Lobengula, 31 August 1887, SE 1/1/1.

3. Speaking of a wealthy American, Paul Rainy, who had killed more than eighty lions; Selous to H.A. Bryden, 10 October 1912, MS57, Brenthurst Library, Johannesburg.

4. F.C. Selous, 'Mr. F. C. Selous's Further Explorations in Matabele-land', *Proceedings of the Royal Geographical Society*, n.s., No. 10 (May 1888), pp. 293–6. The published map also shows the Alluvial Gold Fields.

5. Copy in English of Selous to Lobengula, 31 August 1887, SE 1/1/1.

6. For a detailed analysis of the concession seekers of 1886–8, see A. Keppel-Jones, *Rhodes and Rhodesia: The White Conquest of Zimbabwe 1884–1902*. Kingston, ON: McGill-Queen's University Press (1983), pp. 22–46, on which I have relied in this chapter.

7. Copy in English of letter from Selous to Lobengula, 31 August 1887, SE 1/1/1.

8. Ibid.

9. Even though Fountaine, Cooper and Jameson are named twice in Selous's letter to Lobengula, Stephen Taylor, in his book, *The Mighty Nimrod: A Life of Frederick Courteney Selous, African Hunter and Adventurer, 1851–1917*, London: Collins (1989), pp. 124–5, speculates that Selous wrote the letter on behalf of Frank Johnson and Edward Burnett. According to Taylor, it was not Selous's party that was threatened by Lobengula's man, Mchesa, but Frank Johnson and Edward Burnett of the Northern Goldfields Exploration Syndicate who were camped nearby. Drawing upon his 'imagination', he composes a scenario in which Johnson sends word to Selous that he is in trouble. Selous rides over and calms everyone down by writing a letter to Lobengula explaining that Johnson and Burnett are 'men of consideration in their own country and not dogs to be barked at'. By substituting the names of Johnson and Burnett for Jameson, Fountaine and Cooper, who are named twice in the letter, Taylor gives a totally misleading account of what happened.

 The letter clearly states that Selous sent Malabamba to talk with Mchesa at his main camp on the Umfule River. Johnson and Burnett do not figure at all.

 It appears likely that Taylor was misled by Frank Johnson's account, written when he was over seventy, of a visit from Selous at his camp (their first meeting), when he was experiencing problems with his Matabele escort commanded by Mchesa. Johnson recalled Selous writing a long letter to Lobengula and assumed it was concerned with his troubles. However, as the copy of the letter in Selous's papers does not mention Johnson, this cannot be right. See F. Johnson, *Great Days: The Autobiography of an Empire Pioneer*. London: G. Bell and Sons (1940), p. 55.

10. 'Massacre in Matabeleland', from *Cape Argus*, 25 November 1887; reprinted in *The Field*, 24 December 1887, and *Buck's Herald*, 17 December 1887.

11. Taylor (1989), p. 128.

12. Selous to the editor of *The Field*, Cape Town, 26 January 1888; printed in *The Field*, 25 February 1888, p. 272.

13. Selous, 'Explorations in the North Mashuna Country, Tropical South Africa' *The Field*, 10 April 1886, p. 463.

Chapter 11 Escaped Alone with His Life

1. Selous, 'Mr. F.C. Selous's Further Explorations in Matabele-land, *Proceedings of the Royal Geographical Society*, n.s., (May 1888) No. 10, p. 295.

2. *Pall Mall Gazette*, 16 March 1893.

3. Selous to his mother, 6 April 1884, SE 1/1/1.

4. Heany to Dawson, 16 March 1888, quoted in A. Keppel-Jones, *Rhodes and Rhodesia: The White Conquest of Zimbabwe 1884–1902*. Kingston, ON: McGill-Queen's University Press (1983), p. 59.

5. Robert Rotberg, *The Founder: Cecil Rhodes and the Pursuit of Power*. Oxford: Oxford University Press (1988), p. 209.

6. Reuters telegram from Pietermaritzburg, Natal, quoted in *Morning Post*, 13 November 1888. It is not known whether any of the property was returned to him.

7. See the July 1888 list of trading goods included in the file of correspondence concerned with the RGS article, 'Twenty Years in Zambezia' by R.C.F. Maugham, JMS2/299, RGS.

Chapter 12 Working for Colossus

1. A. Keppel-Jones, *Rhodes and Rhodesia: The White Conquest of Zimbabwe 1884–1902*. Kingston, ON: McGill-Queen's University Press (1983), pp. 105–6.

2. *Nottingham Post*, 1 March 1889.

3. *Pall Mall Gazette*, 7 March 1889.

4. *Glasgow Herald*, 9 March 1889.

5. Ibid.

6. Ibid.

7. 'Mashunaland and the Mashunas', *Fortnightly Review*, 1 May 1889.

8. *London Daily News*, 28 May 1889.

9. *Glasgow Herald*, 9 March 1889.

10. *Western Times*, 17 April 1889.

11. *Bucks Herald*, 25 January 1890.

12. *Glasgow Herald*, 9 March 1889.

13. *Blackburn Standard*, 11 January 1890.

14. Selous to his mother, 27 May 1889, SE 1/1/1.

15. Selous to his mother, 4 June 1889, SE 1/1/1.

16. Selous to his mother, posted from Tete, 16 Aug. 1889, SE 1/1/1.

17. F.C. Selous, *Travel and Adventure in South-East Africa*. London: Rowland Ward (1893), p. 286.

18. Ibid, p. 287.

19. Ibid, p. 311.

20. Keppel-Jones (1983), pp. 151–2.

21. Selous (1893), p. 311.

22. *London Daily News*, 18 January 1890.

23. *York Herald*, 9 November 1889; compare with F.C. Selous, *Travel and Adventure in South-East Africa*. London: Rowland Ward (1893), p. 307.

24. Selous to his mother, 26 October 1890, SE 1/1/1. The idea for the road, he wrote, was entirely his own,

which Rhodes at first rejected.

25. Frank Johnson, *Great Days: The Autobiography of an Empire Pioneer*. London: G. Bell and Sons (1940), pp. 88–93.

26. Ibid, pp. 294–5.

27. Selous to his mother, 22 December 1889, SE 1/1/1.

Chapter 13 Rhodesia

1. Antony Thomas, *Rhodes*. London: BBC Books (1996), p. 217.

2. Frank Johnson, *Great Days: The Autobiography of an Empire Pioneer*. London: G. Bell and Sons (1940), pp. 95–8, 121–3.

3. F.C. Selous, *Travel and Adventure in South-East Africa*. London: Rowland Ward (1893), pp. 369–70.

4. *London Daily News*, 18 September 1890.

5. Johnson (1940), pp. 121–2, 144.

6. See also letter to his mother, 18 May 1890, SE 1/1/1, in which he says that if the Natural History Museum will not buy it, he intends to present it as a gift. Evidently he changed his mind and reserved it for his own collection.

7. Selous to his mother, 26 October 1890, SE 1/1/1.

8. Letter of 13 July 1890, SE 1/1/1.

9. Ibid.

10. Robert Rotberg, *The Founder: Cecil Rhodes and the Pursuit of Power*. Oxford: Oxford University Press (1988), pp. 312–16.

11. Selous to his mother, 16 November 1890, SE 1/1/1.

12. Enclosed with documents relating to the article for the Royal Geographical Society, 'Twenty Years in Zambezia' by R.C.F. Maugham, JMS2/299, RGS.

13. JMS2/299, RGS.

14. Ibid.

15. Ibid.

16. 'An adventurous tour through a wonderful country', *Yorkshire Post and Leeds Intelligencer*, 16 May 1891. Armstrong is identified here only as the son of a Yorkshire tradesman, holding an important position in the BSA Co.

17. Selous (1883), pp. 403 C. Selous, *Travel and Adventure in South-East Africa*. London: Rowland Ward, pp.402–3.

18. T. Ranger, *Revolt in Southern Rhodesia*. London: Heinemann (1967), p. 75.

19. Selous (1893), p. 407.

20. 'A Night Amongst Lions in South-Eastern Mashonaland', *The Field*, 26 September 1891, pp. 484–5.

21. For a description of the farm, which he said 'will grow anything', see *Pall Mall Gazette*, 25 November 1892.

22. Selous to his mother, 20 July 1891, SE 1/1/1.

23. *The Field*, 19 March 1892, p. 413.

Chapter 14 England, Home and Beauty

1. *Pall Mall Gazette*, 19 July 1892; for Henry, see *Liverpool Mercury*, 8 October 1890.

2. J.G. Millais, *Life of Frederick Courtenay [sic], D.S.O., Capt. 25th Royal Fusiliers Selous*. London: Longmans Green (1919), p. 197. Her full name was Marie Catherine Gladys Maddy, but she was always known to friends as Gladys.

3. *Gloucester Citizen*, 2 October 1890.

4. *Bath Chronicle and Weekly Gazette*, 20 August 1891.

5. Selous to his sister Sybil ('Dei'), 30 July 1891, SE 1/1/1.

6. *Sussex Agricultural Express*, 20 January 1893.

7. 'Trophies of the Field and the Forest: A Chat with a Taxidermist', *Pall Mall Gazette*, 24 January 1893.

8. Ibid.

9. *Leeds Mercury*, 4 February 1893.

10. *Daily Gazette for Middlesbrough*, 10 March 1893; *Glasgow Herald*, 9 March 1893; *Edinburgh Evening News*, 8 March 1893.

11. *Nottingham Evening Post*, 27 April 1893.

12. *Review of Reviews*, March 1893, pp. 424–37, reprinted in J.A. Casada, *Frederick C. Selous, A Hunting Legend*. Huntington Beach, CA: Safari Press (2000), pp. 96–126.

13. Ibid, pp.96–7

14. Ibid, p. 100.

15. He recommended the book to readers in F.C. Selous, *Travel and Adventure in South-East Africa*. London: Rowland Ward (1893), p. 8.

16. *Aberdeen Evening Express*, 15 May 1893; *London Standard*, 30 May 1893.

17. *London Standard*, 14 June 1893.

18. J.A. Casada (ed.), *Africa's Greatest Hunter: The Lost Writings Of Frederick C. Selous*, 2nd edn. Huntington Beach, CA: Safari Press (1998), p. 33.

19. The date was 15 June 1893.

20. *Edinburgh Evening News*, 14 June 1893.

21. Selous to the editor of the *London Standard*, 15 June 1893.

22. *Dover Express*, 23 June 1893.

23. Rowland Ward, *A Naturalist's Life Study in the Art of Taxidermy*. London: Rowland Ward, printed for private circulation (1913), pp. 78–9.

24. H.M. Stanley letter to Edward Pease MP, quoted in *London Daily News*, 23 May 1890.

25. Obituary, Canon Henry William Maddy, *Cheltenham Chronicle*, 16 January 1909.

26. Keppel-Jones, A., *Rhodes and Rhodesia: The White Conquest of Zimbabwe 1884–1902*. Kingston, ON: McGill-Queen's University Press, pp. 55 and 97, n.2.

27. *London Standard*, 20 October 1893.

28. Dinner announcement in *Manchester Courier and Lancashire General Advertiser*, 17 June 1893.

29. *York Herald*, 2 September 1893. Millais mistakenly states that Selous's first trip to Lochbuie was made in August 1894.

30. *Pall Mall Gazette*, 21 July 1893.

Chapter 15 Wounded, Lionized and Bagged[PHA}

1. *Edinburgh Evening News*, 27 September 1893.

2. The most analytical and thoroughgoing account is A. Keppel-Jones, *Rhodes and Rhodesia: The White Conquest of Zimbabwe 1884–1902*. Kingston, ON: McGill-Queen's University Press, Chapters 6–8.

3. Ibid, pp. 310–11.

4. Ibid, p. 249.

5. *London Standard*, 19 October 1893

6. Keppel-Jones (1983), pp. 259–60.

7. *The Times*, 6 February 1894, p. 4.

8. *Derby Daily Telegraph*, 3 November 1893; *Yorkshire Evening Post*, 11 November 1893.

9. Rose A. Blennerbassett, and Lucy Sleeman, *Adventures in Mashonaland*. London: Sleeman (1893), as reported in *Derby Daily Telegraph*, 13 November 1893.

10. *London Standard*, 20 October 1893.

11. *Sheffield Daily Telegraph*, 9 November 1893; *Pall Mall Gazette*, 5 February 1894.

12. Selous to his mother, 4 November 1893, SE 1/1/1.

13. *Daily Gazette for Middlesbrough*, 9 December 1893.

14. F.C. Selous, *Travel and Adventure in South-East Africa*. London: Rowland Ward (1893), p. 35; F.C. Selous, *African Nature Notes and Reminiscences*. London: Macmillan (1908), p. 163.

15. *Sheffield Daily Telegraph*, 7 February 1894.

16. *Pall Mall Gazette*, 5 February 1894.

17. Selous to his mother, 27 November 1893, SE1/1/1.

18. *The Times*, 6 February 1894, p. 4; A. Wills and L.T. Collingridge (eds), *The Downfall of Lobengula: the Cause, History, and Effect of the Matabeli War*. London: The African Review Offices (1894), p. 7.

19. *The Times*, 6 February 1894, p. 4.

20. *The Times*, 2 January 1894, p. 3.

21. *Pall Mall Gazette*, 2 January 1894; *Leeds Mercury*, 6 February 1894; *Pall Mall Gazette*, 5 February 1894.

22. *Pall Mall Gazette*, 5 February 1894.

23. *Sheffield Evening Telegraph*, 15 February 1894.

24. *Freeman's Journal*, 22 February 1894.

25. *Evening Telegraph*, 8 August 1894.

26. *Leeds Times*, 17 February 1894; *Derby Daily Telegraph*, 21 February 1894; *Manchester Courier and Lancashire General Advertiser*, 28 February 1894; *Tamworth Herald*, 3 March 1894; *Morning Post*, 6 March 1894; *London Daily News*, 7 March 1894; *Lichfield Mercury*, 9 March 1894.

27. *Morning Post*, 14 March 1894.

28. Reprinted in full in the Maddy family's hometown newspaper, the *Gloucester Citizen*, 14 March 1894.

29. Quoted in *Gloucester Citizen*, 27 April 1894.

30. *Cheltenham Chronicle*, 7 April 1894; see also *Cheltenham Looker-on*, 7 April 1894.

31. *Yorkshire Evening Post*, 1 June 1894; *Edinburgh Evening News*, 16 July 1894.

32. *Manchester Courier and Lancashire General Advertiser*, 6 October 1894. See also E. Chinyamakobvu, *The Farm on Their Land*. USA: Google eBook (2011), p. 47.

33. *Edinburgh Evening News*, 31 July 1894; *Pall Mall Gazette*, 6 Oct. 1894.

34. *Pall Mall Gazette*, 15 September 1894; *Liverpool Mercury*, 19 November 1894. Mrs Selous is mentioned as living in Longford House by 8 December 1894.

35. *Evening Telegraph*, 8 August and 6 October 1894; *Gloucester Citizen*, 20 December 1894; *Sheffield Evening Telegraph*, 6 November 1894; Selous, *Sport and Travel, East and West*. London: Longmans, Green (1900), pp. 44–94.

36. *London Standard*, 8 and 15 January 1895.

37. Selous to Keltie, 30 December 1894, CB 187–1927. Selous file, RGS.

38. *Pall Mall Gazette*, 22 March 1895. Both Millais and Taylor get the date of the Rugby presentation wrong, placing it in 1894 rather than 1895.

Chapter 16 A Rhodesian Idyll and the Rising

1. See prospectus in *Manchester Courier and Lancashire General Advertiser*, 29 April 1895.

2. Notes by Mrs F.C. Selous, SE 1/1/1.

3. J.G. Millais, *Life of Frederick Courtenay [sic], D.S.O., Capt. 25th Royal Fusiliers*. London: Longmans Green, p. 208.

4. *Daily Gazette for Middlesbrough*, 26 November 1895.

5. *Gloucester Chronicle*, 18 April 1896.

6. Notes by Mrs F.C. Selous, SE 1/1/1.

7. Selous to Keltie, 20 February 1896, CB7/Selous, RGS.

8. *New York Times*, 8 March 1896.

9. See, for example, *Sheffield Evening Telegraph*, 13 February 1896.

10. F.C. Selous, *Sunshine and Storm in Rhodesia*. London: Rowland Ward (1896), pp. 7–8. Subsequent accounts of events in the first half of 1896 not otherwise referenced in this chapter are based on this book.

11. Notes by Mrs Selous, SE 1/1/1.

12. Ibid.

13. Selous (1896), p. 24.

14. Notes by Mrs Selous, SE 1/1/1.

15. Gladys Selous to her parents, 28 March 1896, SE 1/1/1.

16. *Gloucester Journal*, 2 May 1896.

17. Reprinted in *Gloucester Journal*, 16 May 1896.

18. Gladys Selous to her parents, 28 March 1896, SE 1/1/1.

19. *Western Gazette*, 10 April 1896; *Wells Journal*, 30 April 1896; *Yorkshire Evening Post*, 14 September 1896.

20. Selous (1896), p. 192.

21. Ibid, p. 193.

22. Ibid.

23. Ibid, p. 67.

24. F.C. Selous, *African Nature Notes and Reminiscences*. London: Macmillan (1908), pp. 229, 251.

Chapter 17 My Dear President Roosevelt

1. Millais, *Life of Frederick Courtenay* [sic], *D.S.O, Cpt 25th Royal Fusiliers*. London: Longmans Green (1919), pp. 221–2.

2. F.C. Selous, *Sunshine and Storm in Rhodesia*. London: Rowland Ward (1896), pp. 245–50.

3. Heany to Rhodes, 7 July 1900, Rhodes Papers MSS Afr. S228/C19, Bodleian Library Manuscripts, Oxford University; *London Gazette*, 22 May 1900.

4. *Hartlepool Mail*, 2 April 1896; *Edinburgh Evening News* and *London Daily News*, 23 January 1897.

5. *Leeds Times*, 23 January 1897.

6. *Pall Mall Gazette*, 27 January 1897.

7. *Aberdeen Journal*, 27 January 1897.

8. *Edinburgh Evening News*, 5 April 1897.

9. The correspondence with Roosevelt has to be pieced together from two repositories. Roosevelt's surviving letters to Selous are collected in file SE 1/1/3 in the Zimbabwe National Archives. Selous's letters to Roosevelt are part of the Roosevelt Papers in the United States Library of Congress, where they are filed alphabetically according to the date received. There is an excellent published *Index to the Theodore Roosevelt Papers*. Washington, D.C.: Library of Congress (1969). This and subsequent references to correspondence are taken exclusively from these two collections.

10. F.C. Selous, 'The Economic Value of Rhodesia', *Scottish Geographical Magazine* (1897) No. 13, pp. 505–14.

11. Selous to Colles, 30 November 1916, file CB8 Selous F.C., RGS.

12. The incidents of this hunt are recounted in considerable detail in F.C. Selous, *Sport and Travel, East and West*. London: Longmans, Green (1900).

13. Roosevelt to Selous 30 November 1897.

14. 'The Preservation of African Big Game', *The Field*, 27 July 1895, p. 172, and 31 October 1896.

15. Roosevelt to Selous, 3 and 15 February 1898.

16. *London Daily News*, 11 January 1898.

17. *Cheltenham Chronicle*, 5 March 1898.

18. *Cheltenham Chronicle*, 5 February 1898.

19. *Gloucester Citizen*, 20 December 1898.
20. Ibid.
21. Selous to Keltie, 20 February 1896, CB7/Selous, RGS.
22. *Morning Post*, 17 January 1900.
23. *Morning Post*, 6 March 1900.
24. M. White to Selous, 5 February 1900, Roosevelt Papers, Library of Congress.
25. Selous to Roosevelt, 4 March 1900.
26. Ibid.
27. Roosevelt to Selous, 19 March 1900.
28. Ibid.
29. Selous to the Secretary, The South Africa Conciliation Committee, 3 August 1900, SE 1/1/2/2.
30. Piet Greyling to Selous, 25 April 1900, SE 1/1/2/2.
31. Roosevelt to Selous, 23 November 1900.
32. Ibid.
33. Selous to Roosevelt, 12 December 1900.
34. Selous to Keltie, 29 January 1900, CB7, RGS.
35. Selous to Keltie, 20 January 1900, CB7, RGS.
36. Reprinted in *Dundee Evening Telegraph*, 2 November 1906. See also Millais (1919), p. 358.
37. They had begun meeting there in 1889. See Selous to Bryden, 12 April 1889 and 21 April 1903, MS 057, FC Selous Letters, MS 57/1-15 Brenthurst Library Johannesburg.
38. J.M. MacKenzie, *The Empire of Nature: Hunting, Conservation and British Imperialism.* Manchester: Manchester University Press (1988), p. 211; Millais (1919), p. 367.
39. Roosevelt to Selous, 18 December 1905.
40. Roosevelt to Selous, 22 January 1906.
41. Selous to Roosevelt, 26 November 1905.
42. Selous to Roosevelt, 20 June 1907; Roosevelt to Selous 20 March 1898.
43. Roosevelt to Selous, 29 April 1908.
44. Selous, *African Nature Notes and Reminiscences.* London: Macmillan (1908), p. 206.
45. Ibid.
46. Selous to Roosevelt, 24 May 1908.
47. Cunninghame to Selous, 11 September 1908; Roosevelt to Selous, 19 August 1908; Selous to Roosevelt, 3 April and 28 October 1908.
48. Roosevelt to Selous, 25 June 1908.

Chapter 18 'Who Could Wish a Better Death?'

1. Roosevelt to Selous, 29 April 1908.
2. Selous to Bryden, 16 March 1909, MS 57, Brenthurst Library.
3. Selous to Bryden, 11 November 1909, MS 57, Brenthurst Library.
4. Comments recorded by a reporter who interviewed Selous as he disembarked in New York, on his way to travel in California, *Dundee Evening Telegraph*, 9 December 1909.
5. Selous to Treasurer, 11 May 1908, RGS.
6. Keltie to Selous 26 May 1908 and Selous to Keltie 29 May and 23 June 1908, CB7/Selous, RGS.
7. J.B. Tyrell, Toronto, to Selous, 30 July 1907, SE1/1/2/2.
8. G.B. Muir, Macmillan & Co. Ltd, to Selous, 7 November 1908, SE 1/1/2/2.
9. J.G. Millais, Life of Frederick Courtenay [sic], D.S.O., Capt. 25th Royal Fusiliers. London: Longmans Green (1991), pp. 10-11.
10. C. Newbury, *The Diamond Ring: Business, Politics, and Precious Stones in South Africa 1867-1947.* Oxford: Clarendon Press (1989), pp. 181-5.

11. *Sheffield Daily Telegraph*, 16 June 1910 and 29 June 1911.

12. R. Baden-Powell, *Scouting for Boys* (1908 edition), Chapter VI (http://www.thedump.scoutscan.com/yarns00-28.pdf).

13. *Cheltenham Looker-On*, 8 February 1913; *Cheltenham Chronicle*, 26 April 1913; *Luton Times and Advertiser*, 10 April 1914.

14. Selous, writing in *The Field*, 5 October 1907.

15. J.A. Casada (ed.), *Africa's Greatest Hunter*: The Lost Writings of Frederick C. Selous, 2nd edn.. Huntington Beach, CA: Safari Press (1998), pp. 122–3, 128–9.

16. F.C. Selous, 'The Romance of the World's Great Rivers: The Zambezi', from *Travel Magazine* (1909), reprinted in Casada (1998), p. 149.

17. E. Selous to Günther, 15 March 1887, Letters In, Zoological Department 1/31, NHM.

18. E. Selous, *Bird Watching*. London: Dent (1901), pp. 333–6.

19. Ibid, pp. 335–6.

20. Roosevelt to Selous, 4 April 1910; Selous to Roosevelt, 16 May 1910; *Chelmsford Chronicle*, 27 May 1910.

21. Millais (1919), pp. 275–9.

22. Roosevelt to Selous, 11 September 1911.

23. Selous, *Travel and Adventure in South-East Africa*. London: Rowland Ward (1893), p. 429; Keltie to Selous, 10 December 1910, CB7 Selous, RGS; *Manchester Courier and General Advertiser*, 25 November 1912; Millais (1919), p.353.

24. Selous to Bryden 21 and 26 June 1911, MS 57, Brenthurst Library.

25. Roosevelt to Selous, 11 September 1911.

26. Selous to Chapman, 26 September 1912, quoted in Millais (1919), p. 285.

27. Selous to Roosevelt, 12 December 1911.

28. Ibid.

29. *Gloucester Citizen*, 15 July 1911; *Gloucester Journal*, 3 September 1910; *Nottingham Evening Post*, 6 September 1910; Millais (1919), pp. 273–4; Secretary of the Saint-Hubert Club de France, 14 September 1910, and Certificate from the National Geographic Society, 6 May 1910, SE1/1/2/2.

30. *Hull Daily Mail*, 1 June 1912.

31. Roosevelt to Selous, n.d., *c.* October 1912. Roosevelt carried the bullet in his body for the remainder of his life.

32. J.A. Balleine to Selous, St Brelade's Rectory, Jersey, 29 December 1898, SE1/1/2/2.

33. Selous to Roosevelt, 9 March 1913; Roosevelt to Selous, 2 April 1913.

34. Selous to Roosevelt, 5 December 1913.

35. Selous to Bryden, 14 February 1914, MS57 Brenthurst Library; *Birmingham Daily Post*, 5 March 1914.

36. *Hull Daily Mail*, 27 June 1914.

37. Selous to Roosevelt, 12 September 1914.

38. Roosevelt to Selous, 5 October 1914.

39. Selous to Abel Chapman, quoted in Millais (1919), p. 301.

40. *Western Daily Press*, 2 February 1915.

41. Roosevelt to Selous, 2 April 1915; *Birmingham Daily Post*, 27 March 1915.

42. Millais (1919), p. 305.

43. Selous, extensive notes on 'personal experiences in the attack', printed in full in Millais (1919), pp. 305–16.

44. Roosevelt to Selous, 28 August 1915.

45. Selous to Heatley Noble, 26 July 1915, printed in Millais (1919), p. 328.

46. For a nuanced, demythologized account of the *askari*, see M.R. Moyd, *Violent Intermediaries: African Soldiers, Conquest and Everyday Colonialism in German East Africa*. Athens, OH: Ohio University Press (1914).

47. Selous to Roosevelt, 12 September 1914; Selous to Millais, 8 December 1915 and 25 February 1916.

48. W.C. Pycraft, 'A Great Hunter: Captain Frederick Courtney [*sic*] Selous, D.S.O.', *Journal of the African*

Society (1916–17), No. 16, pp. 200–15.

49. *The Times*, 27 September 1916.

50. Selous to Colles, 30 November 1916, CB8, RGS.

51. Printed in J.A. Casada, *Frederick C. Selous, A Hunting Legend: Recollections by and about the Great Hunter*, pp. 93–4.

Chapter 19 The Legacies and Afterlife of Selous[PHA}

1. Gladys Selous to Keltie, 5 February 1917, CB 187, RGS.

2. Printed prospectus for the Selous Memorial Committee, DF1004/CP/665, NHM.

3. E.C. Stuart Baker, Honorary Secretary of the Selous Memorial Committee, memorandum 9 April 1918, R.D. Povey to C.W. Fagan, 31 May 1920, DF1004/CP/665, NHM; *Gloucester Journal*, 12 June 1920. Selous, F C. Memorial File, CB8 RGS.

4. F. Harmer to the Trustees, 25 October 1922, Selous Memorial, DF1004/CP/665, NHM.

5. Memorandum on the Selous Collection of Eggs, 26 June 1920; John Guy Dollman, *Catalogue of the Selous Collection of Big Game in the British Museum (Natural History)*. London: Trustees of the British Museum (1921).

6. The entry on Selous in the *Oxford Dictionary of National Biography* reckons the estate at more than £333,441, which would have been an enormous sum in 1917; R.I. Pocock, 'Selous, Frederick Courteney (1851–1917)', rev. Norman Etherington, *Oxford Dictionary of National Biography*. Oxford: Oxford University Press (2004); online edition, May 2006 (www.oxforddnb.com/view/article/36013, accessed 24 June 2015). After inspecting the will I believe an extra 3 was mistakenly inscribed in the handwritten probate declaration. At £33,441 the estate would have been double that left by his brother Edmund a few years later, and more in line with what Selous said about his financial situation in 1908.

7. www.safarilodges.com/index.php?route=information/guide&safari_country_id_6&safari_region_id_59&safari_guide_id=64

8. K. Tidrick, *Empire and the English Character*. London: I.B. Tauris & Co. (2008), p. 59; S. Taylor, *The Mighty Nimrod: A Life of Frederick Courteney Selous, African Hunter and Adventurer, 1851–1917*. London: Collins (1989), p. 130.

9. Selous, *African Nature Notes and Reminiscences*. London: Macmillan (1908), p. 333.

10. Interview for *Windsor* magazine, November 1906, printed in Dundee *Evening Telegraph*, 2 November 1906; *Western Daily Press*, 26 May 1904.

11. R. Baden-Powell, 'The Chief Scout Speaks: Selous the Hunter', *The Argus* (Melbourne) 27 May 1930.

12. Robert D. Madison, 'Hemingway and Selous: A Source for "Snows"?', *Hemingway Review* (Fall, 1988), p. 62.

Select Bibliography

Archived Sources

Archives of the Natural History Museum (NHM), South Kensington, London.

Brenthurst Library, Johannesburg

British Archives, Kew

British Newspaper Archive: www.britishnewspaperarchive.co.uk

Selous Papers (SE), National Archives of Zimbabwe.

Rhodes Papers MSS Africa, Bodleian Library, Oxford.

Roosevelt Papers, Library of Congress, Washington, D.C., USA.

Royal Geographical Society Archives (RGS), London

Publications by Frederick Courteney Selous

African Nature Notes and Reminiscences. London: Macmillan and Co. (1908).

'Explorations in the North Mashun Country, Tropical South Africa', *The Field* (17 April 1886).

A Hunter's Wanderings in Africa, being a Narrative of Nine Years Spent Amongst the Game in the Far Interior of South Africa. London: R. Bentley and Son (1881).

Letter to the editor of *The Field*. Cape Town, South Africa: *The Field* (26 January 1888).

Letter to the editor of the *London Standard*, 15 June 1893.

'Mr. F.C. Selous's Further Explorations in Matabele-land', *Proceedings of the Royal Geographical Society*, n.s., No. 10 (May 1888).

'A Night Amongst the Lions in South-Eastern Mashonaland', *The Field*, 26 September 1891.

'Notes of Travel and Adventure in the Interior of South Africa', *The Field* (23 August 1890).

'Sport and Exploration on the River Chobe, South Central Africa', *The Field* (12 February 1876).

Sport and Travel, East and West. London: Longmans, Green (1900).

Sunshine and Storm in Rhodesia. London: Rowland Ward (1896).

'The Economic Value of Rhodesia', *Scottish Geographical Magazine*, No. 13 (1897).

'The Preservation of African Big Game', *The Field* (27 July 1895).

Travel and Adventure in South-East Africa. London: Rowland Ward (1893).

Books

Beckett, I.F.W., *Riflemen Form: A Study of the Rifle Volunteer Movement 1859–1908*. Barnsley: Pen & Sword Military (2007).

Blennerbassett, R.A., and Sleeman, L., *Adventures in Mashonaland*. London: Sleeman (1893).

Brown, R., *Blood Ivory: The Massacre of the African Elephant*. The History Press: Stroud (2008).

Bryden, H.A., *From Veldt Camp Fires: Stories of Southern Africa*. London: Hurst and Blackett (1900).

Casada, J. A, (ed.), *Africa's Greatest Hunter: The Lost Writings Of Frederick C. Selous*, 2nd edn. Huntington Beach, CA: Safari Press (1998)

—*Frederick C. Selous, A Hunting Legend: Recollections by and about the Great Hunter*. Huntington Beach, CA: Safari Press (2000).

Cody, W., *The Life of Hon. William F. Cody, known as Buffalo Bill: The Famous Hunter, Scout and Guide: An Autobiography*. Hartford, CT: Frank E. Bliss (1879).

Cumming, R.G., *Five Years of a Hunter's Life in the Far Interior of South Africa*, 2 vols. London: John Murray (1850).

Etherington, N., *Preachers, Peasants and Politics in Southeast Africa*. London: Royal Historical Society (1978).

—*The Great Treks: The Transformation of Southern Africa, 1815–1854*. London: Longman (2001).

Fage, J., and Oliver, R. (eds), *Cambridge History of Africa*, Vol. 6. Cambridge: Cambridge University Press (1985).

Finke, J., *The Rough Guide to Tanzania*. London: Penguin Rough Guides (2007).

Griffiths, T., *Hunters and Collectors: The Antiquarian Imagination in Australia*. Cambridge: Cambridge University Press (1996).

Harris, W.C., *The Wild Sports of Southern Africa; being the Narrative of an Expedition from the Cape of Good Hope, through the Territories of the Chief Moselekatse to the Tropic of Capricorn*. London: John Murray (1839).

Hughes, T., *Tom Brown's Schooldays*. London: Cassell and Co. (1907).

Johnson, F., *Great Days: The Autobiography of an Empire Pioneer*. London: G. Bell and Sons (1940).

Kennedy, D., *The Last Blank Spaces: Exploring Africa and Australia*. Cambridge, MA: Harvard University Press (2013).

Keppel-Jones, A., *Rhodes and Rhodesia: The White Conquest of Zimbabwe 1884–1902*. Kingston, ON: McGill-Queen's University Press (1983).

Kerr, W.M., *The Far Interior: A Narrative of Travel and Adventure from the Cape of Good Hope across the Zambesi to the Lake Regions of Central Africa*, Vol. I. Boston, MA: Houghton Mifflin (1886).

Lord, W.B., *Diamonds and Gold*. London: publisher unknown (1871).

Mackenzie, John, *Ten Years North of the Orange River: A Story of Everyday Life and Work among the South African Tribes, from 1859 to 1869*. Edinburgh: Edmonston & Douglas (1871).

MacKenzie, John Macdonald, *The Empire of Nature: Hunting, Conservation and British Imperialism*. Manchester: Manchester University Press (1988).

Mason, P., *Birth of a Dilemma: The Conquest and Settlement of Rhodesia*. Oxford: Oxford University Press (1958).

Millais, J.G., *Life of Frederick Courtenay [sic], D.S.O., Capt. 25th Royal Fusiliers Selous*. London: Longmans Green (1919).

Norton, F. (ed.), *Frank Leslie's Historical Register of the United States Centennial Exposition, 1876*. New York, NY: Frank Leslie (1877).

Parsons, N., *King Khama, Emperor Joe, and the Great White Queen*. Chicago, IL: University of Chicago Press (1998).

Payton, C., *Diamond Diggings of South Africa*. London: Horace Cox (1872).

Ranger, T., *Revolt in Southern Rhodesia 1896–7*. London: Heinemann (1967).

Rotberg, R., *The Founder: Cecil Rhodes and the Pursuit of Power*. Oxford: Oxford University Press (1988).

Tabler, E.C. (ed.), *To the Victoria Falls via Matabeleland: The Diary of Major Henry Stabb*, 1875. Cape Town, South Africa: Struik (1967).

Tallis, J., *Tallis's History and Description of the Crystal Palace, and the Exhibition of the World's Industry in 1851*. London: London Printing and Publishing (1852).

Taylor, S., *The Mighty Nimrod: A Life of Frederick Courteney Selous, African Hunter and Adventurer, 1851–1917*. London: Collins (1989).

Thomas, A., *Rhodes*. London: BBC Books (1996).

Thomas, K., *Man and the Natural World: Changing Attitudes in England, 1500–1800*. London: Allen Lane (1983).

Tidrick, K., *Empire and the English Character: The Illusion of Authority*. London: I.B. Tauris & Co. (2008).

Ward, R., *A Naturalist's Life Study in the Art of Taxidermy*. London: Rowland Ward, printed for private circulation (1913).

Wallis, J.P.R. (ed.), *The Matabele Journal of Robert Moffat, 1829–1860*, Vol. I. London: Chatto & Windus (1945).

Wills, A., and Collingridge, L.T. (eds), *The Downfall of Lobengula: The Cause, History, and Effect of the Matabeli War*. London: The African Review Offices (1894).

Wilmsen, E. N., *Land Filled with Flies: A Political Economy of the Kalahari*. Chicago, IL: University of Chicago Press (1989).

Journals, Articles and Chapters in Books

Grandy, W.G., 'Report of the Proceedings of the Livingstone Congo Mission', Proceedings of the Royal Geographical Society, No. 19 (1875).

Hamilton, C., Mbenga, B.K, and Ross, R. (eds), *Cambridge History of South Africa*, Vol. I. Cambridge: Cambridge University Press (2010).

Hartlepool Mail, 2 April 1896.

Journal of Southern African Studies, Vol. 24, No. 4 (1998).

Mangan, J.A. and McKenzie, C., 'Martial Conditioning, Military Exemplars and Moral Certainties: Imperial Hunting as Preparation for War', *The International Journal of the History of Sport*, (2008) Vol. 25.

Maugham, R.C.F., 'Twenty Years in Zambezia', *Proceedings of the Royal Geographical Society*, JMS2/299. London: Royal Geographical Society.

Morton, F., and Hitchcock, R., 'Tswana Hunting: Continuities and Changes in the Transvaal and Kalahari after 1600', *South African Historical Journal*, No. 66 (2014).

Osborne, H. and Winstanley, M., 'Rural and Urban Poaching in Victorian England', *Rural History*, Vol. 17 (2006).

Online Articles

Chinyamakoobvu, E., *The Farm on their Land*. USA: Google eBook (2011).

The Guardian, online edition (accessed 18 April 2004).

Marketing History of the Piano, www.cantos.org/Piano/History/marketing.html (accessed 5 November 2014).

Oxford Dictionary of National Biography. Oxford: Oxford University Press (2004). See www.oxforddnb.com/view/article/52662 (accessed 11 March 2015).

Sampson, R., *White Induna: George Westbeech and the Barotse*. USA: Xlibris (2008).

Index